QUESTIONS

Couples Ask Behind
Closed Doors

QUESTIONS

Couples Ask Behind Closed Doors

HOW TO TAKE

ACTION ON THE

MOST COMMON

CONFLICTS IN

MARRIAGE

DR. JAMES OSTERHAUS

The stories and situations described in this book are composites of typical situations frequently encountered in marital counseling. No actual person, living or dead, is described in these stories and situations.

For discussion guides and other helpful materials, visit the author's web site at www.jamesosterhaus.com.

Published by Familius LLC, www.familius.com
Familius books are available at special discounts for bulk purchases for sales promotions, family or corporate use. Special editions, including personalized covers, excerpts of existing books, or books with corporate logos, can be created in large quantities for special needs. For more information, contact Premium Sales at 559-876-2170 or email specialmarkets@familius.com

Library of Congress Catalog-in-Publication Data
2014948139

pISBN 978-1-939629-37-1
eISBN 978-1-939629-98-2

Printed in the United States of America
Edited by Aimee Hancock
Cover design by David Miles
Book design by Kurt Wahlner

10 9 8 7 6 5 4 3 2 1

First edition

This book is dedicated to my friend, Joe Jurkowski, who has given me much of the insight that is contained within these pages.

CONTENTS

What Does a Healthy Marriage Look Like?

Rick and Teri came to me with a confused and painful question: "What is a healthy marriage supposed to look like? What does 'healthy' really mean?" It was not hard to see why they felt confused.

Rick's parents were divorced when he was ten. "There was this gigantic tug-of-war going on all the time," he recalled, "and I was the rope. I just wanted to love both of my parents, but they wouldn't let me. They always made me choose between them. Now I'm married with kids of my own, and I'm scared that my marriage may be falling apart. How am I supposed to build a healthy marriage when I don't know what one is supposed to look like?"

"Unlike Rick's parents," said Teri, "my parents never got a divorce—but I sometimes wish they had. Maybe my childhood memories would have been happier if they had split up." Teri remembered going to bed many nights and pulling blankets and pillows over her head, trying to shut out the sound of her parents' fighting. In recent weeks, Teri had begun to realize that she was putting her own preschool-age daughter through the same misery she had gone through as a child.

"Rick and I were in the middle of a fight. I don't remember what we were arguing about—something small and inconsequential, as usual. Suddenly, right in the middle of it all, our four-year-old, Katie, got between us and put her hands on her hips and shouted, 'Stop it!' at the top of her lungs. Well, that stopped the fighting, all right. Rick and I looked at Katie and there were tears streaming down her face. That's when it hit me that we just can't go on like this. I want to have a healthy marriage so we can raise happy, well-adjusted kids. The problem is I don't know what a healthy marriage is."

The "what is 'healthy'?" question is just one of many questions couples ask me over and over again in my counseling practice. The following are some examples of couples and questions they've asked in our counseling. Rod and Amy are in my office because their fourteen-year marriage is in trouble. They seem to have nothing in common anymore—if they ever did in the first place. Rod feels Amy's fiery, tempestuous personality is like fingernails scraping on the blackboard of his soul. Amy complains that Rod is an undermotivated underachiever who needs to be pushed and prodded in order to accomplish anything. Looking back, they both wonder what they ever saw in each other and why they got married—and both admit that they wouldn't marry each other again if they had it to do over. Sitting in my office, they wonder aloud, "How did it happen? How did two such obviously mismatched people ever find each other and fall in love?"

Kristy and Michael visit my office with differing viewpoints. "This is our third year of marriage," says Michael, "and I kept hoping things would get better. But Kristy seems to get more stubborn and unyielding all the time." Predictably, Kristy has a different point of view. "When I married Michael, I loved him for his strong personality," she says. "I'm a tough cookie myself, and I needed to marry someone who was a match for my personality. But something happened after we got married—Michael went into this 'Me Tarzan, you Jane' routine. I mean, I want a partner, not a boss. Most of the conflict in our relationship centers around the question, 'Who's in charge?' How do we resolve this issue?"

Neil and Lori are two people who face an array of problems. At age thirty-three, Lori has decided to go back to school for her master's degree, and that means she has less time and energy for their relationship, their sex life, and their children. As if these pressures weren't enough, Lori also has to put up with continual criticism from Neil's parents, who accuse her of neglecting her family. Lately, it seems that every conversation Neil and Lori have turns into a fight, and they have no plan for dealing with these recurring conflicts. So Neil wants to know, "Why aren't we close anymore? Lori says she needs this master's degree, but what about the kids' needs? What about my needs? What about our sex life? Isn't that important?" And Lori asks, "Why do we keep having the same arguments over and over? How do I get Neil's parents off my back? How do we resolve these conflicts?"

These are the questions I hear over and over again from couples who come to my office for counseling. They come for help because their relationships have become distorted and confused, their lives are in pain, and their marriages are in trouble. So we meet together behind the doors of my office, we shut out the world, we talk, and we listen to one another. In the secure privacy of the counselor's office, a man and a woman face each other, they voice their pain, and they ask their questions. And again and again, I have seen troubled relationships become healthy and satisfying once more. What most people need in order to have a good marriage are the skills and insights for resolving differences, meeting mutual needs, balancing closeness and individuality, and experiencing true intimacy.

The questions that continually recur in my counseling practice are questions about unspoken expectations, unexpressed needs, guilt and forgiveness, intimacy and sex, communication and conflict, in-laws, resentments, resurfacing old issues, decision-making, children, step-children, and personality differences. Often, one partner will share these questions and feelings, and the other partner will look up in surprise and say, "I never knew you felt that way!" And real communication begins—sometimes for the first time in years.

Obviously, no book can take the place of a therapy session with a trained marriage and family counselor. But in this book, I have tried to gather the most common and troubling questions I encounter in my own counseling practice—questions that often reveal the hidden dynamics of a relationship and lead to a major breakthrough in communication and understanding. I have also collected the principles and insights that have produced healing and transformation in so many couples who have crossed the threshold of my office.

As we explore these insights together, the answer to the big question—"What is a healthy marriage supposed to look like?"—will come into focus. This book is designed to give you the hands-on, practical tools and communication strategies so that you and your partner can experience a rich and rewarding relationship.

As you read stories of couples who are much like you and your partner and as you learn new insights and workable principles, you'll find yourself becoming more conscious of your own motivations and of the dynamics that make up your marriage relationship. Wherever you and your partner may be in your life together—newlywed, thirty-something, forty-something, middle-aged, second or third time around, blended family, or golden years—the next eighteen chapters will enable you to acquire powerful insights, skills, and attitudes to help you build a healthy, happy relationship.

I encourage you to think of these chapters not so much as a book to be read, but as a journey to be walked, an adventure to be lived. It is a rewarding journey—the journey of two people spending a lifetime together, growing in love toward each other. By reading this book, you have chosen to move forward, deliberately and consciously, along this lifelong path.

Not everyone makes this choice. Unfortunately, I have seen many couples simply give up without making an honest effort to save their relationship. They think that the work of building a healthy marriage is just too hard and that the process of self-examination and change is too painful. But I believe there is a better future in store for you, because you have chosen to take action to make your marriage better and stronger..

And you have already taken the first step.

ONE

How Did We Find Each Other?

––––––•––––––––––•––––––

"How does that corny old song go?" Terese said. "'Some enchanted evening, you may meet a stranger. . . .' That's how Scott and I met."

"We were at a concert," Scott recalled. "Terese was there with a couple of girlfriends, and I was there with a date. My date and I went through one turnstile and Terese went through the next one. Our eyes met for just a second, and zap! It was *electric*, you know?"

"Electric, absolutely!" Terese added. "It was a fairy-tale moment. Our eyes met and it was like *bam!* Instant attraction!"

"Yeah," Scott said. "But in the next moment, Terese and her friends melted into the crowd, and I didn't think I'd ever see her again. Yet all through the first half of the concert, while I was sitting with my date, all I could think of was this beautiful girl I had only seen for a few seconds. At intermission, my date went to the ladies room and I went out to get some Cokes—and there was Terese again."

"I was at the snack bar," Terese interjected. "Scott came up and talked to me. He seemed really nervous and awkward—"

"I was not!"

"You were, too! But he was also sweet, and we both knew there was something happening between us. It was so exciting. I don't remember what we talked about—just chit-chat about the concert and stuff. The really dumb thing was that neither of us thought to exchange phone numbers or anything."

"But I knew where she worked," Scott added. "The next day, I showed up at her office at eleven-fifty and I found her at her desk, and—"

"And he brought me flowers," Terese said. "We began dating, and the relationship just moved really fast from there. We were together almost every day, and we were married six months after we met."

Stories like that of Scott and Terese—spontaneous romantic combustion—are the exception rather than the rule. Much more common is the experience of Kent and Melina, a couple who met at UC Santa Barbara. Kent was a sophomore, and Melina was a freshman.

"It wasn't love at first sight, exactly," Melina recalled. "Kent was a friend. We both had lots of friends, and we were serious about our studies. We weren't interested in romantic attachments. Kent and I were good friends all through college. We studied together sometimes, we socialized on weekends, and we went to the beach or to the movies, usually in a group with other people. We never thought of it as dating—just hanging out."

"In fact," adds Kent, "I was dating someone else during my senior year. I really expected to marry my girlfriend, Julie—but then she was killed in a car accident. I was devastated. And it was during that time, when Melina really stood by me as a friend, that we just got really . . . close."

"You hear about it all the time," Melina puts in, "that lovers often start as friends. And that's the way it was with Kent and me, in the early part of our relationship. As Kent and I talked and cried together after his loss, our friendship just flowered into romance. We both felt it growing, and at some point we just felt it was right that we should marry."

Romance—this mysterious spiritual, emotional, intellectual, sexual attraction between a man and a woman—sometimes takes place with the explosive suddenness of a lightning strike. Other times, it emerges slowly, almost imperceptibly out of a friendship. Whether your romance was like a bolt out of the blue or the budding of a flower, there are certain psychological and emotional forces that are critical to the healthy functioning of a relationship. These forces are mostly hidden and unconscious in nature. Once you understand how and why you were originally attracted to your partner, you'll be better equipped to communicate clearly, resolve conflicts, and authentically love this person with whom you share your life.

AN AMAZING PIECE OF EQUIPMENT

I hear exasperated questions all the time in my counseling practice, such as "We're so different! What did I ever see in him, anyway?" or, "We have absolutely nothing in common! How could I have ever been in love with her?" In fact, there are a number of ingredients that go into this mysterious mix we call "romantic attraction."

There are, of course, the obvious features that attract the sexes: physical beauty, youthfulness, and other physical attributes that subliminally suggest to us, "This woman would make an excellent lover and mother for my children" or, "This man would make an excellent soul mate and provider." We also tend to select partners who are similar to us in economic/social class, intellect, values, and attractiveness.

But there is an even more fundamental answer to the question, "How did I select this person as my partner?" Most people don't like to hear the answer, but it applies to some degree in almost every marriage relationship: "You selected this person by searching for what you didn't get as a child—and by turning to the wrong source to attain it." Many problems that arise in marriage are due, at least in part, to an unconscious drive on the part of one marriage partner to be "re-parented" by the other. It turns out there's a lot more truth than anyone realized in the old song, "I Want a Girl (Just Like the Girl that Married Dear Old Dad)."

When I suggest this idea to couples in counseling, it often meets with resistance in comments such as, "No way! I don't want anyone to 'momma' me or 'daddy' me! I'm an adult! I entered into marriage because of adult reasons, because I'm mature enough to take on the adult responsibilities of marriage." On one level, the conscious level, this is probably true. But within each of us, there is a hidden, unconscious component of the mind that exerts a powerful influence over our feelings, our thinking, our decision making, and our behavior.

The human brain is an amazing piece of equipment that is designed for a wide variety of functions—from such higher, human functions as thinking, imagining, and creating to the more basic functions such as surviving and procreating. Your brain is not merely a single organ, but a complex assemblage of structures, each performing a specific, specialized function. It's an oversimplification, but I find it useful to think of the brain as consisting of three main divisions:

1. *The Survival Brain* (made up of the brain stem and the limbic system, centered beneath the cerebral cortex)
2. *The Storehouse Brain* (the right hemisphere of the cerebral cortex)
3. *The Logical Brain* (the left hemisphere of the cerebral cortex)

Each of these divisions of the brain plays a unique and crucial role in the way we understand reality, respond to other people, and make decisions. If we understand how these different segments of the brain affect the way we interact with our romantic partners, we will be able to clear away much of the misunderstanding, miscommunication, and distrust that damages our relationships. We will also be able to better understand how and why we selected the person we did, and how those factors continue to affect the marriage relationship today.

THE SURVIVAL BRAIN

First, let's examine the survival brain. Its function is basic—even primitive. The survival brain, located underneath the reasoning areas of the brain, does not think, does not reason, and does not analyze. Instead, it scans; it's wary. Its primary function is to protect you from danger. It continually examines the environment to answer one question: "Is it safe?"

The survival brain receives the bulk of its input from your eyes. Vision dominates the other senses when it comes to safety. As you look into another person's eyes, you may feel as though you have direct contact with that other person. Someone has rightly called the eyes "the window to your soul."

Did you ever notice how you feel anxious or uncomfortable around people who make no eye contact, or who stare too long at you, or whose eyes dart back and forth? Your survival brain is sending you a message (which may or may not be accurate) that you should be wary of this person. People's eyes communicate fear, sadness, arrogance, irritability, and a host of other feelings—and the survival brain has an uncanny (though imperfect) knack for reading emotions.

The survival brain also checks posture, movement, appearance, facial expression, and many other factors to determine if the people around you are safe or threatening. It relies heavily on sounds when determining whether a situation is safe or not. Your survival brain is finely tuned to the voices of other people and can pick up subtle mood changes from the inflection of a single word. (Did you ever notice how much you can pick up about people's mood just by hearing their "hello" when they answer the phone?)

THE LOGICAL BRAIN AND THE STOREHOUSE BRAIN

After the survival brain finishes assessing the safety of a situation, the higher levels of the brain take over. The right and left hemispheres of the cerebral cortex are mounted over the survival brain like two halves of a walnut. Each hemisphere of the cerebral cortex has its own function. The left side is the logical brain—the analytical and verbal side. It is the side that takes in language and processes it to make sense of what people say. The logical brain weighs the information it receives and uses it to make rational conclusions and decisions.

The right side of the brain is the storehouse brain. It is more of a synthesizer than an analyzer. It does not use logic and words, but images and symbols. The storehouse brain is primarily imaginative and intuitive. Whereas the left side is objective, the right side is subjective. I call this part of the brain "the storehouse brain" because this is where images and symbols are stored throughout life to be used as a guide to reality and relationships.

Our relationships are largely made up of messages (both verbal and nonverbal) that we send to each other: "I love you," "I need something from you," or "When you do such-and-such, I feel angry." While the left or logical brain looks at the *content* of a message, the storehouse brain looks at the *context* of the message. The storehouse or right brain synthesizes all the messages coming from the senses by way of the survival brain. The storehouse brain takes into account the circumstances of the encounter with the person and makes a determination of the relationship that exists between you and the other person.

Now let's put all three parts of the brain together and see how they function together. Let's say you are an unmarried young man attending college, and a friend introduces you to a young lady at the campus coffee shop. You sit down across from each other at a table and begin to talk. Here's what takes place from your brain's point of view:

Survival brain: The wary, unreasoning portion of your brain receives sight and sound impressions of this young woman. She smiles. Her eyes sparkle. She is physically attractive. Her voice is soft and pleasing. Your survival brain sees no threat. In fact, since many of the brain's sexual functions are centered there, your survival brain becomes sexually stimulated in a mild, harmless, but pleasant way. Your survival brain signals your higher brain centers that it is safe— indeed, it is desirable—to remain in this person's presence.

Storehouse brain: Over the years, the right side of your cerebral cortex has stored up thousands of symbols and images, most of them related to your primary caregivers in your early life. Your brain seeks the comfort of familiarity, so it compares input of opposite-sex acquaintances with the master template of the opposite sex that is recorded in the storehouse brain—the image of Mom. Those opposite-sex parent images formed by years of time spent with Mom are powerful symbols of what feminine companionship is all about. Here, in the storehouse of the right brain, are all the symbols of what a wife and mother are supposed to be—symbols of nurturing, caring, competence, joy, love, affection, and every other womanly quality.

Logical brain: The left hemisphere or logical brain analyzes the content of what this pleasant young woman says. Being verbal and logical, it interprets her words into meaning. The logical brain is the part of our brain with which we *think* we think. No, that's not a typo. We *think* we think with our logical brains, but we *actually* think with our whole brains. Our storehouse brain also affects our thinking, modifying the meaning of the young lady's words with an overlay of symbols and impressions. And our survival brain affects our thinking—continuously scanning the young lady for safety and sexual desirability.

In the process of attraction and mate selection, all three parts of the brain function together. The logical brain is attracted to her wit, intelligence, and friendly manner. The storehouse brain is attracted by the fact that she is familiar and comforting to be around—something about her voice, her mannerisms, and her eyes remind us of our idealized image of The Perfect Mate. The survival brain finds her sexually attractive and safe. If these favorable impressions continue to accumulate over several months of courtship, there is a good likelihood that a point will come where you, as an eligible young man, would say, "This is the woman for me. I want to spend a lifetime with her."

The process of attraction is virtually the same for a marriageable young woman. All three parts of her brain are engaged, building up impressions and memories that point to a certain young man as "the man for me." Her image of dear old Dad, stored as symbols in her storehouse brain, will form a large part of the template of manhood that she uses in making her selection.

It is important to understand, however, that it is not only the positive traits of our parents that shape our attraction to a given man or woman in the mate selection process. We are also attracted by the negative traits of our parents. Why? Two reasons:

1. *These traits are familiar.* As illogical as it seems, people tend to prefer familiar situations, even if painful, to new and unknown situations. So if one of your parents was an alcoholic and an abuser, you might tend to select an alcoholic, abusive person to marry, because living with an alcoholic is a familiar situation. This is one reason why some people keep getting into one abusive relationship after another. It's not because they enjoy being abused; it's because abusers are familiar. Victims of childhood abuse don't know any other kind of relationship but an abusive one.

   Does it make rational sense for a person to go from one bad relationship to another? Does it make rational sense for people to keep making the same mistakes over and over again? Of course not—but don't ask the symbolic brain to be rational. Reason and logic are functions of the left brain, not the right. As a result, people are repeatedly drawn into painfully illogical situations by their storehouse brains.

2. *These traits represent unresolved struggles of the past.* We may be attracted by the negative traits of our parents because our symbolic right brain—our storehouse brain—continually tries to heal the wounds of childhood, to resolve childhood conflicts, and to compensate for the emotional deficits of childhood. The symbolic storehouse brain confuses the romantic partner of today with the old, stored image of the parent. The storehouse brain says, in effect, "Here is someone like Mom (or Dad). This person is anger-prone, violence-prone, and abusive, just

like my parent. If I marry this person, I can carry on the struggle I began in childhood—a struggle for love and acceptance—and this time I will win."

So the children of alcoholic parents marry alcoholic spouses with numbing regularity. Children of abusive parents find themselves paired with abusive spouses with amazing frequency. Children of unloving, unfeeling parents marry emotionless, uncaring mates again and again. The symbols stored in the storehouse brain compel us in the direction of a potential spouse who unconsciously reminds us of our parents.

Consciously, we tell ourselves that this prospective partner is kind, thoughtful, compassionate, considerate, and the answer to all our prayers. But on an unconscious level, the storehouse brain is thinking, "Here is my parent all over again. Here is a symbolic approximation of the person I struggled with throughout my formative years. If I can just re-create my upbringing, then perhaps I can attain the security, affirmation, and love I was denied in childhood. Finally, I have a chance to get what I never got as a child."

At this point, you may be thinking, "This stuff doesn't apply to me! My parents weren't abusive. They weren't alcoholics. I never felt deprived of love or security. I was never psychologically damaged as a child." The fact is that all of us—even those of us who were raised by the best of parents—experience emotional deficits, psychological scars, shame, pain, and unmet needs.

Even though we consciously look for positive traits in a prospective mate, on an unconscious level we are attracted by both positive and negative traits. Our storehouse brain transfers the feelings and symbols we had for our parents (both positive and negative) onto the spouse, heightening those traits that match the parental traits while ignoring those traits that do not match. Once the storehouse brain is satisfied that the original situation has been restored, it is ready to carry on the old struggles of childhood.

"I DID NOT MARRY MY FATHER!"

Carrie and Tom have been married fourteen years. Though they both profess to love each other, their relationship is frequently punctuated by arguments and periods of mutual withdrawal that seem unsolvable. In the last few years, however, the level of conflict has increased dramatically—and the increased pain of their relationship has finally driven Tom and Carrie into counseling.

In their first counseling session, Carrie explained what initially attracted her to Tom. "I was having a lot of struggles with my father," she recalled. "He was so opinionated, stubborn, and controlling— and he really disapproved of Tom. I'm not saying I married Tom just to get back at my dad—I truly did love Tom—but I saw Tom as a real contrast to my father. My going with Tom just sent my father up the wall! So, in my nineteen-year-old rebellious mind, that made Tom all the more attractive."

Over several additional counseling sessions, however, a different picture of Tom and Carrie's relationship began to emerge. Although Carrie had pictured Tom as a night-and-day contrast to her father, many striking similarities between Tom and Carrie's father began to emerge, similarities such as the fact that both had very strong and similar views on a number of subjects. For example, both men strongly distrusted doctors, lawyers, and other professionals; both were fascinated by guns and were involved in gun owners' organizations; both were fascinated by conspiracy theories and were strongly suspicious of the government.

In addition, both Carrie's father and her husband had limited educational backgrounds (Carrie's father left school after the eighth grade; Tom did not complete his senior year of high school). Both considered women to be intellectually inferior to men.

At first, Carrie was reluctant to acknowledge any similarities between her husband and her father, even though most of the similarities had emerged from statements she herself had made in counseling. When it was suggested to Carrie that she had unconsciously selected a mate in order to continue and resolve her childhood conflicts with her father, she went ballistic!

"I did not marry my own father!" she shouted, her eyes flashing. Such an angry response, of course, is often characteristic of denial, where a person consciously rejects a concept that he or she unconsciously recognizes as a painful truth. It was deeply embarrassing to Carrie to confront the possibility that she had married Tom for an array of hidden and totally mistaken reasons.

"I didn't say you married your father," I replied. "Of course you didn't. You married a man who is very much a distinct individual, and you were attracted to him for a variety of reasons. You were aware of some of those reasons and unaware of others. The more you become aware of the hidden factors that attracted you to Tom, the more clearly you will be able to see him and relate to him."

After a number of counseling sessions, Carrie did in fact begin to see that many of the things about Tom she found so exasperating were also the most unpleasant aspects of her father: rigidity, a judgmental attitude, and a controlling behavior. She realized that she could become unreasonably enraged with Tom whenever he made a disparaging comment about doctors, or when she would find him in his den, oiling and cleaning his guns—and then she flashed on the fact that such incidents reminded her of her father saying and doing those very same things.

Carrie and Tom were able to begin resolving their conflicts when she began to recognize those moments when her unconscious, unreasoning mind confused her image of her Tom with her image of her father. This or that mannerism of Tom's might remind her of her father, but she learned not to judge Tom's intentions or behavior on that basis. She needed to see Tom as he actually was—not as a symbol of her past struggle with her father.

Tom also started resolving his and Carrie's conflicts when he began to work on those aspects of himself that genuinely hurt Carrie. He learned that he needed to respect her as an equal and that his controlling behavior had to end. Tom, not so incidentally, had similar issues in his view of Carrie; to a lesser but still significant degree, he was continuing many of his own childhood struggles in his relationship with his wife.

These struggles can take many forms. Most often, there is an unconscious fusion and confusion of the opposite-sex parent image with the image of one's partner. But there are also situations where it is the image of the same-sex parent or even the image of both parents that is superimposed on the image of one's partner. It should also be noted that the storehouse brain will place any "primary care-givers"—stepparents, foster parents, grandparents, maiden aunts, or whomever—in the place of the symbolic parent.

WHY OPPOSITES ATTRACT

Shanna was an only child who grew up not merely sheltered but truly *smothered* by her mother's love. Her mother coddled her, excused her mistakes, and never let her try at anything—much less fail or get hurt. Shanna was not permitted to change, grow, or form attachments outside of her family. She was homeschooled and wasn't allowed to play with neighborhood children or to go away to camp. In fact, she was rarely out of her mother's sight.

Part of Shanna grew up fearing the perils of the outside world, as her mother continually portrayed them. But another part of Shanna rebelled at the way she was kept a prisoner in her own family. Even as she feared change and the unknown world that her mother shielded her from, she also feared being swallowed up by her mother's possessive love.

Jack's upbringing was the opposite of Shanna's. His parents maintained an emotional and physical distance from each other, from Jack's two sisters, and from Jack himself. They had firmly walled off their own thoughts, feelings, and concerns from Jack and his sisters. The rules of his family were unspoken, yet very strict: "You don't bother me and I won't bother you. Stay out of my space. Mind your own business." So Jack grew up sensing an enormous emotional gulf in his life—a deep hunger for human connection and for someone who would share his need to love and be loved.

When Shanna and Jack grew up, they found each other and got married. This might seem paradoxical—a union of two people from such different backgrounds—but it happens all the time. Shanna grew up emotionally smothered and afraid of being emotionally engulfed by her mother. She was characterized by an excessive resentment of control, intrusion, or involvement by other people in her life. Emotionally cold and distant, she was often antagonistic in conversations with other people. Shanna enjoyed being thought of as "different," and was quick to take offense toward people who tried to get too close to her or make emotional demands on her.

Jack, by contrast, exhibited what psychologists call "a dependent personality," characterized by an excessive and childlike desire to have others provide for him, meet his emotional needs, and interact with him. Because his parents were so emotionally distant and unloving, Jack had low self-esteem and tended to cling emotionally to others. Being alone made him anxious and uneasy, so he had an intense drive to emotionally "fuse" with another person. He tended to behave submissively, and his feelings were easily hurt by Shanna's criticism or emotional distance, which he interpreted as abandonment—much as he had felt emotionally abandoned by his parents. In classic victim style, he put up with Shanna's angry outbursts and her contentious and argumentative conversational style—but he didn't like it. In fact, it was extremely painful for him.

Do you see what brought these two people together? Consciously, Shanna wanted to escape the emotional clutches of her smothering mother —yet unconsciously, she found Jack, who was needy and dependent with a smothering love just like her mother's. Consciously, Jack wanted a wife who would devote herself to him, meet his emotional needs, and always be close to him—yet unconsciously, he found someone as distant and independent as his parents had been.

Both had found the substitute parents their storehouse brains were looking for—and now both were re-enacting the emotional struggles of the past. Both were fighting to achieve what had been denied them in childhood, and they didn't even realize it. The very traits that had brought them together in courtship were now pushing and pulling them in opposite directions in marriage. Jack and Shanna were left wondering how they could have been so wrong about each other when they decided to get married.

But there's another dynamic in Shanna and Jack's relationship that has brought them together and that now brings pain and conflict into their relationship. We all have a tendency to project onto our romantic partners those parts of ourselves that we have disowned and cannot accept. For example, the serious, button-down, uptight businessman learns early in life to repress his carefree, spontaneous, fun-loving side. So when a carefree, spontaneous, fun-loving woman comes into his life, she seems to supply everything he no longer has, everything he has repressed within himself.

In Shanna's case, she recognized in Jack something that she had shut away within herself—a longing for emotional connection, for affection, for dependency. Though she might consciously resent Jack's "clinginess," his "whining," and his "mooning" after her, there's an unconscious part of her that would like to return to childhood, to be smothered by love, to have someone attend to her emotional needs, and to have someone make a fuss over her. She long ago denied and repressed that part of herself in her rebellion against an emotionally overbearing mother. But a part of her feels incomplete without that smothering love in her life. So, though she is often antagonized by Jack's dependent behavior, she unconsciously recognizes in him a part of herself that is missing and that he completes.

So we have an image of our romantic partner that is made up of the image of our parents or primary caregivers from childhood and the parts of ourselves that we have denied and stored away. This image of our romantic partner is kept in the storehouse of our right brain. This is not to say that the image of our romantic partner is totally distorted by the symbols in our storehouse brain. There is usually at least a kernel of objective reality there. But all too often there is far more image than reality in our perception and that image distorts our communication, our behavior, our expectations, and our understanding of the other person.

Then, with our storehouse brains filtering and distorting reality, we jump into marriage. Only after we are married does reality truly sink in. Suddenly, the very traits we found appealing and exciting in this person become irritating and a source of conflict. We find that the denied parts of ourselves are being mirrored back to us by our partner, and we don't like what we see. We also find ourselves caught in the old struggles we thought we had escaped when we emerged from childhood—only these are now adult struggles and they are much more intense.

We look at our partner and think, "I married you so that you could heal these wounds and meet my emotional needs. But instead of healing my wounds and meeting my needs, you are turning out to be just like the absent father who was never available to me," or "You are just like the smothering mother who threatened to overwhelm me," or "You have become that critical stepparent who always belittled me." With each conflict, our focus narrows. We become less and less able to see the complex, varied personality of the other person. Instead, he or she becomes a caricature. We see only a few selected traits. These traits soon feel as if someone were raking a cheese grater across the nerve endings of our souls.

WHAT NOW?

"Okay," you may be thinking, "so now I know how my partner and I came together. I know that my storehouse brain has been manipulating my feelings and my behavior without my conscious awareness. I know that much of the conflict I have with my partner arises because my storehouse brain superimposes the symbolic parental image onto my partner. But what now? What am I supposed to do about it? I guess my relationship is doomed!"

Not at all. There's plenty you can do about it now that you understand the source of the problem. There are many practical pointers for resolving today's problems today, logically and lovingly. One pointer is to recognize the fact that knowledge is power. When you understand the workings of your unconscious, symbolic mind, you have a powerful edge in solving the problem. You don't have to be controlled by your brain's unreasoning force. You have the power to harness your emotional energy for healthy, healing purposes. Whenever you become angry, exasperated, annoyed, or impatient with your spouse, or whenever you become fearful of being abandoned or emotionally smothered by your spouse, ask yourself, "Are these feelings proportionate to my spouse's behavior or are they out of proportion? Are my feelings fact-based and reasonable or am I responding with anger and fear because this is a long-standing 'sore spot' in my soul?"

Another pointer is to take an emotional "reality check." Before responding to your spouse, pause a moment to listen to your feelings and understand what has triggered those emotions. Ask yourself, "Does this situation remind me of the dynamics of my childhood? Do I feel 'small' and powerless right now, as if I were a child again? Do I feel that my partner is treating me like a child or making me feel like a child?" Understanding why we feel the way we do is the first step toward resolving those feelings.

Recognize that your partner has a survival brain and a storehouse brain, too. If he or she is responding to you in a way that seems disproportionate and unreasonable, understand that there may be childhood pain, fear, anger, and resentment underneath it all. That surface issue ("You spent too much on that dress," "Why did you stay so late at the office?") may not be the real issue. It may just be a symptom of a much deeper emotional deficit ("I'm afraid of reliving the stress of my childhood, when my father went bankrupt," or "I'm afraid of being abandoned and alone").

You can also accept the fact that you both have unresolved issues from childhood. They may be huge and traumatic (such as abandonment or incest), or they may be comparatively minor—but they are there. Unresolved childhood issues create distortions in current relationships. Deal with them and discuss them openly with your partner. If necessary, get professional help. Once those issues are resolved, they lose their power to hurt you and your relationship.

Another thing to do is to make a commitment to growth in understanding. Commit yourself to discovering who your partner *truly* is. Replace that mental, symbolic caricature of your partner with his or her authentic reality. Find out what motivates, excites, and saddens your partner. Find out where those "landmines" of childhood pain lie. Find out what makes him or her feel afraid, angry, insecure, or anxious. Work together to replace images and symbols with truth and understanding.

Making a commitment to growth and maturity is another pointer for resolving today's problems today. Instead of making childlike demands on your spouse to meet all your needs, accept the fact that you are an adult. You have some needs that you may legitimately express to your partner, but you also have needs that you should seek to meet out of your own resources or out of your relationship with

God. "When I was a child," the Bible tells us, "I talked like a child, I thought like a child, I reasoned like a child. When I became a man, I put childish ways behind me" (1 Corinthians 13:11).

It's time to put away childish ways. It's time to put away the past and become conscious, aware, and proactive in the present. In the next chapter, we will explore ways to keep your relationship firmly anchored in the present.

TAKE ACTION
Questions of a Marriage

If you and your partner are answering these questions together, first write your answers down separately, then compare your answers— but remember to use covenant-love (see page 31) to deal with any disagreements! Use the information you gather from each other to better understand how each of you look at, and feel about, your love relationship.

1. What is your greatest fear in your marriage relationship?
   - abandonment
   - engulfment
   - invasion
   - Other_____

   How does that fear affect the way you interact with your partner?

2. What do you think is your partner's greatest fear in the marriage relationship?
   - abandonment
   - engulfment
   - invasion
   - other_____

   How does that fear affect the way your partner interacts with you?

3. On a scale of 1 to 10 (below), how would you rate yourself as a person who is honest and keeps promises?

$$1..2..3..4..5..6..7..8..9..10$$

Never keep promises / Sometimes / Always reliable

4. What is a specific situation in your life where someone broke a promise to you? How did that incident affect your ability to trust the other person? Explain.

5. Describe a specific situation in your life where you broke a promise to someone you cared about. How did that broken promise affect the relationship? Explain.

6. Describe a specific situation in your life where you experienced a greater sense of freedom as a result of binding yourself to a promise. What do you think was the source of that sense of freedom?

TWO

How
Do I Know if We're
Really in Love?

———————●————————————●———————

The worst relationship I ever saw was a "marriage made in heaven."

Nathan and Sarah had been married about a year. How did they meet? "God brought us together," they told me. They had met in the singles group at their church. They had a brief, whirlwind courtship and were married in the belief (verging on a religious conviction) that they were not only "in love," but they had been selected by God since before the beginning of time to be joined together in holy matrimony.

Yet, only a year after this "divinely appointed" wedding, they were at each other's throats. "I'm supposed to be the head of the household," said Nathan, "but Sarah won't respect my leadership. She spends money when I tell her we need to save. She won't let me watch football on Sundays because she thinks it's a sin. And she often refuses sex when I want it—she just tells me, 'Take a cold shower and pray about it.'"

"I've had it up to here with his so-called 'leadership'!" Sarah countered. "He's always bossing me around! He doesn't want a wife, he wants a little harem girl to cater to all his wants, but he doesn't care about my needs one bit!"

"Did you love each other when you got married?" I asked.

"Of course we did. God brought us together," they both insisted.

"Then where did the love go?" I asked.

There was a long, confused silence. "I don't know where the love went," Nathan finally said, "but it's gone. All the romantic feelings I had for Sarah were gone a year or two into our marriage. I don't feel anything for her now but anger."

"I keep wondering," said Sarah, "why God allowed us to feel such an intense love before our marriage, then allowed it to die afterwards."

The problem was that, for all their talk about love, Nathan and Sarah didn't know what love truly is.

THE TRUTH ABOUT LOVE

As both a noun and a verb, *love* is perhaps the most overused word in the English language. Most of our books, films, and plays are devoted to the theme of love. Roughly 95 percent of popular music either sings the praises or bemoans the pain of love. We invest a significant part of our lives and our energy searching for love. But, like Nathan and Sarah, few of us really know what love is.

Amazingly, the English language—which has more words and subtle shades of expression than any other language on the planet—offers remarkably little versatility in matters of love. Instead of giving us a spectrum of words to express the nuances contained in that little word *love*, our language gives us a spectrum of meanings and only one, poor, overworked word.

John "loves" Mary. Mary "loves" soap operas and John "loves" football. Their daughter Cindy "loves" Grandpa, but she also "loves" ice cream. Mary "loves" her job. She also "loves" God and "loves" her country. Oh, and she "loves" Matt Damon and Johnny Depp, too. The highest expression of human feeling is fast becoming just another four-letter word.

The ancient Greeks and Hebrews appear to have been wiser in matters of love than we are. They had many words for love, and each word had a specific connotation. The Hebrews used the word *hesed* to denote "covenant-love," a love that is rooted in loyalty and faithfulness to a promise or covenant. This form of love is expressed in commitment.

The Greeks had a parallel word for the Hebrew concept of *hesed*. Their word was *agape*. Although you find this word used only a very few times in classical Greek literature, it is lavished profusely throughout the Greek New Testament. *Agape*-love seeks the good of another person not because of emotional attachment or because that person has earned the right to be loved, but simply because a prior commitment (a promise) has been made. *Agape*-love does not derive from the fact that the other person is lovable or valuable. Rather, it actually creates value in the person being loved.

As you can see, there is no single word in the English language that corresponds to the Hebrews' *hesed* or the Greeks' *agape*. It takes a minimum of a sentence or two in English to convey what a single word instantly connoted in ancient times. That defect in our language is a cultural tragedy because our difficulty in expressing the concept of covenant-love cripples our ability to practice the concept in our everyday lives.

The usual connotation of the word *love* in our culture is synonymous with passion (*eros* to the ancient Greeks). *Eros* is a good word—and a good sensation—but it is not covenant-love. *Eros* derives its power and electricity from the object of that love. *Eros* says, "I love you because you are so lovable." Passion—the physical component of a couple's relationship—is the most exciting dimension of the relationship. It's also the most dangerous. Passion is highly possessive, an actual physical craving of two people for each other. Passionate *eros*-love leads to physical arousal and to the intense desire to unite with the loved one—a desire to penetrate and be penetrated. Passion develops quickly and is much like an addiction. Once a person becomes accustomed to a given level of passion, greater and greater levels of stimulation are required to produce the desired sensations of arousal and satisfaction.

A third kind of love is that which the ancient Greeks called *phileo*-love—friendship-love. This is the love of affection and tenderness. Like *eros*-love, it is rooted in emotions and in feelings.

But whereas the feeling of *eros*-love is one of intense attraction and desire, the feelings of *phileo*-love are feelings of fondness and of wanting to cherish and nurture another person.

All three of these loves—*agape, eros,* and *phileo*—must be dynamically present if a marriage relationship is to be healthy. Passion is essential: the two marriage partners must want each other and must physically bond with each other. Friendship is essential: the two partners must cherish, nurture, and protect each other. Unconditional *agape*-love is essential: the two partners must accept, forgive, and seek the best for each other, choosing to honor promises and commitments even when, emotionally, they want to escape the relationship.

Perhaps the best way to understand these three forms of love is to recognize that each form of love involves a different dimension of our humanness.

Form of Love: *Eros*
Dimension of Our Humanness: Body
Result in the Relationship: Sexual Satisfaction

Form of Love: *Phileo*
Dimension of Our Humanness: Mind/Soul
Result in the Relationship: Friendship/Intimacy

Form of Love: *Agape*
Dimension of Our Humanness: Spirit
Result in the Relationship: Fellowship/Commitment

Phileo and *eros* are both excellent forms of love, and both are necessary to a couple's relationship. But even *phileo* and *eros* together are not sufficient to keep a marriage intact over time. These feelings-centered forms of love need the added strength of committed covenant-love, *agape*-love, in order to endure. Feelings, unfortunately, have a habit of changing. But if we have *agape*-love, rooted in promise and commitment, we can go on loving even if the feelings subside.

"ZAPPED!"—THEN TRAPPED

Annie is getting married. Her fiancé is a handsome, successful young man named Walter. They are making plans to build a life together. Then one night, while Annie is driving alone and listening to the radio, she hears a caller on a late-night talk show. The caller is a lonely man, taking care of his young son all by himself after the tragic loss of the wife he deeply loved. He describes the magical, mystical kind of love he had with his late wife.

As Annie listens to the man tell his story, she realizes two things: she does not have this magical, mystical kind of love for her fiancé, Walter, and she is falling in love with an anonymous caller on a radio show. Problem: How can Annie, who lives in Baltimore, find this unknown man who lives in Seattle?

That's the premise of the film *Sleepless in Seattle.* The rest of the movie revolves around getting these two people—Annie Reed (Meg Ryan) and Sam Baldwin (Tom Hanks)—together so they can meet and fall in love. I "love" this film (there's that word again!). It's a funny, romantic, urban fairy tale. But I also believe this film could ruin a lot of marriages. Why? Because it promotes a hopelessly unrealistic image of love.

When Sam and Annie first meet face to face, their eyes lock and the air crackles with energy—not just sexual energy, but a spiritual energy. Here are two souls whom the stars have literally decreed should be partners for life! (Throughout the film, the stars are actually depicted in the film, astrologically arranging events to bring this man and this woman together.) Love, according to *Sleepless in Seattle,* is a kind of heavenly magic that zaps two people and inexorably draws them into a dreamy world of consuming passion and complete bliss. The perfect, just-right person for you is out there, says the film. Your dream lover's name is written in the stars, and if you want to live happily ever after, just keep searching until you find Mr./Ms./Miss Right.

Annie is a hopeless romantic who really believes that love can be just like a Cary Grant-Deborah Kerr movie. Movie-goers, in turn, are manipulated by *Sleepless in Seattle* into believing that love can be just like a Tom Hanks-Meg Ryan movie.

But love isn't about being magically zapped, nor is it about living happily ever after. It often feels that way, especially in the early stages of a relationship. The passion of *eros*-love feels not only sexual but transcendent, spiritual, and eternal. That's why the passion of *eros*-love has inspired so many films, books, and popular songs. That's why, for example, pop diva Mariah Carey sings about a "vision of love," a dream that she "visualized" and that "sweet Destiny" has brought into being a love "that Heaven has sent down to me."

The result of this kind of magical thinking about love is that people only feel they are "in love" as long as the passion, the magic, and the transcendent emotions last. As long as two people feel they are "made for each other," life is one big honeymoon. But as soon as this haloed image begins to fade and problems and practical realities begin to emerge, these two people with their Technicolor concept of love begin to think, "Hey, what happened to the magic? Oh, no, the magic is gone! I made a mistake! This person isn't my dream lover after all!"

It happens in every marriage, without exception: The day arrives when love's illusions are replaced by disappointing (and downright annoying) realities. When two people wake up and discover that they have not been magically zapped by "sweet Destiny"—and when they begin to feel more "trapped" than "zapped," they start to panic. All too often, this is the moment when one or both partners begin looking for a back door: desertion, separation, divorce, an affair, or even an "emotional divorce," in which both partners maintain the outward fiction of a marriage while living in emotional isolation from each other.

Real love is not about discovering that "dream lover" who is perfectly attuned to your soul. Real love is not about "two hearts beating as one." For better or worse, real love is about hard work and difficult adjustments.

DOES THE PASSION HAVE TO FADE?

Does all this mean that marriage is nothing more than a few months of passion and excitement followed by years of drudgery and toil?

No! The good news is that passion and excitement don't have to fade from a marriage! In fact, all healthy marriages are passionate marriages. I know couples in their seventies and eighties and couples who have celebrated golden wedding anniversaries who are still as passionate as many couples in courtship. The couples who manage to keep passion in their relationships are those who have learned that it takes covenant-love, *agape*-love, to preserve the ardor of *eros*-love.

When two people love each other in a committed way, faithfully keeping all of their marriage vows, they create a nurturing environment for passion. By *agape*-loving each other, they actually make each other more desirable as a source of passion, pleasure, and excitement. Why? Because *agape*-love creates value in the person being loved. *Agape*-love makes people loveable.

But how many couples go into marriage with this view of love? As a psychologist who has spent hundreds of hours doing premarital counseling, I've found that hardly anyone does. For almost every couple contemplating marriage, love is something that occurs in the emotions rather than the will. Each partner views the other as the only person in the world who can excite the senses and stir the hormones until Gibraltar crumbles into the sea. So one of my objectives in premarital counseling is to throw a bucket of cold water on those airbrushed romantic images.

Premarital counseling is different from every other kind of counseling I do. Why? Because couples usually don't feel a need for premarital counseling. They are not coming because they have a problem, so there is no sense of urgency. They are not motivated to listen to my counsel or even to honestly examine their own relationship. Rather, they come because they have been referred by their pastor as part of a requirement for a religious wedding ceremony. It's not easy to get through to people with stars in their eyes.

"What do we need counseling for?" they say. "We've found each other! What more is there to talk about?" So while I'm trying to talk to them about their issues, histories, values, personalities, and motivations, their minds are off dealing with the really important aspects of marriage: the color of the bridesmaids' dresses, the flowers, and the honeymoon arrangements.

"How do you two plan to get along with each other for the next fifty years?" I ask.

"Well," they dreamily reply, "that just falls into place. After all, we love each other! But can we hurry this counseling thing along, please? We've got to order the boutonnieres."

I'll let you in on a secret: the most important tool in a psychologist's black bag is anxiety. If people aren't anxious, counseling usually fails. A couple of starry-eyed young lovers aren't anxious about anything. But people who are anxious and upset are motivated to work and change and listen. So I usually try to stir up a little anxiety. I start by giving the couple a personality inventory, such as the Taylor-Johnson test, which reveals a lot about basic personality traits, beliefs, habits, compatibilities, and incompatibilities. After scoring the test, I may sit down with them and say, "It's clear to me that you two are looking at each other through rose-colored glasses. This tells me you haven't seen the real person you're marrying. This tells me you are each in love with an image you have invented in your own minds."

Sometimes I can cut through all the violin music that's playing in their heads long enough to get across what real love is all about: commitment, promise, sacrifice, hard work, patience, and adjustments. Unfortunately, many about-to-be-married couples aren't buying. They're convinced that they are really in love, and their love is the "real thing." Phil and Renee are a classic case.

MUTUALLY ASSURED DESTRUCTION

Phil was an over-the-road trucker. Renee was a graphic artist. As instructed by their pastor, they came to me for premarital counseling. They sat in my office, casting longing glances at each other, squeezing each other's hands, calling each other pet names. We did the Taylor-Johnson test and I learned that, in each other's eyes, Phil and Renee were more flawless than Ozzy and Harriet and more passionate than Romeo and Juliet.

Yet the test also revealed that they were unrealistic about each other, and they had a totally unrealistic view of love. They were as hopelessly mismatched as any couple I ever met. Moreover, they were both powerful personalities, accustomed to getting what they wanted on demand. I had a feeling that their first disagreement would look a lot like nuclear war: "mutually assured destruction."

I never got through to them, but they did their required three appointments, and then it was adios, sayonara, and happy trails. I was relieved to learn that they would be moving to the Midwest immediately after their marriage. When their passion disappeared and reality set in, I wanted at least six states between me and the war zone.

It's never too late to learn the real meaning of love. I have seen many couples learn about real love, covenant-love, in time to prevent lasting harm to their relationship. Real love doesn't just happen; it takes commitment and hard work. But if you are willing to do that work—the work of communicating honestly, resolving conflicts fairly, and adjusting to each other's needs—you'll make an amazing discovery: you and your partner will find something far better than "movie love."

You will discover a love that lasts a lifetime.

TAKE ACTION
Questions of a Marriage

If you and your partner are answering these questions together, first write your answers down separately, then compare your answers— but remember to use covenant-love to deal with any disagreements! Use the information you gather from each other to better understand how each of you look at, and feel about, your love relationship.

1. From what sources have you derived your conception of what "love" really is?
   • my parents and upbringing
   • movies, TV, books, and popular music
   • talking to friends
   • courtship experiences
   • the Bible
   • other sources: _____

2. On a scale of 1 to 10 (below), what role does *eros* (passion) play in your marriage?

    1 . . 2 . . 3 . . 4 . . 5 . . 6 . . 7 . . 8 . . 9 . . 10

Not important / Somewhat important / Very important

3. On a scale of 1 to 10, what role does *phileo* (friendship) play in your marriage?

    1 . . 2 . . 3 . . 4 . . 5 . . 6 . . 7 . . 8 . . 9 . . 10

Not important / Somewhat important / Very important

4. On a scale of 1 to 10, what role does *agape* (covenant-love) play in your marriage?

    1 . . 2 . . 3 . . 4 . . 5 . . 6 . . 7 . . 8 . . 9 . . 10

Not important / Somewhat important / Very important

5. Are you and your partner comfortable expressing the *phileo*-friendship side of your relationship? Do you enjoy spending relaxing and fun times with your partner? Do you share common interests and pastimes? Is your marriage partner also your best friend? (Note: We will explore the *phileo*-friendship aspect of your relationship in greater detail in chapter 10: "Why Can't We Seem to Get Close?")

6. Are you and your partner comfortable expressing the *eros*-passion side of your relationship? Are you comfortable touching and kissing each other? Are you satisfied with the frequency of your sex life? Are you satisfied with the performance of your sex life? Do your sexual expectations and your partner's sexual expectations match and complement each other? (Note: We will explore the *eros*-passion aspect of your relationship in greater detail in chapter 12: "How Important Should Sex Be?")

7. Do you feel spiritually close to your partner? Using specific examples and incidences (not just vague feelings), explain why or why not.

THREE

Why Do We Get Stuck on the Same Stuff So Often?

"It's the same stupid argument over and over," Martin complained. "It just takes different forms, that's all. For some reason, Lanie feels she has to continually attack my manhood!"

"Oh, puh-leeeze!" Lanie rolled her eyes heavenward. "Martin, why don't you just get over it!"

Instantly, Martin came unglued. "You see! You see! She did it again!"

"Did what?" Lanie fired back.

"You attacked my manhood!"

"Did not!"

"Yes, you did! 'Martin,'" he said, mocking her tone, "'why don't you just get over it!' It's sneaky, but that's what you're doing—trying to make me feel small, trying to make out that I'm some kind of wuss just because I don't like the way you always attack me!"

"It's all in your mind, Martin," said Lanie."I don't attack your manhood. Just because one time, I said—Oh, forget it!"

"No. Let's get it out and deal with it, Lanie. What about that time?"

"That was three years ago!"

Martin folded his arms. "I remember it like it was yesterday! I was at the grocery store, trying to do you a favor, doing your errand, trying to make you happy—"

"I asked you to pick up a few things at the store—some milk, some cereal, and a box of feminine pads. Three lousy items! For that, you had to phone me from the store and pester me with a lot of questions?"

"I wanted to get the stuff you wanted! I didn't know if you wanted whole milk or low-fat. I didn't know if you wanted the cereal with raisins or the cereal without raisins. I didn't if you wanted regular pads, maxi-pads, thin maxi-pads, or extra-ultra-mini-thin pads! I said, 'A man shouldn't have to make such decisions!' And what did you say?"

"Why do you have to drag this up?"

"You said, 'A real man doesn't have so much trouble making decisions.'"

"I also said I was sorry, didn't I?"

"Two days later! After you made a big deal about how I made you miss the most important part of your favorite TV show. I was doing you a favor, and you were attacking my manhood."

"Oh, Martin, if you could only hear how whiny you sound right now!"

"And you're doing it again right now!" Martin threw up his hands and turned to me. "See what I mean, Doc? The same stupid argument, over and over again!"

UNPACKING THE ISSUES

Why did Lanie and Martin get stuck on the same issues over and over again? In fact, why do *most* couples seem to have the same argument again and again, with only slight variations from fight to fight?

Once more, we are dealing with issues, motivations, and emotional symbols that operate at an unconscious level. We're dealing with unresolved feelings from childhood that come back in a disguised form to haunt us in our adult relationships.

Fortunately, it is possible to bring these hidden issues out into the open so they can be consciously examined, unpacked, and disarmed. The hidden engine that drives marital conflict can be shut down only when we begin to understand the maps, symbols, filters, frames, and postures we have accumulated in our storehouse brain. Every marriage is affected by these powerful symbolic forces, and until we understand them, they will cause old issues, old hurts, and old struggles to resurface again and again. In the following sections, we will look at each of these components of conflict.

MAPS

We all have mental "maps" in our unconscious storehouse. Without being aware that we are doing so, we consult these maps continuously on our journey through the landscape of relationships. Our maps are our perceptions, impressions, and conclusions about reality, based on our experience. We tend to confuse the map with the actual territory, thinking our *interpretation* of reality is reality itself.

Most of us draw up our mental maps on the basis of a fairly sketchy sampling of reality. If you go to a restaurant and have one bad meal, you will probably never go back. On your map of reality, you will write, *Bad food—avoid this place* over your mental image of that restaurant. It may in fact be a bad restaurant—or it may be a very fine restaurant that happened to serve one bad meal. But the map of reality you have drawn, based on your limited experience, identifies it as a "bad restaurant," period.

A map is a useful tool. Our maps show us how to act in any given situation. But when our map is wrong or when it doesn't match the territory—watch out! If our map of reality contains false notions about a given restaurant, there's little harm done. There are many other restaurants to choose from. But if our map of reality contains false impressions of our partner, the results can be catastrophic.

How do our mental maps affect our behavior in the real world? There is a three-step process by which each of us interacts with the world around us. Those steps are:

SEE ▸ INTERPRET ▸ ACT

We *see* and sample the world through our experience. Then we *interpret* that experience, give it meaning, place a frame around it, and draw our map. Then we *act* upon that interpretation; we chart our course and base our lives on the map that we have drawn.

Mental maps of reality are not always a bad thing. In fact, they serve a vital function, guiding us through the landscape of life, showing us how to behave in various situations. Our maps are unconscious tools, and we use them without even being aware of them. The more accurate our mental map of reality is, the more helpful a guide it will be in our lives. But if the map is inaccurate, we are much more likely to get lost in our relationships.

Unfortunately, we are rarely aware of these maps in a conscious way. We go through life on automatic pilot, controlled by the unreasoning, symbolic parts of our right brain rather than our thoughtful, analytical left brain. If we fail to periodically review and revise our maps, we will keep doing what we've always done—and we will remain stuck in our pain.

We all tend to assume that everyone else sees the world pretty much as we do and that there is a common agreement as to what constitutes "objective reality." In truth, no two people view reality in exactly the same way. We all perceive and interpret reality differently, and this interpretation becomes an integral part of the situation. Our interpretation of reality prompts our behavior in every situation.

Let's say I have just walked out of a movie theater late at night. I'm walking down a darkened street, heading for my car, when I hear footsteps behind me. I turn and see a strange man silhouetted against the wall. What will my next action be? It all depends on my mental map. If I have been mugged on a dark street before, if the movie I just watched depicted a street mugging, or if I have been reading a lot in the newspaper lately about crime statistics, then I'm likely to have a mental map in mind regarding strangers on dark streets: *danger!* I see the strange man, I interpret him to be a mugger, and then I act by running away as fast as my legs will take me!

Now, is the stranger really a mugger? Or is he a kind-hearted man who followed me out of the theater to tell me I dropped my wallet in the aisle? Clearly, objective reality and my mental map of reality could be two very different things. The map is not the territory. Reality and our interpretation of reality are not the same thing.

SYMBOLS

A major part of our mental map consists of symbols, which we have accumulated in our mental storehouse. These symbols have a strong meaning at an unconscious level of our minds. For example, these symbols may mean "love," "security," "control," "rejection," or "abandonment." An incident that is comparatively trivial to one partner may be powerfully symbolic to another.

For example, Ginny turns to Rob after dinner and says, "Can you help me with the dishes?" Rob replies, "No, not tonight." To Rob's amazement, Ginny explodes! Why? Not because the dishes were so important, but because they symbolized something crucially important in her mental map: *He doesn't care about me.*

Or consider what happens between Ginny and Rob the following Saturday: Rob grabs his keys, heads for the front door, and calls out, "Ginny, I'm going down to the hardware store to buy a shovel. I'll be back in a few minutes." Ginny responds, "Can I come, too?" She just wants his companionship. But Rob instantly becomes annoyed. "What's the matter?" he snaps. "Don't you trust me to buy something as simple as a shovel?" In his mental map, her request symbolizes an attack on his competency.

Our maps tend to magnify isolated actions and incidents into powerful, emotional symbols. A single word, a facial expression, or a gesture can suddenly take on an intense, crushing burden of meaning. Notice these two statements: "You disagreed with me today. You don't respect my opinions or my feelings." The first sentence is an observation of a comparatively common occurrence in all relationships—a minor disagreement. But the second sentence is a conclusion that supercharges the issue, giving it far more emotional energy than the situation demands. Here are some other examples:

- "You turned your back on me while I was talking. Why are you rejecting me?"
- "I just did something nice for you and you didn't acknowledge it. That means you are thoughtless and insensitive, and you don't appreciate me."

- "You were quiet at the dinner table tonight. Your withdrawal means you don't love me."
- "You interrupted me just now. You don't respect my feelings or value my ideas."
- "You want to be alone. You don't want me anymore."
- "You don't want sex tonight. You must think I'm unattractive and unappealing."
- "You were angry tonight. You hate me."
- "You criticized my cooking tonight. You think I'm a horrible person."
- "You criticized my driving tonight. You think I'm completely incompetent."

Our maps are created by memories. Past events have etched the emotional symbols onto our mental maps. Old images lurk beneath the surface of our consciousness, ready to distort present-day relationships with echoes of the past.

Josh's mother was a controlling woman who continually intruded on his life, made his decisions, and chose his activities for him. Now married, Josh goes ballistic any time his wife even makes a suggestion. Because some of his wife's traits unconsciously remind him of some of his mother's traits, his wife's mildest suggestions often symbolize his mother's control and disregard for his feelings. The more resentment he displays, the more she suggests that he needs to change his behavior, which in turn stirs up more resentment—a self-perpetuating cycle of conflict and distorted communication.

In another example, Elaine never felt loved and accepted by her father, an emotionally distant military officer who frequently expressed regret over having a daughter instead of a son to raise in the military tradition. Now married, Elaine constantly pursues her husband for affection and reassurance. Elaine's husband Roy finds her "clingy" behavior off-putting, so he retreats from her. "You come on too strong," Roy tells her.

The more Roy retreats, the more he reminds Elaine of her emotionally distant father. She becomes panicky and pursues her husband all the harder, and he retreats even more—a self-perpetuating cycle. In Elaine's mind, Roy's emotional withdrawal symbolizes her father's lack of love. She's not aware of the childhood source of her fear. All she knows is that she's terrified that she will be rejected by her husband, Roy. Ironically, her own behavior is driving Roy away.

Unresolved wounds of the past are invariably projected into the present. When there are unhealed wounds and unresolved conflicts dotting our mental maps, our storehouse brain attempts to work them out in present relationships. If our mental maps are inaccurate, then our behavior will tend to make matters worse, not better. In order to have healthier, happier relationships, we must bring our unconscious maps out in the open where we can consciously examine them and redraw them to better match the territory.

FILTERS AND FRAMES

How would you punctuate the following line? *that that is is that that is not is not is that it it is*

Properly punctuated, this seeming gibberish becomes a series of intelligible thoughts: "That that is, is. That that is not, is not. Is that it? It is!"

Or take this unpunctuated statement: *Woman without her man is a savage*

Who is the savage in that statement? It depends on how you punctuate it. This sentence could read, "Woman, without her man, is a savage." In which case, the woman is the savage. But the sentence could also be punctuated to read, "Woman: without her, man is a savage." Now it is the man who is the savage in this statement.

Punctuation enables us to make sense of an otherwise meaningless stream of words. Similarly, we "punctuate" our experiences in order to make sense out of life. The difference between the way we punctuate a sentence and the way we punctuate life is that in human experience, punctuation is entirely arbitrary and subjective.

Here's how punctuation works in a marriage: the wife says, "My husband is withdrawn." The husband says, "My wife is a nag." The reality is that when the wife nags, the husband withdraws, which causes the wife to nag even more, which makes him withdraw more. It's a classic case of chicken and the egg. Both share the same experience, but they "punctuate" it differently, they interpret it differently, and they make sense of it differently. Each side, husband and wife, has his or her own interpretation of the event.

This interpretive process is called "filtering" and "framing." When things happen in our lives, we don't attend to every detail of the experience. There is simply too much detail for our memories to contain. Instead, we filter, we pay attention to certain details, we combine bits and pieces of experience, and we ignore other details. Then—patching this filtered information together with the symbols and maps from our storehouse—we form our frame, our unique perspective on the experience.

Everyone's frame on any given situation is bound to be different. John and Jane, for example, go to a movie. They see exactly the same sights and hear exactly the same sounds. John hates the movie while Jane loves it. John says, "What a sloppy, sudsy bunch of mush!" Jane says, "It was so moving and full of emotion. This movie made me feel things I never felt before!" Same experience, same stimuli, completely different frames of the experience. Why? Because each person filtered the experience differently, according to his and her own map of reality.

During the courtship and honeymoon phase of a relationship, we place a golden frame around everything that happens. We highlight and magnify every wonderful aspect of our partner. We dismiss and ignore the little flaws and irritations in our partner's behavior, attitude, and mannerisms.

But as the newness of the relationship wears off and as we begin to accumulate more and more grievances and annoyances, we remove the golden frame and replace it with a grim, black frame. We highlight and magnify the flaws and irritations in our partner, and we dismiss and ignore the positive aspects. Her delightful little laugh becomes reframed as an annoying cackle. His clever gift for witty remarks becomes reframed as a lame, corny sense of humor.

"She's such a shrew." That was Eric's frame for his wife, Susan. Why did Eric view his wife as a "shrew"?

"Because she's always nagging me and ragging me in front of my friends!" he said. Oh? When does she behave this way?

"All the time!" replied Eric. Well, describe an incident of this behavior that happened in, say, the last week or two.

"Well, she. . . . You know, she always. . . It's kind of hard to think of a specific incident right on the spot, but. . . Oh, yeah, I just remembered one! The other night, we were at a Chinese restaurant with friends and she needled me about my tie right in front of everybody!"

Susan looked hurt. "I just said, 'Honey, you dropped a piece of mu shu pork on your tie.' I even offered to clean it off for you."

"Well," Eric responded sullenly, "maybe that's not a good example. But all our friends know she's a shrew. That's why they don't want to spend time with us anymore."

The truth is, many of Eric's friends were feeling uncomfortable around Eric, not Susan. They became embarrassed when he would lose his temper over some completely innocent remark that Susan made. Eric's frame that "Susan is a shrew" drove his behavior, but it was not the truth.

Yes, Susan used to have a habit of criticizing her husband in front of their friends. But she worked hard on this habit. Even though Susan's behavior changed, Eric's frame remained fixed. That's the problem with frames: once we hang a frame on a person, we rarely go back later to see if it still fits.

Frames and filters are necessary parts of our understanding of reality. However, crooked frames and clogged filters distort not only our view of reality but also our relationships. The only way to have a happy, healthy relationship is to continually check and recheck the way we punctuate our marriage experiences.

POSTURES

As a couple's relationship develops over time, both partners come to view each other from the perspective of their own maps, frames, and filters. They tend to narrow the definition of each other. Instead of getting to know each other better over time, there is a real danger that they will actually build up stereotypes and caricatures of one another in their minds. Each side forms assumptions and conclusions about the other that may or may not be true. As a result, each partner takes on a posture toward the other.

What is a posture? It is a position we assume toward our partner—or rather, the range of positions we take toward our partner. We do not assume just one overall posture toward our partner, but a variety of postures, depending on the given issue and situation. These postures change and shift over time.

When two people come together, they relate to each other in terms of two basic postures: the One-Up posture and the One-Down posture. Each of these postures is found in healthy couples, and each has its own risks and benefits. As these two postures are combined in different ways in a relationship, we are able to discern three patterns in the relationship: the Symmetrical Pattern, the Complementary Pattern, and the Reciprocal Pattern.

In a Symmetrical relationship, the postures and responses are similar. If one partner attacks (One-Up), the other counterattacks (One-Up).

In a Complementary relationship, the postures and responses are dissimilar. If one partner attacks (One-Up), the other retreats (One-Down).

In a Reciprocal relationship, the couple alternates between Symmetrical responses and Complementary responses, depending on the requirements of the situation.

Partner A	Partner B	Relationship
One-Up	One-Up	Symmetrical
One-Up	One-Down	Complementary
One-Down	One-Down	Symmetrical
One-Down	One-Up	Complementary

People relate to each other from different postures depending on the issue at hand. It's rare that a couple will always assume the same posture in every situation (although I've seen some extreme cases that certainly seem to be either totally symmetrical or totally complementary). The healthiest relationships are Reciprocal relationships, in which there is a balance of Symmetrical and Complementary dynamics. A relationship becomes unhealthy when it is regularly and typically One-Up/One-Up (Symmetrical), One-Up/One-Down (Complementary), One-Down/One-Down (Symmetrical), or the Flip-Flopped Posture.

In One-Up/One-Up (Symmetrical) relationships, both partners are engaged in a struggle for mastery. This type of relationship can take many forms. For example, one side may use bullying or intimidating tactics while the other uses scheming and manipulating. Both sides are attempting to initiate the action and neither will follow the other. Another form is when both partners are involved in business or professional life and the One-Up/One-Up competition may center on who has the most education, who has the best job, who makes the most money, or who gets promoted fastest. Unless the equality, dignity, and feelings of both sides are respected, the relationship is doomed to be unhealthy.

Another unhealthy relationship is the One-Up/One-Down (Complementary). Normally we think of the word "complementary" as a positive term, suggesting that one side makes up for what the other side lacks. But in the realm of postures, a complementary relationship is one where one side consistently has the most of the leadership role, respect, validation, and emotional energy while the other side has little or none. In these relationships, the energy consistently flows from one partner to the other.

Such was the case of Annie and Dave. Annie and Dave have been married twelve years. Living with a strong-willed wife and two strong-willed daughters, Dave has always been the "odd man out"—and the One-Down partner—in the relationship. Whenever Dave tried to discipline his daughters, Annie would intervene and correct him. Annie had veto power over all of Dave's plans and decisions. He might argue with her, but he invariably gave in when all was said and done. Annie could be harsh with Dave, but sometimes she would also mother him, coddling him and making excuses for his failures, comforting him when he became depressed.

Looking back into Dave's early history, we find a mother who dominated him and made all of his decisions for him. When Dave married, he permitted Annie to assume the role his mother once filled. Annie, who had been raised in a household with a weak, dependent father, was in familiar territory when she married weak, dependent Dave. And yet, deep down, she didn't want a man she could mother, but a man she could respect—and she was continually needling and prodding Dave in the hope that he would somehow rise to the occasion and become a "real man."

Here was a couple in which all the emotional energy (support, love, affirmation, consolation, attention, and encouragement) flowed in one direction—from Annie to Dave. She sensed his weakness and neediness, and she poured her energy into him—sometimes to protect and nurture him, sometimes to discipline and scold him, sometimes to prod him in the hope of making him strong and mature. Annie was in the One-Up posture (dominant and giving), while Dave was in the One-Down posture (submissive and receiving). The unconscious dynamic in this relationship was one in which Annie was the parent and Dave was the child.

A Complementary relationship—in which one partner consistently wields the majority of the control, leadership, initiative, and influence in the relationship at the expense of the other—is invariably unhealthy and painful for both partners. In fact, at this point in Annie and Dave's relationship, they were headed for divorce. Whenever I encounter a couple that is so unbalanced and where there is such a lack of mutual respect and power-sharing, I seek to intervene so that the couple can achieve greater equality and mutuality in their relationship. This is true regardless of whether it is the husband or the wife who is in the One-Up position. While there are different roles and different functions for the husband and for the wife, neither side should dominate or emotionally eclipse the other. The One-Down partner must be allowed to experience a sense of adequacy and respect in the family.

If one side is always the giver in the relationship, I have the couple consciously set aside time to allow the other partner to become the giver. If one side is always the leader in the relationship, I have the couple set aside specific areas where the other side takes leadership responsibility. Though these situations are forced and artificial at first, couples often learn and adopt the new dynamics as part of their way of relating to each other, and the relationship becomes more healthy and mutual.

One-Down/One-Down (Symmetrical) is one of the least common

postures I see in counseling. Here, both partners are waiting for the other to make the first move. There is no leadership, no initiation, and little apparent emotional energy. While there may be little conflict in such a marriage (since there is nothing in the marriage worth fighting for), there is little health in the marriage either. No one takes responsibility for the direction and emotional well-being of the family. No one initiates intimacy, conversation, sex, or even planning a vacation. Both sides need to become more assertive, more passionate, and more involved in the marriage relationship.

The last type of posture is the Flip-Flopped posture. This is when couples experience a situation in their lives that causes the postures in their relationship to radically change. This may be an illness, the loss of a job, a bout of depression, or some other circumstance. Fred and Becca are just one example of this kind of posture. Both Fred and Becca were professionals. Both had master's degrees in related fields and were working on doctoral degrees. Over the course of their eight-year marriage, they had constructed a healthy, functional relationship involving mutual respect and reciprocal roles. If there was any tilt at all in their postures, it might have been to give Fred a bit more responsibility in the leadership department since he was earning a bit more and was acknowledged by Becca to be more savvy and interested in the details of financial management.

But during their respective doctoral courses, problems arose. It's tough enough on a couple when one partner is pursuing an advanced degree, but it can be murder—in terms of stress and strain on the relationship—when both are pursuing the same goal at the same time. Because of some unexpected health problems and some difficulties with his doctoral research, Fred was unable to complete his thesis. While Becca was happily placing a new degree behind her name, Fred was becoming more and more depressed. Finally, he dropped out of the doctoral program altogether.

Fred's professional disaster had a profound effect on their relationship. Before, he had felt highly confident and competent. He had done a good job of responding to his wife's emotional, sexual, intellectual, and spiritual needs. Though their relationship was a mutual and giving one, Fred was frequently the (slightly) One-Up partner in the marriage.

But when he became stuck in his depression and self-pity, Fred suddenly became very needy. Fred was One-Down—big time! He expected all emotional energy to flow in his direction while returning no support or affirmation to his wife. Becca, meanwhile, was unaccustomed and uncomfortable in a long-term One-Up posture toward her husband. As time went on, she felt she could not single-handedly sustain the relationship. Without intervention, they would have ended up in divorce court.

THE KEY TO WHOLENESS: RECIPROCAL RELATIONSHIPS

When our storehouse is filled with distorted maps, frames, filters, and postures, what else can we expect but distorted thinking, perception, communication, and—above all—distorted relationships? Instead of reacting to what actually happens in the relationship, we react to what our minds tell us is happening. We become prone to such distorted thought patterns as:

- Tunnel vision—seeing only what fits our perspective while blocking out other input and information
- Overgeneralization—"She's *always* criticizing me." "He's *never* on time."
- Magnification—the exaggeration of the partner's behavior and traits, either positive or negative
- Polarized thinking—seeing everything in stark black-and-white terms. "Either you do things my way or we get a divorce."
- Biased explanations—automatically assuming the other person's motives are impure. "He's only being nice to me because he wants something from me."
- Negative labeling—"He's a bully." "She's a slob."
- Mind reading—"I know what he *really* means by that."
- Subjective reasoning—If one partner has negative feelings, he or she automatically assumes the other partner

is responsible. "I feel depressed; it must be because my husband is never home."

- Selective abstraction—taking an event out of context and arriving at the wrong conclusion. For example, a couple is at a dinner party. The wife relates a funny story about going to a restaurant, getting lost, and the food being bad; the husband becomes angry because all he "hears" in his wife's story is criticism of himself.
- Arbitrary inference—having a strong mindset and making negative judgments with little or no basis in fact. For example, a wife sees her husband sweeping the porch. He is thinking, "I have some spare time, so I'll help out a little." She thinks, "He's only doing that to criticize me for not keeping the house clean."
- Personalizing—believing that the actions of one's spouse are directed personally at oneself. "She's running the vacuum cleaner just to annoy me!" "He bought Diet Coke at the store just to let me know that he thinks I'm fat!"

These distorted forms of thinking will continually, repeatedly get us stuck in the same pointless conflicts and unproductive behavior patterns. By becoming consciously aware of the maps, frames, filters, and postures we use, we can correct our map of reality, readjust our frames, unclog our filters, and improve our posture. Then we can respond to our partner with love, clarity, and realism.

One of the most unhealthy and unhappy features of Symmetrical (One-Up/One-Up or One-Down/One-Down) and Complementary (One-Up/One-Down) relationships is that they tend to be static and self-reinforcing. These relationships do not grow. Unless there is conscious intervention, the only change these relationships experience is change for the worse. What, then, does a healthy relationship look like?

A healthy relationship is a Reciprocal relationship. In a Reciprocal relationship, both partners take turns in the One-Up and One-Down postures. Both partners get a turn at being the giver or the taker. Leadership roles are mutually agreed upon and periodically reassessed. Duties and chores are shared. Affirmation, encouragement, and emotional support are freely exchanged. As a result, the relationship changes over time; it grows in joy, maturity, and depth. Both partners experience fulfillment and a sense of adventure in a relationship because every day is a new and fresh experience, not just a numbing repetition of unhealthy patterns.

For some of us, simply understanding how these dynamics work in a marriage gives us enough insight to make constructive changes so that we can move toward a Reciprocal relationship. Others, however, need help in understanding their maps, frames, filters, and postures. Professional marriage and family counseling can be helpful in providing this personalized insight. A psychologist has many tools at his or her disposal that can help to bring hidden dynamics into view. For example, the Meyers-Briggs personality profile helps couples to see themselves and each other with greater clarity.

Once these hidden dynamics are brought out into the open, they begin to lose their power to lock us into repetitive patterns of conflict. Our sense of frustration and helplessness is replaced by a new and exciting sense of growth, healing, and progress toward wholeness.

In the next chapter, we will see how we can maintain the unity of a relationship while safeguarding our individuality.

TAKE ACTION
Questions of a Marriage

If you and your partner are answering these questions together, first write your answers down separately, then compare your answers—but remember to use covenant-love to deal with any disagreements! Use the information you gather from each other to better understand how each of you look at, and feel about, your love relationship.

1. Make a list in the table below of several issues that you and your partner regularly get stuck on.

2. After each issue, write what that issue seems to symbolize to you.

Issues we get stuck on	What this issue symbolizes to me
Accompanying my husband to the store and he says 'no'	Rejection

3. See if you can remember back to the early years of your relationship. Think of one or two characteristics that drew you to the other person (e.g., She was so willing to go along with my suggestions). Write the characteristic from the past in the left hand column and how you now see that same characteristic today.

Characteristic from the past	Way I know see this same charactaristic
He was so funny	He never takes life seriously

4. What posture(s) do you take with one another? Is the posture always the same (e.g., I always go One-Down to him, giving in on all occasions), or does your posture vary according to the situation?

My Posture	The Situation
I'm One-Down	We're trying to decide what to do for entertainment

FOUR

How
Can I Be Married and
Still Be My Own Person?

They used to call her Patti. Her given name is Patricia, and her friends all call her Trisha, but to her mother, father, and siblings, she has always been Patti. She came from an upper-middle class family and married a young man named Ethan. While it's true that "opposites attract," Patti and Ethan were so completely opposite that they had almost nothing in common. In terms of cultural background, socioeconomic status, religion, career goals, interests, values, and education, these two came from different worlds.

"I was attracted to Ethan because he was different," she recalls. "He was different from me, different from my background—and he was really different from my parents! They *hated* him! Ethan really set my dad's teeth on edge. The more my folks told me how wrong he was for me, the more I wanted to be with him. It was really a rebellion thing. My parents never let me have a life of my own, never let me make my own decisions, and never gave me any privacy or freedom. To me, Ethan symbolized freedom from my parents and my upbringing."

Unfortunately, the sense of "freedom" Patti sought by rebelling against her parents and marrying Ethan was short-lived. Soon after the wedding, she began to feel trapped in the marriage. "Ethan has no sense of responsibility about money," Patti says. "Give him a dollar and it just burns a hole in his pocket. He just has to spend it, even if we don't have it. He never stays with one job very long. So he goes out and has a great time while I get stuck with the bills, past-due notices, cutoff notices, and phone calls from creditors."

But that's not all. Patti discovered that by marrying Ethan, she had not gotten rid of one set of intrusive parents—she had actually added a second set. Ethan's mother would drop by unannounced, walking in the back door without even knocking. She would proceed to "hint" about how Patti should cook, clean, and care for her son Ethan (her "hints" were about as subtle as an M-1 Abrams tank).

What's more, Ethan's brothers and sisters were constantly borrowing things without permission—CDs and DVDs, clothing, and even Patti's car. "When I married Ethan," Patti seethed with bitterness, "I never imagined I was marrying his whole annoying family! We don't have any privacy—none!"

In their own way, Patti's parents were every bit as intrusive as Ethan's family. "I know that husband of yours doesn't provide for you," her father would say, pushing a wad of money into her hands, "so here's something to get you through the month." If Patti refused it, he would leave it in Patti's refrigerator or cookie jar when she wasn't looking.

Patti's mom, meanwhile, made a habit of stopping by every now and then to make sure that Patti kept a clean house . "You know how messy your room at home always was!" Patti's mother would run her finger across the woodwork, checking for dust. She would even rearrange Patti's furniture. No subject was off-limits to her mother's prying curiosity—not even Patti's sex life.

Through counseling, Patti discovered that a large part of her problem with parents and in-laws was that neither she nor Ethan had any boundaries in their family relationships. Both families considered Patti and Ethan as children who were just "playing house" and who hadn't really moved away from home. Since "we're all just one big happy family," Patti's parents and in-laws saw no need to give her and her husband any privacy. Patti and Ethan urgently needed to draw some clear boundaries between themselves and their families of origin.

AN EMOTIONAL FENCE

A boundary is anything that marks a limit or border. The term implies a restriction and a defensive barrier. Boundaries say, "Certain people, certain actions, and certain intrusions are not permitted here. This is who I am, this is how I should act, and this is how you should act toward me. Anything that falls outside of these limits is not allowed."

Boundaries draw clear, healthy distinctions between one individual and another. They are like fences with a gate, and you have the key to the gate. You decide whether to let anyone else into your boundaries or not. (For Patti and Ethan, these fences had fallen down and were being trampled on daily.)

An emotionally healthy couple is a well-bounded couple. Healthy couples are composed of people who have left their respective families and have established clear physical and emotional "out-of-bounds" lines between themselves and their childhood families—and between themselves and the rest of the world.

There's a beautiful paradox in the process of separating from family and forming boundaries: it is our separateness that allows us to fully enter into a close and permanent bond with another person. In a healthy marriage relationship, two separate, well-defined people enter into a relationship so intimate that it borders on emotional fusion—yet each remains a unique and distinct well-bounded individual.

Healthy couples are composed of people who have left their respective families of origin to form a new family unit. When children become adults, their parents must release old emotional claims on them. Unfortunately, parents often cling to their adult children out of a sense of insecurity. They sometimes project their own feelings of inadequacy onto the child. This, in turn, causes that adult child to be hindered in taking responsibility for him- or herself.

The adult child must step out of the parents' shadow and away from the parents' grasp. Unless both partners in a marriage are able to separate from their respective families, they won't be able to establish a healthy boundary around their marriage. Without healthy boundaries, couples are vulnerable to repeated interference from dysfunctional family members.

There are several different kinds of boundaries that contribute to a happy and healthy marriage relationship, including control, time, emotional, and financial. The first is control boundaries. As an adult, you have a duty and a right to make your own decisions regarding your career choice, your finances, your friends, your marriage, your leisure time, where you choose to live, and how you choose to live. If you like, you can ask for the opinions of other people regarding those choices, but no one—not even a parent—has the right to manipulate or control you. When other people try to control you, it's time to lay down some boundary markers.

Another boundary is time. If you have a parent who continually monopolizes your time, you need a firmer time boundary in your relationship. These boundaries may take the form of ground rules, such as "Mom, please call first before coming over to visit", "Dad, please call at certain times," "This isn't a good time to talk; could we talk later?" or "I only have ten minutes to talk right now." Avoid making phony excuses for getting off the phone. Just tell the truth, such as "Mom, I've got to get this laundry done. Call me tomorrow morning, and you can finish telling me about Aunt Sophie's funeral."

A person with healthy emotional boundaries is able to say to family members, "My sense of well-being doesn't depend on you, and yours shouldn't depend on me. I care about you, but I can't be the answer to your emotional needs. I can't allow you to intrude into the private places of my marriage." Family members who do not have clear boundaries between each other are said to be "enmeshed." They unconsciously consider other family members to be extensions of themselves. That is why they don't even realize that it is wrong to intrude on the lives of other family members.

Parents who are emotionally enmeshed with their children have trouble letting go. They don't recognize or respect the maturity and separate personhood of their children. At the same time, however, the adult children of enmeshed parents have some responsibility for the lack of emotional boundaries. Often, in the painful or confusing dealings they have with their parents, they unconsciously allow or invite intrusions because it is emotionally comforting to retain some vestiges of being a child.

How do you draw emotional boundaries where they have not existed before? You do this by communicating clearly and firmly that you need to have boundaries in the relationship. It's not necessary to say, "I need to pull back from you." Instead, say, "I want to improve our relationship. I think it would be healthy for us both to find more time for our own goals and our own interests. You and I have taken too much responsibility for each other's happiness and well-being, and I'd like to see us have a more balanced relationship. The fact that I feel a need for a greater sense of my own individuality doesn't mean I don't love you. Instead, I love you enough to be honest with you. This is going to be a great new chapter in our relationship."

If there are specific areas of intrusion that need to be confronted, address them firmly yet graciously. Stay focused on the issue and avoid accusing or bringing up side issues and past grievances. Be firm, yet positive, such as "Mom, I know you love me, but I don't want you to ask me questions about my sex life or to rearrange my furniture anymore."

The last boundary is financial boundaries. Money is a big issue in many families. Sometimes the financial needs of parents can strain the resources of their married kids, and sometimes it's the other way around. Parents occasionally use money (either consciously or unconsciously) as a way to control their adult children. Whenever you accept money from your parents, you incur a debt, and that financial debt makes you vulnerable to being emotionally manipulated or becoming emotionally dependent. A financial debt to a parent can diminish our sense of mature personhood and self-esteem, making us feel like children again.

One sign that we have achieved full and healthy adulthood is that our financial life is completely separate from that of our parents. This doesn't mean that one side can't help the other with an occasional gift or loan. But the normal situation is for finances to be completely separate—that means we must set financial boundaries. To have healthy financial boundaries means that we take personal responsibility; we don't expect our parents to continue providing for us. We prefer to put off purchases and scale back our lifestyle in order to live independently from others. Another way to have healthy financial boundaries is that we accept sacrifices in order to maintain our independence. If we find we are not succeeding financially, we take the necessary steps to cure the problem ourselves: an extra job, a tighter budget, cutting up credit cards, getting financial counseling, and so forth.

Remember, you have no obligation to impoverish yourself on your parents' behalf, nor are they obligated to impoverish themselves or endanger their retirement in order to bail you out. If you or your parents have trouble with spending, saving, investing, or debt, seek professional help and counseling. Your counselor can usually provide help or direct you to the resources you need. In the meantime, maintain clear, healthy financial boundaries between yourself and your parents.

AN ENCLOSURE OF SAFETY

Boundaries enable us to maintain our selfhood and individuality within a relationship. The boundary a healthy couple builds around their relationship serves a double purpose. First, it keeps some things out. Second, it keeps other things in.

A well-bounded couple recognizes that certain people, certain actions, and certain words are off-limits. A person with clear boundaries does not flirt or respond to flirting with people outside the relationship. A person with clear boundaries does not act disloyally toward a partner by criticizing, ridiculing, or embarrassing him or her in front of others. A person with clear boundaries does not reveal secrets of the marriage relationship—sexual intimacies, shame issues, and so forth—to other people (except, when appropriate, to a counselor).

Boundaries create zones of protection and safety within and around the relationship. Just as each marriage needs a boundary around it, so each partner within the marriage also needs a boundary around him- or herself, a sense of protected individuality and identity. Each person in the relationship must be able to say to the other, "This is who I am as opposed to you. These are my thoughts, my feelings, my desires, my goals." Personal boundaries within the relationship enable both partners to feel that their unique needs, abilities, and convictions are recognized and respected. These inner boundaries protect the identity, security, and individuality of both partners.

When you talk to a couple with healthy boundaries, you should be able to distinguish differences between them—different likes, goals, interests, wants, needs, ideas, convictions, and so forth. There are always real distinctions between people with healthy boundaries. If you find a couple consisting of two people who are virtually identical and inseparable in every way, then they probably don't have adequate personal boundaries.

When there are clear boundaries *within* the relationship, it's easier to build clear boundaries *around* the relationship. With a foundation of mutual trust and respect, both partners can work together to maintain a clear boundary separating their own marriage relationship from the outside world. In every healthy marriage, there must be boundaries *within* the relationship and boundaries *around* the relationship. Boundaries within the relationship protect the individuality of each partner. Boundaries around the relationship protect the integrity of the relationship against intrusion from the outside.

While it's important for each partner in the relationship to have individual boundaries and individual "space" within the relationship, it's perfectly normal for couples to experience an enmeshment-like fusion in the early stages of the relationship. In the emotional hothouse of the courtship and honeymoon phase, couples commonly experience such an intense emotional bonding that they tell each other, "You are me and I am you." Over time, however, the relationship cools down to a point where each partner sees the other as a distinct individual with unique differences and a need to be respected as a distinct first-person singular "I."

Though healthy boundaries between partners are important, it's possible to take boundaries too far. The couple that maintains separate finances and routinely takes separate vacations has erected walls of isolation instead of protective boundaries. Many couples live in a state of "emotional divorce"—they live under the same roof and eat at the same table, but they do not share any genuine intimacy. If you want to be married and still be your own person, you have to continually seek that delicate balance—two well-bounded individuals, distinct but not too separate, joined but not enmeshed, two partners unique in their intellect, creativity, ability, and viewpoint, but joined at the heart for life.

WHAT HAPPENED TO PATTI?

As we saw at the beginning of this chapter, Patti's parents and siblings used to call her Patti even though her given name is Patricia. Not anymore. "Patti" was Patricia's childhood name, but now she has put away childish things. She has drawn the clear boundary lines of adulthood in all the relationships of her life. To symbolize the new boundaries in her life, she has asked her parents to call her Trisha, just as her friends do.

When a poorly bounded man and a poorly bounded woman come together, they create a relationship in which there are continual encroachments and trespasses against each other's individuality. The relationship that results is painful and dysfunctional. But when a well-bounded man meets a well-bounded woman and they form a well-bounded relationship, they create a safe and nurturing enclosure where their relationship can thrive and grow.

The paradox of the marriage relationship is that our well-bounded separateness actually allows us to enter into a close bond with another human being. When two people join to become one, both become more fully themselves than when they were single.

In the next chapter, we'll explore ways that two separate, distinct individuals can learn to trust one another.

Questions of a Marriage

If you and your partner are answering these questions together, first write your answers down separately, then compare your answers— but remember to use covenant-love to deal with any disagreements! Use the information you gather from each other to better understand how each of you look at, and feel about, your love relationship.

1. Have you truly separated from your family of origin? How well-defined are the emotional boundaries between you and your parents? To find out, take the brief Emotional Boundaries Test below:

(Check true or false.)

T ☐ **F** ☐ I often feel guilty about spending too little time with my parent or parents.

T ☐ **F** ☐ When I see or sense that my parents are hurting, I feel responsible and feel I need to do something about it.

T ☐ **F** ☐ My parent or parents rely on me as a source of happiness and emotional support.

T ☐ **F** ☐ My parent or parents discouraged me from moving away from home.

T ☐ **F** ☐ My parent or parents frequently shared intimate confidences and secrets with me.

T ☐ **F** ☐ I feel closer to one parent than the other.

T ☐ **F** ☐ I have been my parent's best friend.

T ☐ **F** ☐ I often share information with my parents (about my social life, finances, career decisions, and so forth) that is really none of their business.

T ☐ **F** ☐ One of my parents preferred my company to that of his or her partner.

T ☐ **F** ☐ One of my parents told me or conveyed to me that I was his or her favorite or "special" child.

T ☐ **F** ☐ My parent or parents did not want me to date or marry.

T ☐ **F** ☐ One of my parents seemed overly interested in my sexuality and my body.

T ☐ **F** ☐ I often find myself explaining or defending my parents to other people.

If you scored four or more "True" answers in this quiz, then there is a strong likelihood that you have a problem with emotional enmeshment with your parents and need to define clearer boundaries with your parents in the emotional dimension of your relationship.

2. On a scale of 1 to 10 (below), how much do you allow other people to control you?

1 . . 2 . . 3 . . 4 . . 5 . . 6 . . 7 . . 8 . . 9 . . 10
Never   Sometimes   All the time

What is a specific area of your life which you have allowed someone else to control during the past week?

What could you have done differently to maintain a healthy boundary in that area of your life?

3. On a scale of 1 to 10 (below), how good a job have you done in separating yourself from your family of origin so that you can be your own person in your marriage?

1 . . 2 . . 3 . . 4 . . 5 . . 6 . . 7 . . 8 . . 9 . . 10
    Poor   Fair   Good

What is a specific area of your life which you have allowed a family member to intrude across the boundaries of your marriage in during the past month?

What could you have done differently to maintain a healthy boundary in that area of your life?

4. On a scale of 1 to 10 (below), how satisfied are you with the level of individual boundaries in your marriage? In other words, how satisfied are you with the zone of safety and secure personhood you have in your marriage? To what extent do you feel your partner respects your individuality—your thoughts, your personality, your beliefs, your convictions, your abilities, your feelings?

1 . . 2 . . 3 . . 4 . . 5 . . 6 . . 7 . . 8 . . 9 . . 10
Very Dissatisfied / Somewhat Satisfied / Very Satisfied

How would you describe the present state of the boundaries between you and your partner?

1 . . 2 . . 3 . . 4 . . 5 . . 6 . . 7 . . 8 . . 9 . . 10
No boundaries / Just right / Too much separation
(Enmeshed) (Balanced)   (Isolated)

5. In what specific area of your marriage do you feel you need stronger, clearer boundaries?

What would you like to do differently in order to maintain a healthy boundary between you and your partner?

FIVE

How Can We Learn to Trust Each Other?

● ⋯⋯⋯⋯⋯⋯⋯⋯⋯⋯⋯⋯⋯⋯ ●

Clarice was sick with worry. In twenty-two years of marriage, Bill had never been late without calling—until tonight. When she tried calling his cell phone, the calls went straight to voice mail; she had never been unable to reach him before. She had fed the kids their dinner and sent them to her sister's house for the weekend. While clearing the table, she planned Bill's funeral in her mind and tried not to picture him bleeding and broken in the wreckage of their car.

She was ready to start phoning hospitals and the Highway Patrol when she glanced out the window and saw his car pull into the driveway. Instantly, her mood swung from concern to anger. *He's got a lot of explaining to do!* she thought.

Clarice waited in the living room, glaring coldly, as Bill came in and shed his coat. "Why didn't you call?" she demanded.

"Don't start with me, Clarice," he shot back. "I'm not in the mood."

"Don't start with *you!* Bill, you're two hours late! Where have you been?"

"Driving around. Thinking."

"Thinking about what?"

Bill sighed and looked away, not meeting her eye. "I'm confused, Clarice. There's this woman—"

Suddenly, her anger was overtaken by panic. She felt an eerie sensation, like insects crawling up and down her spine. "A woman—?" she whispered hoarsely.

"Look, do I have to spell it out?" Bill said. "There's someone else in my life now. She makes me feel things I haven't felt in years. I've got to keep seeing her. The only thing is, I don't know what to do about you and me. Should we split up, make a clean break? Or should we stay together, at least until the kids are older?"

Clarice felt as if her heart was beating against her rib cage. She couldn't breathe.

Bill looked directly into her eyes for the first time. "Why are you acting so surprised, Clarice? You must have known this was coming."

Clarice could hardly find her voice. "I had no idea. . . . No idea."

This seemed to anger him. "Come on, Clarice! Our marriage has been disintegrating for years! How dumb can you be?"

As Clarice sat in my office and told me this story, she repeatedly went back to some words spoken twenty-two years earlier at a church altar. Those words were very important to her. "Bill promised," she said emphatically. "He said, 'Till death us do part.' When I asked him about that promise, he just shrugged and said, 'That was then.'"

Why should a few words said in a ceremony twenty-two years ago loom so important for Clarice today? Obviously, those words weren't important to Bill anymore.

It was Jonathan Swift who said, "Promises and piecrust are made to be broken." Swift's observation is some 250 years old, but it has not gone out of date. We have to ask ourselves, "What's so important about promises? Aren't promises made to be broken?"

TRUST: THE FOUNDATION OF A HEALTHY RELATIONSHIP

Like most people entering into marriage, Clarice never expected trust to be a problem. She assumed that her ability to trust her husband was just a natural part of their marriage vows. He loved her, and he had promised to be faithful; it didn't even occur to her to doubt his commitment. She *should* have been able to rely on his promise because that's what the marriage vows are all about: sealing a commitment, creating an enclosure of safety, and enabling a relationship to grow in an atmosphere of trust.

But Clarice's husband, Bill, placed a lower premium on trust and commitments. He saw the marriage vow as being a conditional contract rather than a sacred commitment. When conditions changed, so did Bill.

Trust is built upon commitment, upon the ability to make and keep a promise. Trust is the foundation on which a solid relationship is built, and it is also the protective canopy beneath which a relationship unfolds. The two crucial ingredients of trust are predictability and dependability.

Predictability plays a large role in trust. In order to trust one another in the marriage relationship, we must be able to foretell each other's behavior with a certain degree of reliability. For example, you must be reasonably assured that the person you married is not a bigamist, an axe murderer, a mobster hiding out in a federal witness protection program, a playboy (or playgirl), or an alien from outer space. You could not feel safe if your partner fell into one of those categories. You could not be sure what such a person might do to disrupt your marriage or your life.

Dependability also plays a large role in trust. In order to trust one another, you have to be able to rely on each other. You have to be assured that this person is available to you in times of need or crisis. You have to know that this person keeps agreements, respects boundaries, and cherishes you. You have to know that this person is able to make and keep promises.

The ingredients of predictability and dependability draw from past behavior to create certainties regarding the future. That's one reason why it's so important to know a person well before you get married. When you have a certain depth of experience with another person, you can rely on your knowledge of that person to predict how he or she will react under certain circumstances. There is a safe level of predictability and dependability in a relationship that has had time to grow rich and deep.

A DAMAGED CAPACITY FOR TRUST

Many people find it hard to trust even when their partners are perfectly trustworthy and committed to their marriage vows. I've counseled many couples whose marriages were being torn apart by suspicions and doubts—even when it was clear to me that the "suspect" was innocent. Unfortunately, some people come into a marriage with a severely damaged capacity for trust.

Adult experiences can play a major role in determining our ability to trust. Charlie, for example, continually watches Andrea. He closely monitors every check she writes, demands to know where she's been whenever she comes home a little later than usual, and even eavesdrops on her phone calls. Why? Because Charlie was married once before. His previous wife drained their bank account and carried on an affair shortly before she walked out on him. If he doesn't learn to trust Andrea—who has been perfectly faithful—he's going to tear their marriage apart with his suspicions.

In most cases, however, a diminished ability to trust is the result of childhood experiences. The ability to trust is learned in childhood, but some grow up with an impaired ability to trust due to hurts inflicted at an early age by parents or other primary caregivers (stepparents, foster parents, other adult role models and authority figures, and so forth). There are many childhood wounds that can hinder one's ability to trust. One wound is an enmeshed relationship with a smothering parent. Despite the stereotype of the over-involved "smothering mother," there are smothering dads as well. Smothering parenting produces a child who is overprotected and overindulged. Such children are never allowed to experience the disappointments, frustrations, and problems that are a normal part of growing up and developing character. They are never allowed to make their own decisions or to take normal childhood risks. They never learn to trust their own feelings and perceptions because Mommy or Daddy is always there to smother those feelings and reinterpret those perceptions, such as "You don't really feel sad; you just need a piece of pie or a new bicycle and you'll feel all better!" Smothering, overprotective parents often teach their children to view the opposite sex with suspicion and distrust, such as "Watch out for girls, son. They're just after your money" or "Just stay away from boys, honey. They only want one thing from you."

Another childhood wound that can hinder the ability to trust is an emotionally distant mother or father. Emotional distance can take many forms. Most alcoholic parents are emotionally unavailable to their children. So are most depressed or mentally ill parents. Some parents are emotionally distant from their children simply because that's the kind of people they are: cold, self-absorbed, and emotionally sealed off from others. A child can become hindered in his or her ability to trust simply through a lack of parental touch. Children need physical affection—a hug, a pat, a loving touch on the hand or face—from both Mom and Dad. When parents touch their children, they invite their children to emotionally bond with them. The parent who does not touch his or her child actually communicates a silent message of distance and rejection to the child. Though the child may have no conscious awareness that he or she failed to receive parental touching in childhood, the hidden and silent pain of that message of rejection will be carried by the child into adulthood as an inability to trust others.

An emotionally deprived childhood due to parental absence is another wound. A mother or father may be absent because of death, divorce, or illness. Children often take these events very personally and even feel responsible for the death, divorce, or illness of their parents. Sometimes there is anger, either open or repressed, that may seem illogical from an adult point of view, but which is very real to the child, such as "Why did Daddy get cancer and leave me to go away to heaven?" or "I can't forgive myself for causing my parents' divorce."

Sexual or physical abuse can also hinder the ability to trust. The most extreme damage to a child's ability to trust occurs when a parent, stepparent, or other caregiver (such as a teacher, camp counselor, baby sitter, or childcare worker) violates that child's boundaries by engaging in sexual abuse or violence against the child. It's the most egregious violation of trust imaginable. A child has a right to feel safe and protected, emotionally and physically. Abuse violates the core of a child's being, often making that child feel vulnerable and incapable of ever trusting again.

LACK OF TRUST = FEAR

People who are unable to trust are haunted by fears. The person who grew up with a smothering parent is haunted by a *fear of engulfment,* of being smothered by excessive, destructive "love." I place the word "love" in quotes because it is really not an authentic form of love, focused on the well-being of the other person. Rather, the smothering parent has a selfish obsession with the child, treating that child as a possession to be preserved in amber rather than a person to be respected, nurtured, and (when mature) set free to live as a separate and mature individual. "Love"-smothered children often grow up into adults who create distance between themselves and others. They are careful to keep other people from getting too close because they fear being smothered again.

Those who grew up with distant or absent parents are haunted by *fear of abandonment,* of being left alone. As adults, they often pester their partners for reassurance that they will not be abandoned. Those who fear abandonment are often attracted to those who fear engulfment and vice versa. This sets in motion a dynamic where one partner is continually seeking reassurances and trying to edge closer to the other partner; that partner, meanwhile, is wary of engulfment. One side advances, the other retreats, the one side advances even more aggressively, the other side retreats even more frantically, and the fears on both sides are stoked to a dangerous pitch.

Those who grew up with abusive parents are haunted by a *fear of invasion*—either sexual invasion or violent invasion. They live in fear of the dangerous or unpredictable behavior of others.

The key to resolving all these fears, of course, lies in rebuilding broken trust. Once trust is cemented into a relationship, those fears evaporate.

HOW TO BUILD
(OR REBUILD) TRUST

As we have already seen, people tend to unconsciously use the marriage relationship as a place to work out the unresolved conflicts of childhood. So, if you had an emotionally smothering parent, a distant or absent parent, or an abusive parent, there's a good chance you will seek out a partner who symbolically represents that parent. In time, the pain of the marital conflict (which is largely a replay of childhood pain) will become so intense that you will take action to end the pain. For example, you might choose to read a book on marriage, such as this one, hoping to gain some useful insights. You might also choose to seek marriage counseling, hoping that a counselor can resolve the problems (or at least point the way to a resolution). You could even end the relationship—a very common approach, unfortunately, especially among those who do not know how to break the cycle of conflict or who do not want to take on the hard (but rewarding) work of making the relationship healthy.

So what's the answer? What can we do to build or rebuild trust in a relationship? How can we put an end to fears and insecurities—both those that arise from childhood and those that stem from adult experiences?

First, both partners must decide that they want to trust and be trusted. A willingness to trust another person cannot and should not be built upon a wish or a whim; it must be built upon the reality that the other person is trustworthy.

Second, both partners should make sure that old issues and wounds are flushed out and dealt with so they can no longer hinder the present relationship. The partner who is haunted by fears of engulfment or abandonment, or who was raised by smothering, distant, absent, or abusive parents, should deal with those powerful emotional issues. That person needs to resolve old hurts and forgive the offending parent in order to get on with life. Professional counseling may be required in order to gain the insights and healing to resolve those issues.

Third, both partners should recommit themselves to the original promise they made on their wedding day. Moreover, both partners should commit themselves to becoming people who are uncompromisingly truthful and who make and keep promises. Truthfulness goes hand in hand with trustworthiness and reliability. If we are not truthful, trustworthy, and reliable, we will not be people who keep promises, and we will not be people who can be trusted. A promise is framed in words, and in order for the promise to be trustworthy, our words must be backed up by consistent, honest behavior.

Let's face it: honesty isn't easy. In *The Day America Told the Truth* (New York: Prentice Hall, 1990, p. 45), James Patterson and Peter Kim reported that fully 91 percent of respondents said they found it hard to get through a single week without lying; only 31 percent said that they believe that honesty is the best policy. You may identify with those results.

So what can we do to build trust and to become more trustworthy people? What are some practical, workable steps we can take toward becoming people who make and keep promises?

MAKING AND KEEPING PROMISES

First, let's take a look at what a promise really is. A promise is a declaration of intentions. It's a statement of assurance regarding what one will or will not do. A promise looks to the future and is intended to overcome the unpredictability of tomorrow. Promises reach ahead in time to create certainty and trust.

We make promises in every arena of our lives, in even the most mundane circumstances and transactions. Unless certain assurances are in place in our business, social, and marital relationships, chaos results. On any level—personal, social, business, or governmental—the more that's at stake in a relationship, the more formal the promise must be. In our own culture, the solemnity of a promise ranges from a casual statement ("Hey, no problem, consider it done") to a handshake to a sworn oath to a written contract. Promises are a necessary part of our lives for three fundamental reasons.

The first reason is that human society is impossible without promises. Promises bind us together. Without promises, all human relationships would instantly dissolve. As we look around us, it seems society is unraveling right before our eyes. The reason? Fewer and fewer people place a premium on keeping promises. Why do we see such growth in the number of attorneys in our society? One reason is that the precious commodity of trust is deteriorating in our society. As fewer and fewer people demonstrate a commitment to keeping their word, you need more and more attorneys to enforce covenants.

The commitment of a promise is foundational to a marriage. A strong marriage bond is foundational to a family. The family is foundational to the community, to the nation, and to the society at large. When the promise that binds and secures the family begins to crumble, it threatens all of our other institutions with collapse as well, for they are supported on the foundation of the family.

Another reason that promises are a part of our lives is that human identity is impossible without promises. We derive much of our sense of who we are from the promises we keep. People don't exist in a vacuum, but are interconnected by a network of relationships. We are defined by our relationships, and our relationships are largely defined by our promises and commitments. Other people understand who we are by the promises we keep—or *fail* to keep.

When a person demonstrates integrity by making and keeping promises, he or she gives a reason for us to have confidence in that person's reliability. We learn that this is a person we can trust. An antisocial personality is, by definition, a person who cannot keep promises. Antisocial people ignore legal, financial, social, and family obligations. They are totally untrustworthy because trust is a by-product of promises made and kept. They break relationships and bleed society. The more people demonstrate a willingness to disregard promises, the faster society weakens and dies.

The last reason we need promises is that human freedom comes alive within the confines of a promise. Like most deep truths, this one comes wrapped in a paradox: "If I bind myself to a promise, I actually set myself free." At first glance, that sounds like nonsense. Most people see "freedom" as the state of having no limits or rules. Obligations make us feel like slaves, so many people simply shrug them off. In reality, however, the boundaries of a promise give us the freedom to truly be ourselves. A network of promises, faithfully kept, delineates the boundaries of the playing field. The game is no fun to play unless we know the rules. The game isn't even comprehensible unless we know where the yard lines, sidelines, and goal lines are marked off.

True freedom is not the absence of a master, but is having the right master. The anti social, promise-breaking people are not people without a master, but people whose master is their animalistic self. They are slaves to to his most basic drives and impulses and has little true freedom or intentionality in life. On the other hand, people who are committed to making and keeping promises have the power to set a course in life and consciously stick to it.

Lies and broken promises destroy trust, generate fear, drive marriage partners apart, and shatter the foundations of the relationship. If you find it hard to be truthful and to make and keep promises, here are some practical suggestions:

- Every morning, commit yourself to being a truthful, trustworthy person throughout that day. Make your commitment to truthfulness one day at a time. Commit yourself to a "zero-tolerance" policy toward dishonesty in your life.
- Seek God's help. In prayer, ask God to convict you whenever you are on the verge of telling even a "little white lie."
- Become involved in an accountability group, such as a small group Bible study, a support group, a men's or women's fellowship group, or a small circle of trusted friends. Find a group of people who believe as you do, who struggle in some of the same areas you do, and who truly want to live lives of honesty and integrity. Hold each other accountable on a regular basis (preferably weekly). Share the fact that you struggle with being honest and trustworthy, and ask your friends in the accountability group to check in with you on a regular basis and ask you tough questions about your progress in that area of your life.

The marriage commitment binds two people together in a relationship, making them feel safe and protected. When we make and keep promises, we declare ourselves to be reliable and unchanging, even in the face of unpredictable events and circumstances. We slay fear whenever we generate trust. We build a healthy, durable relationship that can last a lifetime.

In the next chapter, we will examine the issue of expectations in marriage and answer the question, "What do I have a right to expect from my partner?"

TAKE ACTION
Questions of a Marriage

If you and your partner are answering these questions together, first write your answers down separately, then compare your answers—but remember to use covenant-love to deal with any disagreements! Use the information you gather from each other to better understand how each of you look at, and feel about, your love relationship.

1. Find a quiet place and relax. Let your mind drift back to your early childhood. Picture the house you lived in, the various rooms—your bedroom, the kitchen, the living room, the back yard. Who are the people you see there? What would you like to say to them? What do you wish they had given you that you never received from them?

    Write your answers down or speak them into a tape recorder. Describe your feelings and your thoughts.

2. Think back to a painful episode in your childhood. What feelings did you experience at the time?

    What feelings do you feel now as you think about that situation?

3. Recall a recent struggle or argument with your partner. What feelings did you experience at the time?

   What feelings do you feel now as you think about that situation?

4. What contrasts and similarities do you see between the two situations—the episode of childhood pain and the recent episode of marital conflict?

5. Relax again. Picture the house you live in today. Picture the various rooms of your married life—your bedroom, the kitchen, the living room, the back yard.

   Are you happy in this house? If not, why not? What do you lack to make you happy? In other words, what are your emotional needs which are currently going unmet?

6. Picture your partner. What would you like to say to him or her? What do you wish your partner had given you that you have never received?

7. Share your impressions and feelings with your partner. Then, listen to your partner's impressions and feelings. What did you learn about your partner's past history and present feelings that you never knew before? How has your image of your partner changed as a result of this exercise?

SIX

What
Do I Have a Right to Expect
From My Partner?

●━━━━━━━━━━━━━●

"We've been married six years," Jay said in exasperation, "and I still don't know what Shannon expects of me. Take last month. We were on vacation, having the time of our lives on St. Croix. We had saved for years to take a Caribbean vacation, and it was finally happening. Everything was perfect—the flight, the hotel, the beach, the food, the weather, everything.

"Then, during the last three days of our stay, something went wrong. Shannon started giving me the silent treatment—answering in words of one syllable, if at all; sitting through a fabulous dinner without saying a word; and giving me icy stares. And whenever I tried to find out what was bugging her, she'd just say, 'Nothing,' but she said it in that tone that means, 'Figure it out for yourself, stupid!' I finally decided to do my best to ignore it and wait for her mood to blow over. It eventually did—about a week after we got home! No matter what was bothering her, she should have been willing to talk about it. Giving me the cold shoulder was just plain stubborn and selfish."

"Stubborn!" Shannon exploded. "Selfish! What about you, Jay?"

"Well, what about me?"

"I waited and waited for you to apologize and you never did."

"Shannon, I would have *loved* to apologize! I begged you to tell me what I did wrong so I could apologize! But you refused to tell me!"

"You knew what was bothering me!"

"I didn't!"

"You mean to tell me you don't remember telling me I was fat?"

For a moment, Jay was completely speechless. "Shannon, what in the world are you taking about? I never said you were fat!"

"Oh, yes you did, Jay, and you remember it as clearly as I do!"

"Shannon, I don't remember any—Oh, wait a minute!"

"Ah-hah!"

"Do you mean out on the beach, when I asked you about the swimsuit?"

"Don't remember, eh? You pointed to that sleek, slinky Vogue model in the white two-piece and said, 'Why don't you look like that anymore?'"

"I did not! I said, 'You have a bathing suit like that at home. Why don't you wear it anymore?' I wasn't implying you were fat!"

"Same thing."

"It is not! My gosh, is *that* what this is all about?"

That's what it was about, all right. And Shannon's expectation was that Jay should know—as if by mental telepathy—why she was angry and what he should do to make up to her. Jay and Shannon had stumbled into one of the most common pot holes of marriage: hidden expectations.

MAINTAINING CLEAR EXPECTATIONS

We all have expectations of our marriage partners. Some are up-front and on the table. These are *spoken expectations*. Examples of spoken expectations include: "I'd like you to be more friendly and outgoing when my parents come to dinner." Or, "I'd like you to take out the trash and clean the bathrooms once a week without being asked."

But many of our expectations are *unspoken expectations*—the kind that Shannon had toward Jay. These are much more difficult to deal with than the spoken kind because people are not mind readers. Some examples:

> "If he loved me, he'd know I want to go out to dinner tonight."
>
> "I shouldn't have to tell her what I want. If she doesn't know after twenty years of marriage, then she just doesn't care."
>
> "I want him to be able to enjoy all the things I do, and as much as I do. I mean, he should want to share these interests with me. Is that too much to ask?"

When these expectations are not expressed verbally and clearly so they can be discussed and negotiated, the stage is set for conflict because one way or another, these expectations *will* be expressed. They'll most likely be expressed in a destructive, hostile way: the "silent treatment," subtle digs and sarcasm, open attacks and criticism, or hostility that is "stuffed" until it explodes without warning.

Uncommunicated, unrealistic, and unreasonable expectations are dangerous to a relationship. These expectations lurk just below the surface—a minefield of hidden agendas that the other partner finds impossible to fulfill or even understand. Until these agendas and expectations are forced to the surface, they will continue to create wariness, distrust, and open conflict in the relationship.

Our goal should be to *identify* those unspoken expectations and *speak* them. Many people, for example, have unspoken expectations about sex. They find it embarrassing to talk openly about what they would like their partner to do during lovemaking. As a result, many people end up thinking, "If he (or she) really cared for me, I wouldn't be lying here feeling hurt and unsatisfied." It would save so much unhappiness if they would turn their unspoken expectations into spoken requests: "I'd like you to take sex slowly and gently. I want you to spend time holding me and talking before the lovemaking begins."

In the case of Shannon and Jay, Shannon eventually did give voice to her unspoken expectation as the two of them sat in my office. But in many cases, these unspoken expectations *never* get spoken, and the partner in the relationship never gets a chance to learn what is expected. The relationship becomes a series of bewildering conflicts, and the partner is left wondering, "What have I done this time?"

UNCONSCIOUS EXPECTATIONS

In addition to spoken and unspoken expectations, there is a third class of expectations: unconscious expectations. These are the most difficult to deal with. Our unconscious expectations are tucked away in our storehouse brain.

For example, without even realizing it, you may have entered into marriage in the belief that your partner would meet all your emotional and sexual needs, provide you with non stop intellectual stimulation and excitement, provide for you, cook for you, maintain your house for you, build up your ego, and be patient with you, and on and on. It was to obtain all these attributes that you selected your partner because these attributes represented your image of what a partner is supposed to be.

Over time, however, you discovered that your partner behaved in ways that did not conform to that idealized image in your mind. You became frustrated, impatient, and angry when the reality of your partner contradicted your unconscious expectations of how he or she was to behave.

Meanwhile, your partner has been undergoing a similar process of disillusionment about you, and the stage is set for conflict. Because neither of you fully understands why you are frustrated with each other—your expectations are, after all, unconscious—you continually find yourself in conflict for seemingly irrational or trivial reasons.

Many unconscious expectations we have are simply the baggage we carry into the marriage from our family of origin. Tim's dad always ordered Tim's mom around, and she always accepted this treatment and scurried around, trying to make the old man happy. Now Tim is married, and he can't understand why his wife stands up to him and says "No!" when he gives her an order. Tim is convinced there's something wrong with his wife. It never occurred to him to consider that maybe his unconscious expectations are out of whack and that he has brought certain assumptions into the marriage that are simply not valid.

Barry comes home from work and talks about his problems at the office. Renee listens patiently as Barry talks—then she begins suggesting solutions to his problems. Barry gets aggravated. "Stop trying to fix my problems!" he growls. "I can run my own life, thank you very much!" Renee is bewildered. "I just wanted to help," she laments, very hurt, "like my mom always helped my dad!"

What Renee doesn't realize is that her parents ran a mom-and-pop store together, so her mother was her father's business partner. Naturally, they would discuss business problems together. But Barry sees Renee's offer of solutions to his problems as interference in his business life. He wants to be able to share his struggles at the workplace, but he wants to solve his problems on his own.

Unconscious expectations are often conflicting and inconsistent. For example, you may want your spouse to become more independent and assertive—yet you become frustrated when your spouse holds views that conflict with yours. The inconsistency in your expectations may not even be apparent to you until it is pointed out.

MONITOR AND RECALIBRATE

The goal of an emotionally healthy couple is to continually bring hidden expectations out into the open, to make sure that all unspoken expectations are spoken, and that all spoken expectations are fairly and mutually negotiated between both partners. Here are some suggestions for monitoring and recalibrating your own and your partner's expectations:

- Set aside time on a regular basis or as the need arises to communicate honestly and openly about your mutual expectations. It's best not to attempt this immediately after a conflict since the act of discussing expectations can be stressful and could renew the conflict if tensions are still running high.

- Practice being a good listener. When your partner proposes an expectation that you find unacceptable, avoid immediately countering or objecting to that expectation. Instead, consider if this expectation is reasonable or unreasonable. Can it be modified to the satisfaction of both parties? Can an alternative be found?
- When stating your expectations, use "I" statements—"I need more time to myself," "I want you to be more romantic," or "I would like you to help more with the children." Avoid "you" statements, which are threatening and confrontational—"You need to give me more space," "You need to be a better lover," or "You need to be a more involved parent." A "you" statement sounds accusatory, and it immediately puts the other person on the defensive.
- Consider writing out a "Contract of Expectations" between yourself and your partner. Give the contract an expiration date—say, six months or a year away. Then, on that expiration date, come together and renegotiate the deal. A contract may include some or all of the following:

1. A statement of mutual faithfulness, devotion, fidelity, and support.
2. Spiritual expectations: "I expect Joe to lead our family in evening prayer on a consistent, nightly basis," Or "I expect Sandra to support me as I struggle to launch this new business."
3. Emotional expectations: "I expect Sandra to treat me with respect, without name-calling or criticizing me, either in private or in front of the children," or "I expect Joe to turn off ESPN every night at nine so I can have twenty minutes to talk to him about things that are important to me."
4. Sexual expectations—including the recognition of needs—a goal for frequency (if frequency has been a problem), and steps for improvement or exploring new sexual techniques.

5. Practical expectations, such as household chores, taking care of the children, finances, and so forth. Sometimes, in the process of negotiating our expectations, we begin to see that some of our expectations are not realistic. So, in the process, we discard some expectations, we modify others, we make trade-offs and compromises, and we mesh our expectations with those of our partner. The result is a mutually satisfying, stable relationship that can grow and thrive over the coming years.

In the next chapter, we will discover why marriage relationships change—for better or worse—over time.

TAKE ACTION
Questions of a Marriage

If you and your partner are answering these questions together, first write your answers down separately, then compare your answers—but remember to use covenant-love to deal with any disagreements! Use the information you gather from each other to better understand how each of you look at, and feel about, your love relationship.

1. How open are you with your partner? In a few sentences, describe the areas of your life where you have maintained open, clear communication with your partner.

2. How has your partner disappointed you in the past few weeks? Refer to a specific situation or situations.

   Now ask yourself: Have you openly communicated your expectations to your partner regarding that situation where he or she disappointed you?

3. In this chapter, we have seen three kinds of expectations: spoken expectations, unspoken expectations, and unconscious expectations. Below is a chart on which you

may list your expectations of your partner and identify them as either spoken or unspoken (we will deal with unconscious expectations in the following exercise). Here are some examples of expectations to help jump-start your thinking:

- "I expect my partner to meet all my emotional needs. Unspoken."
- "I expect my partner to help get the kids washed and dressed on Sunday mornings so we can get to church on time. Spoken."
- "I expect to have great sex with my partner every day. Unspoken."

Husband's Expectations	
Expectation	Spoken or Unspoken
1.	
2.	
3.	
4.	
5.	
6.	
7.	

Wife's Expectations	
Expectation	**Spoken or Unspoken**
1.	
2.	
3.	
4.	
5.	
6.	
7.	

4. But what about unconscious expectations? How do we become aware of the expectations we have that we don't even consciously know we have? The following exercise is often very helpful in bringing people's unconscious expectations out into the open.

Take a sheet of paper and write a few paragraphs entitled "The Ideal Partner." Write quickly, and write what comes easily to mind. Allow a limited amount of time to do this exercise—say, five minutes—and don't mentally "edit" as you go. Just let it flow out of you, honestly and spontaneously. Be specific, not general. When you are finished, you will probably be surprised at the all the unconscious expectations you have already placed on your partner. Finally, ask yourself, "How many of these expectations are reasonable? How many should I discard? How many should I clarify? How many should I turn into open, clear spoken expectations?"

SEVEN

Why Are Things Different Than When We First Got Married?

<hr />

"Karl tells everyone we have the perfect marriage," Glee says, her eyes red rimmed and puffy. "I look around at our lives and think, 'What marriage?'"

She falls silent for several long seconds, gathering her thoughts. Then she explains, "Here we are in our early fifties with all this time on our hands—time we could be spending together. After all, Karl sold the hardware business and retired early, and I'm not working outside the home. We could be doing things together. We could be going places. We could just sit and talk like we used to.

"We used to dream about this time in our lives. He always planned to build up the business to a point where he could sell it at a big profit—then he'd retire and we could do all the things we dreamed of. Well, the dream has come true, and I've never been more miserable.

"It's not like we live separate lives, exactly. We eat together, we sleep together, we take trips and vacations together, we have sex—two, three times a week, in fact. His lovemaking technique is good. But I feel like our sex life has become mechanical—he does what has always worked. It's not an act of intimacy; it's just one of those things that has to be taken care of, like brushing your teeth.

"We never really talk anymore. Not like we used to. Not about feelings. Not about hopes and dreams and what we want out of life. If I try to engage him in conversation, he answers in monosyllables and finds some excuse to cut off the conversation. We don't fight. We don't argue. He just has his life—his friends, the golf course, the lodge—and I have my life, such as it is.

"Every day, I wonder, 'What happened to us?' I don't understand it. Why does a relationship change so much over the years? Why are things so different from when we first got married?"

Glee asks questions that many people ask. They can be very painful questions.

You are not the same person you were yesterday or ten years ago. Neither is your partner. We sometimes assume that two people who find each other and love each other ought to be able to come together as husband and wife, and everything should click into place automatically. Many people assume that, after an initial settling-in period, conflicts should smooth out, intimacy should deepen, the friendship should strengthen, and things should get better and better with time.

The fact is that the marriage relationship is a very complicated transaction at the beginning, and it remains a complicated transaction throughout its various stages.

THE SEVEN STAGES OF A MARRIAGE

Every marriage is as individual as the two people who make up that marriage. Yet there are also certain features and stages of marriage that are common to virtually all marriages. Because couples are constantly growing and changing—both as individuals and as a unit—it's important for every couple to consider where they are in life's journey. By understanding the pressures and stresses that are common to each of these stages, a couple can better respond when these natural pressures and stresses arise. The seven stages of marriage are:

Stage 1: Courtship
Stage 2: Two Become One
Stage 3: Two Become Three

Stage 4: The Children Go Off to School
Stage 5: Mid-Life
Stage 6: The Empty Nest
Stage 7: The (Supposedly) "Golden" Years

Of course, not all marriages follow these chronological stages with precision. These stages are sometimes skipped or reshuffled, especially in remarriages, blended families, couples without children, or couples where one partner is significantly older than the other. But most couples will recognize the general outline of the chronological development of their relationship in these seven stages. Let's take a closer look at each one.

STAGE 1: COURTSHIP

Marriage begins with separation—the separation of parent and child.

As a child matures, his or her parents gradually turn over more and more freedom and responsibility to that child. In time, the child reaches young adulthood and is ready to separate from his or her family of origin, find a partner, and build a new family unit.

Upon leaving the family of origin, an emotionally healthy young adult has established a strong sense of self, a sense of boundaries, a sense of "this-is-who-I-am." Now he or she is ready to develop a deep and intimate relationship with another human being. This person goes out into the world, making friends, gaining experiences with the opposite sex, and ultimately becoming strongly attracted to one other special person.

Unfortunately, the powerful forces that drive sexual and romantic attraction have little to do with sustaining a relationship over the long haul. To lay the foundation for a lasting relationship, each partner in the courtship must quickly learn to make promises and must be able to trust the other to keep promises. Both partners must develop emotional and intellectual intimacy during this initial phase of the relationship. Both partners must also form healthy boundaries—that is, they must separate physically and emotionally from their families of origin.

Eventually, the journey of courtship reaches its ideal destination—the wedding day. And now the real adventure begins!

STAGE 2: TWO BECOME ONE

Rex is a youth pastor and Donna is a preschool teacher. They met and became best friends at college. In time, their friendship became a romance. They married and moved to Rex's hometown where he took a position in the church where he was raised. Rex is outgoing and has many friends and an active ministry life. He frequently takes the kids in his youth groups on skiing outings, hiking outings, or other outings. Donna is shy, has very few friendships, and is not interested in the outdoorsy activities of her husband.

At the end of each day, Donna waits for Rex to get home from church. As soon as he gets home, Donna pounces on him, starved for adult companionship and conversation. Rex, however, withdraws into his newspaper, walling himself off from her with a barrier of newsprint.

The problem is that these newlyweds, Donna and Rex, have not yet made the transition from two "I"s to a single "we." Rex is an independent young man who enjoys the freedom of the outdoors, the freedom to run his youth ministry, and the freedom to be himself. After the wedding, he feared losing himself in the marriage. So, to maintain his individuality, he put up a shield—the newspaper—between himself and Donna. This only made her more desperate to connect with him, which in turn caused him to barricade himself even more.

When they came to me for counseling, I told them they would need to begin talking openly about their feelings and struggles with each other. This open communication would help reduce Donna's fear of rejection and abandonment. But I also suggested that they construct a boundary around their discussion times—limiting those times at first to a firm twenty minutes a night; this boundary reduced Rex's fear of losing himself in the marriage.

Rex and Donna's experience illustrates the delicate balancing act that both partners must perform at the beginning of a marriage.

Each partner must remain an "I" while both partners together become a "we." It's easy to tip too far one way or the other in search of that balance.

The most common problem that arises in the "Two Become One" stage of a relationship is conflict. When couples experience disagreements in the courtship phase, they are usually smoothed over with a heaping helping of sugary courtship affection. But once the honeymoon is over, the couple is in the crucible of marriage, from which there is no escape (except divorce, which for most couples—at least at first—is The Unthinkable). Whenever two people must share the same living space, disagreements are inevitable.

What many couples fail to understand is that disagreement is a good thing in a marriage. Each partner should bring a different perspective to the relationship. In this way, both partners learn from each other, adjust to each other, and grow to understand each other. A healthy relationship is not a relationship without disagreements, but one in which disagreements are monitored and negotiated in a healthy way.

Whenever a couple tells me, "We never argue," I get nervous. A lack of conflict usually means a lack of resolution. Healthy couples say, "We disagree about many things, but we learn about each other and we adjust to each other during those times of disagreement. Ultimately, we grow closer by understanding and appreciating each other's differences." When approached in a healthy way, disagreement in a marriage relationship enables two people to do the following:

- Construct healthy boundaries around their relationship
- Learn to love in a committed, covenant way—a way that is focused on the other person's welfare rather than on one's own needs and wants
- Learn how to be both passionate (sexually bonded) and intimate (intellectually and emotionally bonded) with each other
- Develop mutuality in giving and taking, in leading and following
- Negotiate closeness and distance, especially in regard to sex

- Learn how to manage and resolve conflict

During this stage, each partner must learn to see the other as the "primary resource person" in his or her life—friend, lover, confidant, counselor, cheerleader, business partner, protector, and emotional supporter.

STAGE 3: TWO BECOME THREE

When children come, the challenge becomes one of maintaining a strong marriage relationship within a well-managed family relationship. Often, the addition of children to a marriage causes the parents to forget that they are still a couple. The couple's relationship must continue to be nourished even as the family expands.

Ashley came into counseling completely distraught, saying, "My husband says he wants to date other women! He says he wants to stay married to me, but he wants to have what he calls an 'open marriage'! I don't want my marriage to be 'open'!"

Probing her situation, I learned that Ashley thought she had adequately met her husband's needs, and she certainly felt he had met hers. This declaration of his intention to date around came as a complete shock. "A complete shock?" I asked. "You didn't have any clue?"

"Well," she hesitated. "He has been kind of stand offish lately— well, actually for a few years. I remember one time, a couple years ago, he said the strangest thing to me, right out of the blue."

"What was that?"

"He said, 'Ashley, I don't know why you stay married to me.' I was floored. I've always wanted to be married to him. I love him."

It was a clue. I thought I had an insight into the problem. I pursued my hunch with another question. "Can you think of anything that has changed in your marriage in the last two or three years?"

She thought for a moment, and her brow furrowed. "Well," she ventured, "our daughter was born a little less than three years ago. You don't think that has anything to do with it, do you?"

"Why don't you have your husban come in with you next time?"

A week later, Ashley was back, along with her husband, Rob. Talking to Rob, I learned that my hunch was correct: he had lost a sense that he was "special" to Ashley when their daughter was born. He saw Ashley devote all of her attention to their child, and he felt not only ignored and unwanted, but unneeded. It seemed to him that Ashley received all the emotional sustenance she needed from their daughter, and it made him feel inadequate to meet his wife's needs.

"So," I said, "you've been feeling like you're not enough of a husband for your wife. And that's why you want to date other women."

He nodded. And with this issue out in the open, Ashley and Rob were able to communicate, to rebuild understanding, and to repair the damage done to their relationship by neglect and misunderstanding.

When a couple becomes three, new pressures are added. The child becomes the focus of both parents' attention, especially the mother's. Husbands often feel left out of their wives' love; they sense competition from the new infant. Many men take the birth of a child as a signal to become more involved at work.

The child takes up so much of the mother's energy and time that intimacy and passion get squeezed out. Sex may take on new dimensions as the wife's body changes and is used in feeding and nurturing the child. Both partners must be aware and intentionally focused on these issues so that adjustments can be made and feelings can be monitored by both sides.

When a couple neglects the marriage relationship during the child-bearing years, the results range from increased tension and conflict to sexual dysfunction to major communication breakdowns. Both partners must maintain a focus on each other as their primary love relationship. Unless both partners work on maintaining their intimacy and passion, they will tend to drift into separate corners of the marriage. They may even drift apart—permanently.

This can be a time of greatly increased conflict as both partners need to renegotiate their expectations of each other. If Mom is a working mother, she is likely to feel overwhelmed by assuming the heavy obligations of parenting on top of the obligations of her career. She will naturally expect her husband to help out more with parenting and household chores, and it is a natural male inclination to be rather insensitive and oblivious to his wife's expectations and needs.

At this stage of the marriage, wives often find themselves in a needy position, wanting considerable help, support, and nurturing from their husbands. Can the husband make this adjustment? Is he listening to her needs, to her spoken and unspoken expectations? Are both sides monitoring and recalibrating their own and each other's expectations? Even though a child has been added, both partners need to carefully maintain the crucial elements of a marriage relationship: boundaries, romance, intimacy, and passion.

STAGE 4: THE CHILDREN GO OFF TO SCHOOL

As children start school, they make friends and encounter outside influences. These influences are brought into the home by the child and sometimes create conflict—a clash of values or ideas. Especially in a very close family, children going off to school and returning with new ideas can be threatening.

Disagreements between spouses over child rearing tend to intensify, especially as children become old enough and sophisticated enough to play one parent against the other. There is a tendency for one parent to be a "hard-liner" in discipline issues and the other to be a "soft-liner." Each parent reacts to the other's parenting-style extremes, and conflicts often arise as one parent attempts to rescue the child from the other parent (who is either "too lenient" or "too tough"). The tendency is for the tough parent to compensate by becoming even tougher while the soft parent becomes even more lenient.

During this stage, the conflicting demands of family and career can make intimacy harder to maintain. Children are becoming more active and heavily scheduled (music lessons, dance class, soccer practice, Little League), and all of these activities siphon time and energy from the relationship. The more kids in the family, the harder it becomes for parents to create privacy for resolving their mutual conflicts and for expressing their sexual passion.

Both partners must learn to focus special attention on the needs of their marriage relationship—boundaries, romance, intimacy, and passion—or the marriage can begin to deteriorate due to stress and neglect.

This stage is a rehearsal for the separation to come—the mid-life stage—when children leave home for good.

STAGE 5: MID-LIFE

As their children become more independent, both parents must negotiate new ways of dealing with the children. At this stage, couples often "triangle," making the teenager the focus of their drama while avoiding the task of resolving their own conflicts. As long as we keep focusing on our teenager's grades, friends, taste in music, body piercing, Internet and cell phone use, strange attire, and the like, we don't have to face the fact that, as a couple, we are drifting apart. We don't have to acknowledge that we are losing intimacy, neglecting passion, and letting romance die.

At the same time, just when teenagers start cranking up the wattage of family stress and tension, the couple's parents often become more needy. If infirm, Grandma and Grandpa may move in with the family, upsetting household routines, making demands, and hindering the honest resolution of conflict. Grandparents sometimes side with the teens against the parents, creating disciplinary havoc.

It's also the time of life when both partners in the marriage begin to face questions of adequacy, fulfillment, and direction in their lives. Both partners are asking themselves, "Who am I?" Perhaps some dreams have died or some aspirations have been delayed or have gone unfulfilled. The husband may make a radical career change ("This may be my last chance to fulfill my dream of being a hog farmer in Iowa") while the wife may wish to re-enter the work force after years of homemaking. As a result, she may place new expectations on her husband: "I can't do as many of the household chores; you need to pick up some of the slack."

Mid-life is a crucial passage for the marriage, and both partners should make a conscious effort to monitor expectations and renegotiate roles as needed. Issues of intimacy and passion are as important in this stage as in every previous stage, and both partners need to devote time and energy to making the relationship work.

STAGE 6: THE EMPTY NEST

Ben and Lisa's youngest daughter just left home for college. Now they can do all the things they planned to do once the kids had all "flown the coop," right? Wrong! As Ben and Lisa discuss plans for the coming years, they discover they have very different agendas. Ben plans to pursue more hunting and fishing, the kinds of activities he likes to pursue—*alone.* Lisa kind of figured they were going to spend more time traveling—*together.* He expected more time separated while she expected more togetherness and intimacy.

The problem Ben and Lisa have is a common one for couples in this stage of marriage: "Can we let our children go and still deal with each other as marriage partners? Or, having raised our kids, have we discovered we no longer have anything in common? What do we do with each other now that our kids are no longer our focus?"

This problem is particularly acute among couples who have neglected their marriage relationship during the child-rearing years. Some couples find they have nothing to share together and nothing to talk about. As a result, this stage often catches couples off-guard. They never realized how perilous this stage of marriage can be.

The pain and peril of this stage is magnified if one or both parents maintain an unhealthy attachment to the children. As children approach maturity, they must be allowed to "leave by the front door"—that is, with the full blessing and support of the parents. There is an old saying: "Back doors are revolving doors." In other words, if the child does not leave via the "front door" of parental support and blessing, then that child will not be able to make a healthy transition to adulthood. Instead, that child will be back, again and again, triggering the return of old unresolved conflicts.

In a healthy family, children are encouraged and able to leave home at the proper time, but they remain positively involved with their family of origin. They maintain healthy contact even after moving into a career and establishing their own families.

STAGE 7: THE (SUPPOSEDLY) "GOLDEN" YEARS

Hal is driving June nuts. He's only been retired for a month, and already June can't stand to have him around. He follows her around all day, asking what she's doing. When she's ironing, he stands over her shoulder, observing the back-and-forth motion of June's steam iron as if it were an instant replay on ESPN.

Clearly, Hal has not made a very good adjustment to retirement. He needs to take responsibility for finding satisfying activities of his own before June runs screaming out of the house. The last stage of a marriage can be a golden stage, but there are also adjustments to be made in the culminating years of a relationship. Both part-ners have to adjust to being home together more, to changes in health and vitality, to financial changes, and to the loss of friends and family members. Leadership issues may re-emerge: the primary leader-provider in the relationship may become incapacitated and become a follower-receiver. Expectations may need to be reassessed and readjusted.

Eventually, one partner must cope with the biggest change of all: the death of a spouse. When this loss occurs, the survivor often feels that life has become empty and meaningless. Somehow, the surviving spouse must learn to make a new life and to find new meaning in it. Where do you see yourself and your partner in these stages of marriage?

Wherever you are in your journey with your partner, it is im-portant to be attentive to the issues and dynamics of that particular stage. Never take your relationship or your partner for granted. No matter how long you and your partner have been together, there are always new depths in your partner to be explored, new levels in the relationship to be discovered. Continue to focus your love and attention on the relationship and you'll find that your marriage can remain healthy and rewarding at every new stage along the way.

In the next chapter, we'll examine the issue of changing emotional needs.

TAKE ACTION
Questions of a Marriage

If you and your partner are answering these questions together, first write your answers down separately, then compare your answers—but remember to use covenant-love to deal with any disagreements! Use the information you gather from each other to better understand how each of you look at, and feel about, your love relationship.

1. What chronological stage of marriage are you in right now?
   - Stage 1: Courtship
   - Stage 2: Two Become One
   - Stage 3: Two Become Three
   - Stage 4: The Children Go Off to School
   - Stage 5: Mid-Life
   - Stage 6: The Empty Nest
   - Stage 7: The (Supposedly) "Golden" Years

2. On a scale of 1 to 10 (below), how satisfied are you with the level of intellectual and emotional sharing in your marriage?

   1 . . 2 . . 3 . . 4 . . 5 . . 6 . . 7 . . 8 . . 9 . . 10
   Very Dissatisfied / Somewhat Satisfied / Very Satisfied

3. Think back to a time when you were at the previous stage of marriage. Remember how you related to your partner. How satisfied were you with the level of intellectual and emotional sharing in your marriage at that time?

   1 . . 2 . . 3 . . 4 . . 5 . . 6 . . 7 . . 8 . . 9 . . 10

Very dissatisfied / Somewhat satisfied / Very satisfied

    Has your level of satisfaction improved or worsened over the past few years?

    To what do you attribute the change?

    What specific, practical steps can you take to improve the intellectual and emotional dimension of your marriage?

4. On a scale of 1 to 10 (below), how satisfied are you with the level of passion and romance in your marriage?

    1 . . 2 . . 3 . . 4 . . 5 . . 6 . . 7 . . 8 . . 9 . . 10

Very dissatisfied / Somewhat satisfied / Very satisfied

5. Think back to the previous stage. Remember how you related to your partner, sexually and romantically. How satisfied were you with the level of passion and romance in your marriage at that time?

    1 . . 2 . . 3 . . 4 . . 5 . . 6 . . 7 . . 8 . . 9 . . 10

Very dissatisfied / Somewhat satisfied / Very satisfied

    Has your level of satisfaction improved or worsened over the past few years?

    To what do you attribute the change?

    What specific, practical steps can you take to enhance the passion and romance in your marriage?

6. What issue or issues in your marriage do you feel a need to focus more attention on?

- communication
- intimacy
- passion (sex)
- boundaries
- time alone

- time together
- trust
- expectations
- keeping promises
- managing conflict
- mutuality in giving and taking
- negotiating closeness and distance
- mutuality in leading and following
- balancing parenting roles and marriage roles
- practical duties, chores, maintenance, etc.
- doing things together (exercise, travel, vacations, etc.)

7. What issues in your marriage do you feel your partner needs to focus more attention on?

- communication
- intimacy
- passion (sex)
- boundaries
- time alone
- time together
- trust
- expectations
- keeping promises
- managing conflict
- mutuality in giving and taking
- negotiating closeness and distance
- mutuality in leading and following
- balancing parenting roles and marriage roles
- practical duties, chores, maintenance, etc.
- doing things together (exercise, travel, vacations, etc.)

8. Share your answers with your partner, and listen carefully to his or her answers. Note the differences between your perception of your marriage and your partner's perception. Avoid arguing with those perceptions; instead, try to see the relationship from your partner's point of view.

Negotiate changes in roles, expectations, boundaries, intimacy requirements, sexual expectations, and so forth. Work together to make the marriage more mutually satisfying. Make genuine love—seeking the welfare of the other person—your goal.

EIGHT

Why
Do Our Emotional Needs
Keep Changing?

Will and Gail had been married for more than twenty years. "Will hides behind his job during the day," Gail complained, "and he hides in his workshop at night. I never see him, and he refuses to talk to me! I don't have anyone else to talk to, I never go anywhere, and I just want to have a little quality time with my husband. But noooo! He shuts himself out of my life! Is it any wonder I'm depressed?"

"I no sooner walk in the door," Will countered, "and she's all over me with things she wants to do, things she wants me to do, things she wants to discuss with me! I work hard all day, I'm tired, and I just want a few minutes to relax before dinner. Instead, I'm overwhelmed with all these demands! I just can't take it!"

"Will," I said after a few moments' reflection, "I think you're too close to your wife. You need more distance in your relationship."

Gail hit the roof. "What?!"

Even Will seemed surprised. "I do?"

"Yes," I said. "Until you put a little more space between yourselves in this relationship, you'll never be able to truly help and support Gail in the marriage."

Gail was stunned. "But that doesn't make any sense! I just told you, Will walls himself out of my life as it is. How much more distance can he put between us? Should he move to another state?"

"What I'm suggesting," I explained, "is that by putting some healthy space into the relationship, Will can be even more available to you than he is now. The way things are now, he runs from you because you cling to him, and the more he runs, the more you cling. You will never be able to enjoy his friendship and receive his support as long as you keep clinging and he keeps running."

"But when we were married," Gail said, "the minister said something about 'the two become one.' We're not just two people who happen to live at the same address! We're married, and that means we're supposed to be close!"

"Yes, there should be closeness," I replied. "But in a healthy marriage, there should also be two intact, distinct personalities. If those two personalities become too close, then one person can easily begin to feel absorbed or smothered by the other. Will sensed that was happening in your relationship, and he ran and hid to keep from being smothered."

Gail shook her head. "No, that's not right. That's not it. I think you've misunderstood the situation."

"Maybe so," I said, "but I'm basing what I said on what you told me. Earlier, you said, 'I don't have anyone else to talk to and I never go anywhere.' In other words, you don't have any outside interests. You depend completely on Will for all of your social interaction. In a healthy relationship, each partner should have a few outside interests, a few friends and activities—an individual life. Then, when both partners come together in a committed relationship, they can give themselves to each other, confident that each remains intact as an individual."

Gail seemed dubious, but Will said, "Sounds paradoxical, but it makes sense."

We hammered out an agreement whereby Gail would become involved in outside activities, doing volunteer work and becoming more involved at church. She made friends, developed new interests, and, within a few months, the entire dynamic of their relationship had dramatically improved.

By putting more space into their relationship, Gail and Will actually became closer.

THE FOUR EMOTIONAL STAGES OF A MARRIAGE

Will and Gail were "stuck" in the first stage of a four-stage emotional process in their relationship. In the previous chapter, we examined the seven chronological stages of a marriage. Now we look at the four emotional stages every marriage relationship goes through. Although these stages are more subtle and difficult to recognize than the chronological stages, they are more predictable.

Every enduring relationship must negotiate this four-stage emotional journey. The four emotional stages are:

Stage 1:   Stuck
Stage 2:   Unstuck
Stage 3:   I-ness
Stage 4:   We-ness

Here are four truths to keep in mind as we examine these four emotional stages:

Truth No. 1: The order of the stages never varies.
Truth No. 2: You can't skip any stage.
Truth No. 3: Each succeeding stage is more complex than the stage before.
Truth No. 4: Each stage grows from the preceding stage and prepares for the stages to follow.

Let's look at each of these stages in order.

STAGE 1: STUCK

Occurring early in marriage, this stage involves intense bonding between two people. The purpose of this stage is attachment, and it entails a great deal of passion, giving and receiving, and nurturing.

Neither side makes many demands for the other side to change. Both sides accommodate to each other. Conflict is avoided and minimized. Both sides sacrifice individuality in order to perpetuate the sense that "we are one." Anxiety emerges when one side glimpses the other as a different self.

Counseling couples in the Stuck stage can be very difficult—especially couples who are in the courtship phase. I once did premarital counseling with a couple in their upper forties. It would be his second marriage and her third. Both were competent, intelligent, and successful professionals—yet around each other, they behaved like giddy fifteen-year-olds. They refused to see any problems in their relationship, and they were certain that everything was coming up roses for the rest of their lives. These two were stuck like superglue!

I never got through to them. For all I know, they may both be married today, but I wouldn't bet they're married to each other. When both partners experience a kind of symbiotic intermingling, I call it a "stuck/stuck" stage. He is stuck, she is stuck; both partners are stuck on each other, fused together in this stage of the relationship.

It is not unhealthy for a couple to be stuck during the courtship and newlywed phases of the marriage. But if a couple remains stuck for years or decades, then they are not progressing and growing in their relationship.

The stuck stage can take an alternate form. This is the "Stuck/Fighting" stage. The partners are hostile and dependent at the same time. Each says, "I can't live with you, I can't live without you." Conflict and aggression are used to maintain both distance and contact—simultaneously. One partner fails to see the impact of his or her behavior on the other. There are strong projections of feelings and assumptions from one partner to the other: "I know what you're thinking!" They are like two boxers in a clinch: the referee tries to separate them, but they are locked together in a struggle, their gloved hands flailing and punching ineffectually, hurting each other but unable to disengage from each other.

In most marriages, sooner or later, the stuck stage eventually runs its course and a new stage emerges.

STAGE 2: UNSTUCK

The couple now enters a stage of differentiating, of establishing boundaries, and of becoming unique individuals again. In a healthy relationship, partners develop the capacity to tolerate differences and to define clear areas of responsibility and authority. The purpose of this stage is to enable both partners to re-establish their own boundaries, their own sense of self, and their own uniqueness. They shift from an obsession with the other partner to a process of internally defining themselves and their own independent thoughts, feelings, goals, and needs.

In relationships between emotionally immature or insecure people—people who have never understood the role of clear boundaries, clear expectations, and covenant-love, and who have never learned to manage conflict well—the Unstuck stage is perilous. It is at this point that many marriage partners mistakenly assume, "We've fallen out of love," or "We were just incompatible." In fact, the two people in the relationship are simply passing through a normal process of differentiating and rebalancing after the emotionally intense Stuck stage.

Sometimes—as in the case of Will and Gail—one partner will enter the Unstuck stage alone, leaving the other partner stuck. The stuck partner, having no one to stick to, panics. This situation creates the crisis that often brings people into counseling. In counseling, the stuck partner learns to grieve the loss of the intense, fused, symbiotic relationship. Once the loss is grieved and the reality of this new phase of the relationship sinks in, the stuck partner is usually able to make the transition to unstuck.

The task of the person who is moving into the unstuck stage is four-fold. This person must:

1. Identify his or her own thoughts, feelings, and desires.
2. Express those thoughts, feelings, and desires to the other partner.
3. Understand and accept the other partner as separate, distinct, and different.
4. Learn to respond effectively to those differences.

STAGE 3: I-NESS

Dan had spent the last few years trying to help his wife, Alice, deal with her anger, self-pity, and depression. She had been sexually abused as a child—something Dan had only recently found out. Until Alice revealed the abuse, Dan was baffled and hurt by years of sexual dysfunction and teary episodes over issues he couldn't understand.

After learning of Alice's childhood pain, Dan tried everything to make Alice happy. But instead of getting better, she grew progressively more depressed. Worst of all, she refused to seek counseling. She shut herself in her house, cried, stared, or sometimes just slept through the day.

In desperation, Dan came to counseling alone. "I'm not really the one who should be here," he said. "Alice is the one who was molested as a child, but she just won't deal with it. I've tried to make her happy, but nothing works. What should I do?"

"You know something, Dan?" I said. "It's not your job to make Alice happy. It's Alice's job to make Alice happy. She has to take responsibility for herself. And as hard as it may be, you need to take responsibility for yourself and quit trying to carry Alice's burden for her."

As this idea sank in, it was as if a light came on in Dan's eyes. At that moment, Dan began the transition into the I-ness stage. From then on, he communicated to Alice, "I love you, but I can't be responsible for your feelings. You have to take that responsibility on yourself. If you really love me and care about this relationship, you'll get out of this gloomy house and get yourself into counseling. You'll get these issues out of your way and get on with your life."

In time, Alice did just that—and she experienced the I-ness stage as well.

I-ness is a healthy stage of development in the life of a couple. In the I-ness stage, each partner experiences a time of intense individuality, explores activities and friendships outside of the marriage. The attention of each partner is directed to the external world as both seek to consolidate their self-esteem and individual power, while learning to express themselves creatively in the world.

Once both partners have securely established their own identity, they can look to each other once again for intimacy and emotional support. As they begin to reconnect, there is a re-emergence of vulnerability, the tender balance between "I" and "we" is cemented into place, and both partners begin to respond to each other more consistently and comfortably.

STAGE 4: WE-NESS

The final stage is the goal of marriage: mutual interdependence.

This is a comfortable, peaceful, and productive stage of marriage. At this stage, two individuals in a healthy relationship have found satisfaction in their own lives and have developed a deep, mutually satisfying bond. Two people, comfortable and secure as individuals, have arrived at a place where they can satisfy each other's needs without losing a sense of self. It takes work, commitment, caring, and covenant-love to reach this stage, but once you arrive at a place of we-ness, you know it has been worth the journey.

Here we see one of the great truths about relationships. When couples persevere through the four emotional stages of a relationship, they usually reach a place of peace, security, and satisfaction with each other. They find that, day by day, year by year, stage by stage, they have built a love relationship that has grown rich and deep and has stood the test of time.

In the next chapter, we will examine the critical issue of needs.

TAKE ACTION
Questions of a Marriage

If you and your partner are answering these questions together, first write your answers down separately, then compare your answers—but remember to use covenant-love to deal with any disagreements! Use the information you gather from each other to better understand how each of you look at, and feel about, your love relationship.

1. Which emotional stage of marriage are you in right now?
   - Stage 1: Stuck (or Stuck/Fighting)
   - Stage 2: Unstuck
   - Stage 3: I-ness
   - Stage 4: We-ness

2. Are you and your partner at the same stage together? Why or why not? Explain your answer.

3. Do you sense progress and growth in your marriage relationship over the past few years? Why or why not?

4. You and your partner are two very different people. Is that fact hard for you to accept? What is it about your partner's differences that make you uneasy?

   Take a piece of paper and divide it into two sections, labeled *alike* and *different*. Then take a few minutes and write down at least ten ways you and your partner are alike and ten ways you and your partner are different.

   What does this exercise tell you about the stage of emotional development you and your partner are in?

5. What interests, activities, and friendships do you enjoy outside of the marriage relationship?

6. Have you ever stepped back, taken a look at your marriage, and said to yourself, "We've fallen out of love," or, "We were just incompatible"?

   Have you ever verbalized such thoughts to your partner, or has your partner verbalized them to you?

   Could it be that you and your partner are simply going through the Unstuck stage of emotional development? Are there other signs that your marriage is entering the Unstuck stage? Does it help you and put you at ease to know that this is simply a passage your marriage goes through?

NINE

What About My Needs?

⊷━━━━━━━━━━━⊶

Oliver and Joanie have reached the unstuck stage in their relationship, and Oliver is becoming uncomfortable with their unstuckness. He sees Joanie developing friendships and activities outside of their relationship. Oliver needs reassurance that Joanie still considers their marriage to be of primary importance. He wants Joanie to be more affectionate toward him.

But when Oliver asks Joanie to spend more time with him and demonstrate more affection to him, she blows up. "Why are you so demanding?" she snaps. "Back off and give me my space!"

Why is Joanie so upset?

What is at stake here is the issue of needs. Joanie needs to experience more validation of herself as an individual. Oliver needs reassurance that Joanie still values him and validates their relationship. He fears losing his connection with Joanie as she is developing interests and friendships outside of their relationship.

Joanie has never told Oliver much about her childhood, but even if she had, he probably would not have put two and two together to understand why Joanie was so sensitive. During her childhood and adolescence, Joanie's father had often made demands on her and demonstrated little respect for her rights as an individual. He had tried to keep her at home when she wanted to attend a university in another state.

So when Oliver reasonably set forth a request for more connection with Joanie, she perceived it as a demand that she pull away from her newfound friends and interests and that she stay home with Oliver. In her mind, Oliver's request was an unreasonable demand—a demand that symbolized not love but a lack of respect for her needs.

Later, Joanie felt bad about shouting at Oliver. She couldn't understand why she became so angry with him. She went to Oliver and apologized. Oliver accepted her apology, but for days afterward, he was wary and withdrawn. Though he was once eager for connection with Joanie, he then pulled into a shell and shut Joanie out.

What's happening between Oliver and Joanie?

AN UNEQUAL TRANSACTION

We previously discussed the role of symbols, maps, filters, frames, and postures in a relationship. Using these terms as our reference points, here is how this episode appears from Joanie's emotional perspective:

> Joanie's symbol: Oliver is demanding (like Dad).
> Joanie's frame: Oliver disrespects me (like Dad).
> Joanie's posture: One-Up; attacks.

Oliver has his own childhood history, a history that places an entirely different symbolic frame around this episode. During Oliver's early childhood, his mother was a volatile woman who lashed out in anger at him for the smallest reasons or for no reason at all. Then, when Oliver was ten, his mother abandoned the family and ran off with another man. Oliver never saw her again.

Today, Oliver carries a deeply etched fear of abandonment. Symbolically, he sees Joanie behaving toward him the same way his mother did—lashing out at him for no reason other than that he sought affection from her. Now he wonders, *Will she abandon me, too?* Here, then, is the way this episode appears in Oliver's emotional frame:

Oliver's symbol: She's uncaring (like Mom).
Oliver's frame: She abandons me (like Mom).
Oliver's posture: One-Down; withdraws.

Now, neither Joanie nor Oliver is consciously aware of these symbols and frames. Neither is consciously thinking, *Oh, Oliver's being demanding like Dad* or, *Joanie's behaving just like Mom before she abandoned me.* Somewhere below the level of their awareness, both Joanie and Oliver sense a familiar and threatening pattern—but they don't consciously understand what this pattern reminds them of.

Next, notice how Joanie's and Oliver's postures relate to each other: Joanie's posture (One-Up, Attack) and Oliver's posture (One-Down, Withdraw) are different. This dynamic in their relationship is complementary, unequal, and unhealthy. What if Oliver counterattacked instead of withdrawing? Then his posture would be One-Up, Attack. Their postures would match and the dynamic in their relationship would be symmetrical, explosive, and just as unhealthy.

What is the solution? How can Joanie and Oliver both get their emotional needs met in the relationship when their needs are so different?

THE SEQUENCE FOR GETTING NEEDS MET

At this point, you may begin to see why it is often so hard for us to get our emotional needs met in marriage. Many of us have been taught since childhood that it is wrong and selfish to express our needs, to say, "I want . . ." or "I need. . ." But the fact is that we all have needs. A marriage relationship should be a safe, nurturing enclosure where both the husband and the wife can have their needs met, including their need for support, partnership, consolation, affection, sex, love, affirmation, and protection.

In a healthy relationship, those needs are met in a mutual, reciprocal way. One partner asks and the other provides. Then they switch. Our goal, as we become more consciously aware of our own needs and the needs of our spouse, is to learn how to productively express those needs to our partner, how to negotiate, how to give, and how to receive.

There is a sequence we must follow in order to get our needs met within marriage. If we break this sequence, the result will be frustration (the need will go unmet) or misunderstanding (which leads to conflict, resentment, and hurt feelings). The next few paragraphs will outline the sequence.

The first item in the sequence is to know your needs. If you cannot identify and articulate your own need, it cannot be met. Many of us have a vague sense that we need something from the relationship that we are not getting, but we don't stop and think through what that "something" is. If you try to ask your partner to meet a need before you fully understand what that need is in your own mind, trouble and misunderstanding will surely result. How can your partner know what you want if you don't know yourself?

You should be able to state your need very specifically. For example, "I need more support from you now that we have a new baby. It would help me tremendously if you could take it upon yourself to do the dishes every evening and clean the bathrooms once a week."

After you have thought your need through and can articulate it to your spouse, another problem often arises: you feel inhibited about expressing that need. You think, *That sounds so selfish.* But remember: you and your partner are a team, a partnership. Clear communication and mutual support are essential to any team effort, including marriage. What goes around, comes around, and you can make it clear that you are ready to reciprocate in meeting your partner's needs whenever the occasion arises. It's your turn now; it'll be your partner's turn soon.

The next item is to ask for your needs to be met. State your needs clearly, and tell your partner exactly what you want him or her to do. Don't hint around. Don't be subtle or cute. Ask. All too often, one or both partners takes the stance, "If my partner really loved me, I wouldn't have to ask." Nonsense. People are not mind readers. The only place you find ESP is in science-fiction novels and supermarket tabloids. In real life, to make your needs and feelings known, you have to communicate verbally and clearly. This can be difficult if you are talking about sensitive, personal needs in the area of sex, for example, but the old saying is as true: you don't get if you don't ask. If you will not be verbal and clear about your need, then your need will go unmet.

Then you need to make sure your message is clear. This means you may have to state and restate your needs more than once, and in several different ways. There is a common misconception about communication: many people think, *If I said it once, it has been communicated.* The problem is that what you think you said may not be what your partner thought you said. Your partner's mind may have wandered. He or she may have filtered your message through a personal or emotional bias, or you may have been ambiguous in your choice of words. There are hundreds of things that can go wrong when one person communicates with another, and the message, as a result, can easily become distorted.

Once you have communicated your need, it may be helpful to ask your partner to repeat back to you in his or her own words what you have just said, to make sure that what your partner heard is what you intended to convey. When your partner communicates a need to you, then you should mirror back his or her message so that you can be certain you have heard it correctly. If there is distortion in the message when it is mirrored back, the speaker can fine-tune the meaning: "No, that's not exactly what I meant. What I really need is. . ."

This kind of mirrored and monitored communication is called "reflective listening," because as you listen, you reflect the message back to make sure that the communication is taking place without distortion.

Again and again, I counsel couples who are locked in an argument based on a complete misunderstanding of what is being asked or said on both sides. One side states a need, the other side completely misinterprets that need, and World Wars III, IV, and V all erupt at once. As soon as both partners are able to accurately hear each other and agree on what they are actually fighting about, the fight often disappears and peace unexpectedly breaks out. That is why clear communication is so crucially important in a relationship.

The following step is that your partner agrees to meet your need. If your partner does not agree to meet your need, then the sequence is aborted at this stage. Your partner may respond, "I can't meet your need; it's beyond my power to meet." Or, "I don't want to meet your need; bug off!" Either way, your needs will go unmet and you will probably feel frustrated at this point. If your partner is able and willing to meet your need, then you proceed to the fifth step in the sequence.

The fifth step is to be willing to receive from your partner. Oddly, many people will follow this sequence and make it all the way from Step 1 to Step 4 and then find that they are unable to receive from their partner. "I don't want to bother you," they say, or "I'm not worthy of having this need met."

Marriage is all about giving and receiving. Complete the sequence, ask and receive, and then turn around and reciprocate for your spouse. When both partners give and receive—meeting needs and having needs met—then the marriage functions as it was designed to, and both partners experience a deep, fulfilling sense of satisfaction in the relationship.

BARRIERS TO GETTING YOUR NEEDS MET

There are a number of common barriers people experience that keep them from getting their emotional and practical needs met in the marriage. The following paragraphs offer some examples of barriers.

Low self-esteem is one barrier people run into. Many people can focus on other's needs, but not their own. They feel unworthy. Or unhappy childhood experiences have taught them to focus on others at the expense of themselves. When you ask them to identify their own needs, they don't know where to begin. They can't even acknowledge that their own needs are legitimate. Those who are hindered in identifying and asking for their own needs to be met should consider counseling to resolve their self-esteem issues.

Conflicting needs is another common barrier. It happens all the time: We are torn by conflicting, inconsistent needs. One part of us wants one thing while the other part wants the opposite. For example, "I need you close. However, I fear closeness because I don't want to lose my individuality." These conflicting needs have to be sorted out, resolved, or balanced, so that you can send a consistent message to your partner. If conflicting signals are sent, your partner will be confused and frustrated. Counseling is often necessary to clarify a person's needs and resolve his or her inner conflicts.

Another barrier is taboos. People are often taught from childhood not to express their needs, not to be "selfish," and not to say, "I want. . ." These prohibitions or "taboos" are ingrained in us during childhood and can have a powerfully inhibiting effect on our adult lives. If you go through life pretending you have no needs yet hoping someone will notice and meet your needs, you can count on one thing: your needs will go unmet.

I once counseled a taboo-ridden man who found it impossible to express his own needs. He would come into the kitchen while his wife was cleaning up, and he would just stand around. His wife would ask what he wanted, and he would shrug. Then she'd ask if he wanted X, and he'd shake his head; she'd ask if he wanted Y, and he'd say, "No. . ." With luck, she'd hit on what he wanted, and he would brighten and she'd know she got the right answer. Sometimes he would call his wife from work, and he'd just hang on the phone, breathing; his wife would pose question after question until she finally got a positive response. But the man could never bring himself to simply state his needs. As you can imagine, she soon tired of having to play this game with him, which is why she dragged him into counseling.

Unhealthy patterns of relating also create barriers. Couples often run into trouble over needs when they have settled into unhealthy patterns of relating to each other. One unhealthy pattern is the rigidly complementary pattern. This pattern is when one spouse always asks for his or her needs to be met while the other always provides. Another is the symmetrical pattern. This pattern is when either both partners try to give to each other and no one receives, or both withhold from the other. It is often difficult for us to recognize these patterns ourselves—we're right in the middle of them, after all. We sometimes need someone who will stand outside of our situation (such as a counselor) to see it more clearly and to point it out to us.

Couples also run into the barrier of timidity and indirect communication. Direct communication produces clarity; indirect communication produces confusion and misunderstanding. Indirect communication is frequently the result of timidity—the fear of confronting an issue squarely and directly. Timid people often behave as if to say, "I won't ask you directly for what I need. Instead, I'll show you by giving to you what I actually need. I have a need, but I don't want to express it, so I'll give it to you in the hope that you'll take the hint."

Mark and Michelle were a middle-aged couple who came to me for counseling. They had a pattern of behavior in which he would withdraw and she would pursue. As I probed their situation, I learned that he tended to withdraw whenever she wanted him to do something. Here's how their little marital drama would play out:

Michelle would ask, "Mark, do you want to eat out tonight?"

Mark, not looking up from his smartphone, would shrug and grunt noncommittally.

Michelle would pursue, asking, "Does that mean yes or no?"

And Mark would murmur incoherently, "Uhhh, mmm-uhm." Fact is, Mark didn't really know if he wanted to eat out or not, but the simple laws of inertia ("a body at rest tends to remain at rest unless acted on by an outside force") dictated that he probably preferred to remain at rest. However, because his wife—the "outside force"—had suggested it, he assumed *she* wanted to eat out—so he vaguely and grudgingly agreed. This pattern was repeated over and over in their relationship.

I told Mark and Michelle that the core problem was that the ownership of needs was in doubt. Mark didn't really know what he wanted, and Michelle wasn't sure what she wanted. When Michelle said, "Do you want to eat out?" she wasn't trying to maneuver him into going out. She just wanted him to voice a need—any need. She hoped he would make a commitment for both of them. Instead, he just went along half-heartedly with her half-hearted suggestion.

I directed Michelle to say to Mark, at least once a day, "I want . . ." and then she should make a simple request of her husband. Through this exercise, Michelle soon learned to express her needs in clear, direct terms. As Michelle began communicating directly instead of indirectly with Mark, their communication and their relationship dramatically improved.

The last barrier is pride. Some people feel that by stating a need, they are giving up a piece of themselves. "If I need something from you," they seem to think, "that means I am weak. If I maintain a façade of total self-sufficiency, then I am strong." Others feel that if someone else meets their needs, they lose control over their own lives. "I hate to receive," some people say, "because then I'm in someone else's debt. I feel controlled."

In the area of emotional needs, as in so many areas of life, pride goes before a fall. Couples need a sense of healthy, mutual interdependence. Pride must be punctured and deflated so that you can receive from your partner and your partner can receive from you. In a healthy relationship, both partners trade postures. Sometimes, the wife will ask (One-Down) and the husband will provide (One-Up). The next time around, the husband will ask (One-Down) and the wife will provide (One-Up). A healthy couple shares the joy of giving and the joy of receiving.

"WE'VE FOUND EACH OTHER AGAIN!"

Matt and Deena were married for twelve years and had two pre-school-age children. "We're not communicating," Deena said when they came in for counseling. "Matt isn't even trying. He spends all his time at the office, leaving me at home with two little kids and no one to talk to. He's totally closed, emotionally. I feel like I'm seventy-five percent divorced."

Slumped in his chair, Matt shrugged.

"Matt?" I said. "Any response?"

He frowned. "I don't even want to be here."

"You see!" said Deena. "Like a clam! Totally closed!"

"How do you usually try to get through to him, Deena?" I asked.

"I just keep talking to him! I keep trying to drag him out of his shell!"

"You increase your demands on him."

Deena looked stunned. "I wouldn't put it like that."

"How would you put it?"

She thought for several moments. "I guess you're right. I guess I do increase my demands. I keep turning up the heat, trying to get a response out of him."

"It seems to me," I said, "that you've both lost your place with each other. You are no longer important to each other."

I was trying to frame the situation to see if I understood it, and if they would buy it. They both bought the frame. Matt nodded. So did Deena. "I think that's it," Matt agreed aloud. "We're not important to each other."

"Is that the way you want to leave it?" I asked. "Or would you like to do something about this situation?"

There was a long silence. A tear slid down Deena's cheek. "I want to do something. I don't want our marriage to end. Honey?"

"I dunno," said Matt. "You think it can be saved?"

"If you both want it to be," I answered. It was true. It was up to them.

The next time we talked, I gathered data. I learned that Deena was a perfectionist. She liked to "keep the car on the road." Matt was impulsive and adventurous. "I'm a four-wheeler," he said. "I like to go off-road."

Deena and Matt were opposite personalities, and they had kept each other in balance until their first child was born. With the arrival of the baby, all of the order and predictability went out of Deena's world. She was once very involved in meeting Matt's needs, and he had always counted on that—but suddenly, when two became three, that was over. She lacked the time and the energy to meet his needs, so he withdrew to the office.

Deena became bitter and demanding. At first, Matt felt guilty over the rupture in their relationship, and he said "yes" to her demands, but his "yes" was empty. She asked him to supply various emotional and practical needs for her, and he agreed to her requests, but he broke most of those promises.

I gave them an assignment: when Deena made demands on Matt, Matt was to consider her request and answer honestly. Instead of saying "yes" and not meaning it, he would say "no" and stick to it. If he answered "yes," he would consider it a promise, and he would keep his promise.

The next time I saw them, they both agreed they felt closer, and they believed they were on the right track. Still, Deena felt Matt spent too much time away from her, "hiding" at the office. She framed his behavior as being a trait of a child of alcoholics (Matt's mother had died of alcoholism). Matt strenuously rejected Deena's frame. The more Matt argued, the more Deena tweaked him about being "in denial."

Finally, I stepped in and said, "Deena, instead of arguing with him about why he stays at the office, just tell him, 'I need you.' Why don't you just avoid mentioning his mother's alcoholism anymore?"

"I should just say, 'I need you'?" said Deena, her brow furrowing.

"I'd like to hear that," said Matt. "If I knew that you wanted me home because you needed me, I think I'd be home more."

Deena agreed not to mention alcoholism anymore. Instead, she would express her need for Matt.

The next visit, they both reported that things were still better. But Matt had a problem. Now that he was spending more time at home, he wanted Deena to be with him, to do things together, sharing affection. But Deena was often unavailable. She was washing or ironing or cleaning the kitchen when he wanted to be near her. This made him feel rejected.

At first, this made no sense. Deena had wanted, even demanded, that Matt come home. Now that he was home, she kept him waiting while she ran the vacuum cleaner! It was difficult to get to the bottom of this issue, but finally we were able to make sense of it. Deena wanted to spend time with her husband, but she wanted everything just so. All of this cleaning was an effort to bring order to her world so that everything would be perfect for her time with Matt.

Why was it so difficult to get to the bottom of this issue? Because Deena had chronic trouble expressing her needs. "My female friends can read me like a book," she finally said. "They always know what I need, and they supply it without me saying a word. If they know me that well, then I surely shouldn't have to explain everything to my own husband! He should be able to read me, too, and to adjust himself to my needs."

"I can't do that!" Matt protested. "I'm not a mind reader!"

So I gave them another exercise. They were to alternate expressing needs. On odd days, Matt would express a need for Deena to provide; on even days, vice versa. I also gave them a written exercise. I had them each take sheets of paper and write out:

1. Five things we used to do for each other during courtship that we no longer do.
2. Five things my partner does to please me (specific, positive, regular acts that meet my needs such as calling from work just to chat, taking over my household chores for a day to give me a break, or placing a love note in my suitcase when I go away on business).
3. Five things I wish my partner would do for me that I've never been able to ask for (from simple chores to private fantasies).
4. Complete this sentence: "Honey, I would like you to . . ."

After they completed this exercise, I had them exchange papers. Each partner was permitted to place a check mark in front of any item on the list he or she was unwilling to do at this time. Then, for the next month, each spouse was to attempt to meet one of the remaining needs on the list every day. Each spouse could add more items to the list, and was encouraged to do something extra for the other as a gift, expecting nothing in return.

After doing this exercise for a few weeks, Deena and Matt came back full of excitement and enthusiasm. "Remember when we said we were no longer important to each other, that we'd lost our place with each other?" Deena said, her eyes sparkling. "Well, we've found each other again!"

In the next chapter, we will examine the issue of closeness.

Questions of a Marriage

If you and your partner are answering these questions together, first write your answers down separately, then compare your answers—but remember to use covenant-love to deal with any disagreements! Use the information you gather from each other to better understand how each of you look at, and feel about, your love relationship.

1. List five needs—practical, emotional, sexual, etc.—that you would like your partner to meet for you.

   After listing those needs, place a check mark in front of each need which you have verbalized to your partner.

   Consider those needs which do not have check marks. Why haven't you verbalized those needs to your partner? What holds you back from asking for what you need or want?

2. The sequence for getting needs met is:

   (1) You must know what your need is and be able to articulate it.
   (2) You must ask for your needs to be met.
   (3) You must be willing to make yourself clearly understood.
   (4) Your partner must be willing and able to meet your need.
   (5) You must be willing to receive from your partner.

   At which of these steps does communication tend to break down between you and your partner?

   What can you do to repair the communication process so that you and your partner can effectively and mutually meet each other's needs?

   Are you willing to commit yourself in an active, committed, daily way to following this sequence so that you and your partner can experience greater satisfaction in the area of needs? If so, express that commitment to your partner. Consider writing out a written agreement between you to focus on those problem areas in the sequence.

3. Do you "mind read" your partner?

Do you expect your partner to read your mind and meet your needs without having to verbalize them?

What are some problems that arise between partners when one partner expects the other to "just know what I need without my having to say anything"?

Make a commitment to verbalize your needs, clearly and openly, without relying on "ESP" to get the message across. Ask a counselor, marriage support group, or trusted friend to hold you accountable for verbalizing your needs to your partner.

4. Do you feel inhibited about sharing your needs with your partner?

What is the source of this inhibition? (Check as many as apply.)

- My needs are too private and personal.
- If I say "I want . . ." I'm being selfish.
- I don't want to impose on my partner.
- I'm afraid of how my partner might respond.
- I don't deserve to have my needs met.
- My needs are inconsistent and conflicting.
- I'd rather show my partner by giving to him or her than verbalize my needs.
- If I express needs, then my partner will think I'm weak.
- If I express needs, I will feel weak.
- Other _____

Name three specific things you are going to do this

week to free yourself of your inhibition or inhibitions so that you can become more verbal and proactive in getting your needs met. Recognize that by actively asking for your own needs, you liberate your partner to do the same. The issue is not selfishness, but mutually giving to one another, which is the way God intended marriage to function.

TEN

Why Can't We Seem to Get Close?

———————○———————

"I don't get it," said Alan. "I just don't get it! She keeps telling me she wants intimacy. I try to give her what she wants!"

"No you don't," said Jennie. "You try to get me in the sack! You just want sex!"

"But that's what you want!" Alan responded, genuine astonishment in his voice.

"No! I don't want sex!" Jennie fired back. "I mean, I want sex *sometimes*, but when I want intimacy, I don't want sex!"

"Same thing!" says Alan, spreading his hands.

"It's *not* the same thing!" Jennie wailed, shaking her fists in the air.

Alan looked stricken. He hesitated, then ventured, "So—like—are you telling me you want more foreplay?"

Jennie slumped in her chair and her eyes rolled heavenward. "Clueless," she groaned. "Totally clueless!"

THE FORMULA FOR INTIMACY

Alan's confusion is understandable. Our culture often uses such words as "intimate" and "intimacy" to denote sex. But when I use the word "intimacy" in this book, it refers to a dimension of the marriage relationship that is much deeper and more fundamental to the relationship than sex. In its truest sense, intimacy is the emotional and intellectual component of the relationship. Intimacy is the intersection at which two human souls connect. Intimacy has many facets, including:

- emotional intimacy (the level of deep feelings)
- intellectual intimacy (the sharing of ideas)
- aesthetic intimacy (the sharing of experiences of beauty and pleasure)
- creative intimacy (the sharing of creativity and imagination)
- spiritual intimacy (the sharing of spiritual meaning and nurture)

Intimacy doesn't just happen. We achieve intimacy through conscious, deliberate effort. The formula for intimacy is:

$$Safety + Honesty = Intimacy$$

Safety is created by promises that are made and kept. Ideally, our sense of safety and security begins in childhood. We develop our sense of self in a safe environment, created by parents who make and keep promises. Our sense of self continues to unfold with our marriage partner, who is also expected to make and keep promises. If we have difficulty experiencing intimacy in marriage, it may be due to a lack of safety and security, either because our parents or our marriage partner (or both) have broken important promises in a significant way.

Honesty is crucial to intimacy because another person cannot know you intimately unless you are willing to pry the lid off the deep recesses of your life and honestly reveal who you are. To be honest with another person, you must first be honest with yourself. You must *know* yourself; that's not as easy as it sounds. Most of us are, to some degree or another, not fully aware of our feelings and emotions. We are in denial about some of our bad habits and traits. We have blocked out painful memories. We reject the knowledge of our worst behavior and try to pretend we have no dark side.

As we become progressively more honest with ourselves (and such honesty often requires involvement in counseling, account-ability groups, recovery groups, or support groups), then we become progressively more capable of sharing our true selves with our marriage partner. We move through deeper and deeper levels of intimacy over time.

FACTORS THAT AFFECT INTIMACY

As we progress in the relationship, we encounter barriers to inti-macy. Those barriers include such thoughts as *What will he or she think of me if I reveal this part of myself?*, *Will he or she accept me or reject me?*, and *Is it safe for me to reveal my true self?*

Our attitudes and postures toward each other play an important part in our ability to share intimacy with one another. We must see our partner as an equal in order to be intimate. We are not inclined to open up and become intimate with someone we feel is beneath us or "One-Down" in the relationship. Nor are we inclined to be intimate if we feel inferior or "One-Down" ourselves.

We may feel it is safe to be intimate in one area of our lives but not another. The dynamics of intimacy have a tendency to change over time, varying with the different chronological stages of life.

During the courtship phase of the relationship, the drive for intimacy will be intense. The couple will want to be together con-stantly, unfolding and exploring each other's mysteries with an al-most obsessive fascination. Both partners feel heightened emotions during the initial learning and exploring phase of a relationship because there are so many exciting unknowns to discover.

During the newlywed phase, the intense drive for intimacy in-creases steadily, then levels off and recedes as both partners become more comfortable and familiar with each other. Soon, distractions begin to creep into the relationship. Much as these two people would love to be together every waking moment, gazing into each other's eyes, sharing histories and secrets, they have jobs to go to and paychecks to collect.

When the first child comes, the couple has a new distraction. The relationship is no longer bipolar, a matter of him and her. It is now a triangle, and much of the emotional energy must now be focused on that new, third corner of the triangle.

In mid-life, distractions accumulate. One or both partners become immersed in a career, the drive for success, church activities, community activities, and leisure activities. Some of these activities may exclude the other partner. It's easy for couples to let intimacy wither and die in this stage.

The empty nest stage of marriage, when the kids are grown and moving into their own adult lives, is a critical passage for intimacy between two marriage partners. It can be the best time of a couple's married life now that they have more freedom to reconnect, to travel together, to do things together as a couple instead of as a family, and to talk together without interruptions and distractions. Or it can be a time when two people face each other and discover they have been neglecting intimacy for decades. Suddenly, they confront the question, "What do we do with each other?"

Intimacy is as important in the retirement years as it ever was, but by this time, many people have settled into familiar (but not always healthy and intimate) ways of relating. There are many things couples can do to build intimacy and to deepen the friendship of a lifetime. They don't have to simply rattle around in an empty old house together. It can be as simple as watching favorite old movies together or as exciting as a second honeymoon in Europe.

Whatever they do, they should share their feelings and their thoughts with each other. No matter how many years two people have lived together, there are still mysteries to be explored and hidden facets of the soul to be revealed.

THE INTIMACY GAP

Another word for intimacy might be togetherness. To be intimate with another person means to be together with that person in a deep, vulnerable way. Men and women tend to be very different in their need for intimacy. They have different mental definitions of what it means to be together. They differ over what constitutes a satisfying, intimate relationship. They differ in the intensity of intimacy they require. A woman tends to expect a deep level of feeling, emotional vulnerability, sharing, and disclosure. Many men consider themselves to be sharing at a deep level if they are talking about the point spread in Sunday's game.

Tom considers himself a sensitive, caring guy. He tells Nicole about his ambitions in life, his joys, and his feelings. He never lets a day go by without telling Nicole that he loves her. Whenever Nicole has something to tell him, he hangs on every word. He figures he's operating at about a 100 percent intimacy level. How much more intimacy could she want?

But that's not the way Nicole sees it. She's hurt. She wonders what's wrong with their relationship, and why Tom always holds back. Why isn't he more honest and open with his feelings? Why doesn't he tell her how he really feels about her? Why doesn't he ever talk about the things that make him happy, the things that make him cry, or the dreams he has of their life together? Maybe he doesn't have any dreams! Maybe he doesn't love her anymore! Otherwise, why would he stop at 25 percent instead of giving her 100 percent of his thoughts, his emotions, and his story?

There's a big disparity here. Tom's 100 percent equals Nicole's 25 percent. He frames himself as wide-open, honest, and sensitive—completely maxed-out in the intimacy department. Nicole, however, frames him as closed, hiding something, insensitive, guarded, and possibly losing his love for her. Poor Tom—he's not hiding anything, he's just clueless! He simply can't imagine a deeper level of sharing than what he's already doing. There's a big gap between Tom's perception and Nicole's, as you can see in the chart below. I call it "the intimacy gap."

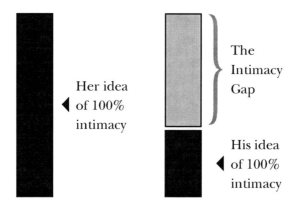

So while Nicole sees Tom as holding back, he says, "Me? I'm an open book!" There's a level of intimacy that's completely off his graph and beyond his scope, and it's right there in the intimacy gap. So what can Tom do to bridge the gap and move toward a level of intimacy that would satisfy both himself and Nicole? The following paragraphs offer some ideas of how to bridge the gap.

One way to bridge the gap is to recognize that being together means more than just "being together." Couples often spend time together without being truly engaged and open with one another. Two people can hold hands, look deeply into each other's eyes, and carry on a conversation that is completely meaningless. Yet some of the most mundane marital experiences can take on a sense of excitement, wonder, and depth when approached with a desire for genuine intimacy.

If you are doing a remodeling project together, don't work in opposite ends of the house; work room by room together, and use the time that would otherwise be spent just slapping paint on the wall as an opportunity for conversation about thoughts, dreams, fears, feelings, and histories. Find creative ways to turn mundane chores—a long drive, a wait at the doctor's office, a shopping trip—into opportunities to explore a deeper relationship. When you go out to dinner or a movie, treat it as a date, and use the occasion as an opportunity to explore each other's mysteries, just as you did during courtship.

You could also learn to accept each other's feelings. This is a problem especially for men. Intimacy has to do with disclosing feelings—emotions such as fear, sadness, pain, regret, joy, and anger. When women express feelings—particularly unpleasant feelings—their husbands tend to want to "fix the problem." Men are not comfortable, by nature, with their wives' emotions. Instead of allowing their wives to simply express and work through their emotions, most men try to turn off the spigot and solve the problem so that everyone can be okay again. This, unfortunately, closes the door to intimacy.

True intimacy requires that we allow our partner to unpack those emotions and share them with us. Instead of fixing, we need to simply listen and empathize. When men learn to be comfortable around their wives' emotions, then intimacy is enhanced. Husband

and wife are drawn closer when they know they are understood and their feelings are accepted. When you try to "fix" another person's emotions (even with the best of intentions), the message your partner receives is, "I don't accept your feelings." At that point, intimacy grinds to a halt.

Creating a zone of safety in the marriage can also help bridge the gap. There are two continuums in the marriage relationship that could be called "Intimacy Indicators." By rating your marriage on these indicators, you can get an accurate sense of the level of intimacy in your marriage. The first indicator is "The Safety Indicator." On a scale of 1 to 10, how do you feel around your partner? If you feel fearful and anxious around your partner, and if you feel you must walk on eggshells and watch what you say because your partner is unpredictable and could blow up at the slightest provocation, that's a 1. If you feel safe and secure, and if you feel you can share any thought, any feeling, any idea, and your partner will always listen, love you, and accept you, that's a 10. And, of course, there are many possible gradations between 1 and 10.

The second indicator is "The Honesty Indicator." On a scale of 1 to 10, do you feel communication between you and your partner is characterized more by anger and defensiveness or by honesty and openness? If you feel there is great anger and defensiveness between you and your partner (whether on your part, your partner's part, or both), that's a 1. If you feel that there is honest, open, candid communication between the two of you at all times, that's a 10. Again, there are many possible gradations of honesty and openness between 1 and 10. Try to base your response on actual incidences and behavior patterns in your relationship.

If you and your partner both rate your relationship on these two scales and you find a significant disparity between your rating and your partner's, that indicates a crucial difference between your perception and your partner's perception. Often, the person who rates the marriage lower in these areas feels intimidated by the anger of the other partner. The person who rates the marriage significantly higher in these areas is often not clued in to the emotional needs and feelings of the other partner. The level of intimacy in a marriage cannot rise above the level of anger or fear in the marriage.

Anger generates fear, and fear shuts down intimacy. A marriage that rates only a 5 on these two scales rates only a 5 on the intimacy scale.

Intimacy is a function of honesty and openness. Honesty and openness are the results of a sense of safety and security. If you feel you cannot share your real self, your real thoughts, or your real feelings, then you will not be honest and open, and no intimacy will take place. This doesn't mean there's no place for anger in an intimate relationship. In fact, in order for us to reach the full depths of intimacy, the marriage must be a place where all of our feelings, including anger, can be safely expressed. But anger should be expressed in a way that respects the feelings of the other person.

There is a difference between *aggressive* anger and *assertive* anger. Anger should only be expressed assertively, never aggressively. Aggressive anger includes shouting, ranting, accusing, screaming, swearing, name-calling, threatening, frightening behavior, throwing things, hitting things, and committing acts of physical violence. Whenever you act angrily in a way that demonstrates a lack of respect and caring for another person's feelings, you are demonstrating aggressive anger. Aggressive anger generates fear and shuts down intimacy.

In contrast, assertive anger involves verbalizing your feelings in a way that is meant to communicate, not intimidate. Assertive anger says, "When you do such-and-such, I feel angry." Assertive anger owns the emotion rather than blaming the emotion on someone else; it says, "This is what I feel," not "You make me feel this way." When both sides in the marriage learn to express anger in an assertive, respectful way rather than by means of naked aggression, then the marriage becomes a safe place and intimacy is enhanced.

Many of the intimacy problems couples experience are related to fear, such as a man's feelings of panic in the face of his wife's anger. It is common for men to worry about keeping their wives happy—or, at least, not angry. Men often feel responsible (rightly or wrongly) for their wives' emotional states. Out of fear, men often work hard to keep the general mood in the family upbeat, to stay away from known problem areas in the relationship, and to generally walk on eggshells around their wives.

For some reason, few men think to ask themselves, "Why am

I so afraid of her? Is it really my responsibility to keep her from getting mad? Shouldn't she be allowed to be angry, if that's how she feels? Can I deal with her anger?" These questions should come with the question of responsibility: "Maybe it really is my fault that she's angry. She may be angry because I've been a jerk, and if that's the case, then I need to take responsibility. I need to apologize and try to reconcile."

If your partner expresses anger, you should listen to that anger and attempt to understand it. Allow your partner to express those feelings, and decide whether or not you are in any way responsible for provoking those feelings. If you are not responsible for your partner's anger, you can still listen, hear, and understand. When you do that, intimacy is enhanced, not shut down.

Women are sometimes angry for reasons that have nothing to do with their husbands. Unfortunately, many men feel responsible anyway. They swing into action and try to fix their wives' emotions even though they had nothing to do with the problem and can't fix it. In fact, by trying to fix it, they only make things worse. For intimacy to grow, husbands need to allow their wives to feel and express their feelings. We shut down intimacy when we try to "fix" our partner's feelings instead of listening and understanding.

Another idea of how to bridge the intimacy gap is to accept the natural gender differences between you and your partner. In general, men tend to initiate sex and women tend to initiate conversation. This is normal, and we don't want to erase the differences between men and women. But as we accept those differences, we should also try to bridge those differences and move toward each other. Both partners should continually try to create a more balanced, mutual, and reciprocal arrangement. Sometimes, the wife should be sexually assertive; sometimes the husband should be more conversational. In this way, both sides take the initiative in bridging the intimacy gap. If one side initiates all the time, then the relationship is out of balance.

Being aware of the role of filters in your communication can also help bridge the gap. Filters are the result of many factors in our lives, including past experiences, personality traits, and gender. When we listen to each other or observe each other's behavior in marriage, we assume that we perceive objective reality. In fact, we are *interpreting* reality through our internal mental filters.

A person who grew up loved and affirmed in a secure home filters people and experiences differently than a person who grew up abused in an insecure environment. A person who is open and optimistic by nature filters people and experiences differently than a person who is wary and negative. Women filter experiences differently than men. Couples continually filter each other throughout their life together.

I can also illustrate this principle from my own marriage. My wife, Marcy, and I once took the Meyers-Briggs Personality Inventory, and we discovered that we are opposites in virtually every personality indicator. One of the significant ways in which we are different is that I am an "E" (or External Thinker) while Marcy is an "I" (or Internal Thinker).

An Internal Thinker, like Marcy, works through an idea silently, mentally testing it, working out all the angles, doing all the calculations, and exploring all the possibilities before ever verbalizing it. Only when the idea is very well formed is the Internal Thinker ready to voice it. Once an Internal Thinker voices an idea, he or she is frequently ready to go to the wall to defend it. After all, it has been carefully thought out and now has the force of a conviction.

An External Thinker, like me, does his or her thinking out loud—verbalizing half-baked ideas and letting them bounce off the walls like Ping Pong balls, watching them collide with other ideas, and waiting to see which ones fly and which fall flat. This is sometimes called "brainstorming" or "spit balling." An External Thinker frequently voices ideas or opinions without feeling any great allegiance to them or ownership of them.

External Thinkers drive Internal Thinkers crazy! During discussions with Marcy, I would sometimes make a statement, thinking, *Here's a possibility, let's run it up the flagpole and see if anyone salutes.* Well, Marcy, being an Internal Thinker, would hear my nutty, off-the-wall, half-baked idea and think, *He's stating a core conviction—and it's the craziest doggone thing I ever heard of!* She would look at me absolutely aghast and say, "You can't possibly believe what you just said!" And, of course, I didn't. It was just an idea I tossed out into the middle of the room.

Meanwhile, Marcy had just stated one of the core convictions of her being, and she had done so with absolute feeling and intensity. But being the External Thinker that I am, I figured she had merely tossed out an opening gambit, a spitball, just like most of my half-baked ideas.

So Marcy and I were filtering each other's communication through the storehouse of our own experiences, our personality traits, and our gender. Until we began to understand each other's thinking styles, these differences often caused some very tangled communication patterns. If we are not aware of how these factors can filter and distort communication in a relationship, they can produce serious damage to intimacy and to the relationship.

Another idea for bridging the communication gap is to beware of the cycle of pursuit and withdrawal. This cycle is a common cause of the breakdown of marital intimacy. Usually, the wife is the one who pursues intimacy and togetherness while the husband tends to withdraw. This is often due to the fact that men have been conditioned to be "cool," non-emotional, and unexpressive. A woman will pursue intimacy with her husband for a while, but she eventually tires of the chase. She can't get her husband to enter into her idea of intimacy and togetherness, so—frustrated and helpless—she finally gives up.

When intimacy fails, a divorce of some kind invariably results. It may be a *legal* divorce, with attorneys, a judge, and a written decree. Or it could be an *emotional* divorce—a hollow shell of a marriage in which two people live separate lives and direct their emotional energies away from the marriage relationship. The partners find alternatives to intimacy. He turns to work, hobbies, outside activities, drinking, golf, or another woman. She turns to work, female friends, outside activities, children, compulsive overeating, compulsive overspending, or another man.

Maintaining a continual and vigilant emphasis on relationship building is another way to bridge the gap. Couples must periodically ask themselves, "Where are we as a couple right now? Where have we been successful? When were we most successful at practicing intimacy, and what did we do right in those days that we don't do anymore? Where are we emotionally—stuck, unstuck, I-ness, or we-ness?" The marriage relationship must continually be checked for vital signs.

It's a good idea to set intimacy goals and monitor your progress toward those goals on an annual basis—say the night before each anniversary. (Why the night before your anniversary? So you can spend your anniversary celebrating!) Sit down together and have a serious talk about the state of your relationship.

Re-evaluate and recalibrate your goals for the marriage. Set plans for vacations, mini-honeymoons, days out, evenings out, and Sabbaths (rest days). Brainstorm inventive ideas for spending quality time together. Think of favorite old places and brand new places for togetherness getaways. The soul of a relationship is intimacy, so make time for building a truly intimate relationship that will last a lifetime.

In the next chapter, we'll take a closer look at gender differences in marriage communication.

TAKE ACTION
Questions of a Marriage

If you and your partner are answering these questions together, first write your answers down separately, then compare your answers—but remember to use covenant-love to deal with any disagreements! Use the information you gather from each other to better understand how each of you look at, and feel about, your love relationship.

1. Make a list of your "exits"—alternatives you use to avoid spending time with your partner (overeat, stay at work late, play golf, or even something as seemingly positive as spending a lot of time with your kids). You may have never thought of these activities as "exits." You may be thinking, "Sure, I do things like that, but not because I'm avoiding intimacy!" You may be right, or you may not be fully aware of all the reasons why you do these things.

2. Make a list of your partner's "exits." Share your lists with each other. Place a check mark beside "exits" you want to eliminate. Place an X by those you feel will be difficult to eliminate. Pray together for wisdom and power to make constructive changes in the way you use your time in the marriage. Covenant to be accountable to each other and to check in with each other at least once a week as you close your "exits" and move closer together in your relationship.

3. Tonight, write a covenant statement: "During the coming year, we agree to work on _____ (area of intimacy) in the following way."

   Sign the statement and check in with each other on a weekly basis to see that you are making progress in this area of your marriage.

4. Evaluate the various facets of the intimacy dimension of your marriage on a scale of 1 to 10. Each partner should fill out this evaluation separately. Afterwards, compare your responses and discuss your responses, both the responses where you agree and disagree. In areas where there is divergence of opinion, seek specific instances which lead you and your partner to respond as you did. As you discuss, try to lower your defenses, listen carefully, and try to see the relationship from your partner's point of view.

   On each of the items below, circle the number which you feel approximates how you view that particular aspect of togetherness in your marriage relationship.

NEGATIVE   POSITIVE

Communication

                1 . . 2 . . 3 . . 4 . . 5 . . 6 . . 7 . . 8 . . 9 . . 10
The lines have been cut.   The lines are open.

Listening

1..2..3..4..5..6..7..8..9..10

All right, I admit it.   I listen attentively
I'm a lousy listener.   to my partner.

Being Heard

1..2..3..4..5..6..7..8..9..10

My partner is a   My partner is
a lousy listener.   terrific listener.

Feelings

1..2..3..4..5..6..7..8..9..10

I don't accept or understand   I welcome and under-
my partner's feelings.   stand my partner's feelings.

Affection

1..2..3..4..5..6..7..8..9..10

We never touch.   We're as cuddly
               as teddy bears.

Sex, Frequency

1..2..3..4..5..6..7..8..9..10

What sex?   We can't keep our
         hands off each other.

Sex, Satisfaction

1..2..3..4..5..6..7..8..9..10

I'd rather watch paint dry.   Pure ecstasy!

Growth Together

1..2..3..4..5..6..7..8..9..10

Intimacy is stagnant.   We grow closer daily.

Spiritual Togetherness

As my partner and I relate to God, we:

1..2..3..4..5..6..7..8..9..10

Have nothing in common. Worship and believe as one.

My Goals

1 . . 2 . . 3 . . 4 . . 5 . . 6 . . 7 . . 8 . . 9 . . 10

I feel my partner doesn't understand what I want out of life.

My partner is in perfect sync with me about my life goals.

My Partner's Goals

1 . . 2 . . 3 . . 4 . . 5 . . 6 . . 7 . . 8 . . 9 . . 10

I don't understand what my partner wants out of life.

I fully understand my partner's life goals.

Encouragement

1 . . 2 . . 3 . . 4 . . 5 . . 6 . . 7 . . 8 . . 9 . . 10

I discourage my partner.   I encourage my partner.

Time

1 . . 2 . . 3 . . 4 . . 5 . . 6 . . 7 . . 8 . . 9 . . 10

I avoid my partner.

I spend quality time with my partner.

Self-Esteem

1 . . 2 . . 3 . . 4 . . 5 . . 6 . . 7 . . 8 . . 9 . . 10

I hate myself.   I like myself.

Optimism/Pessimism

1 . . 2 . . 3 . . 4 . . 5 . . 6 . . 7 . . 8 . . 9 . . 10

The glass is half empty.   The glass is half full.

Responsibility for Feelings

1 . . 2 . . 3 . . 4 . . 5 . . 6 . . 7 . . 8 . . 9 . . 10

It's my partner's fault I feel the way I do.

I take personal for my own feelings.

Fairness

1 . . 2 . . 3 . . 4 . . 5 . . 6 . . 7 . . 8 . . 9 . . 10

One partner carries the whole load.

We share marriage responsibilities fairly.

Conflict, Part I

1 . . 2 . . 3 . . 4 . . 5 . . 6 . . 7 . . 8 . . 9 . . 10

I fight to win.   I resolve conflict.

I have to be right.   because I love my partner.

Conflict, Part II

1 . . 2 . . 3 . . 4 . . 5 . . 6 . . 7 . . 8 . . 9 . . 10

My partner fights to win.   My partner resolves conflict

He or she has to be right.

Crises

When problems, pain, or tragedy strike, what happens to
your marriage relationship?

1 . . 2 . . 3 . . 4 . . 5 . . 6 . . 7 . . 8 . . 9 . . 10

We fall apart.   We pull together.

Leisure

1 . . 2 . . 3 . . 4 . . 5 . . 6 . . 7 . . 8 . . 9 . . 10

Separate vacations,   Leisure time with my

please.   partner is an adventure!

Fun—My marriage is:

1 . . 2 . . 3 . . 4 . . 5 . . 6 . . 7 . . 8 . . 9 . . 10

Dull as dirt.   More fun than human beings
should be allowed to have.

The higher the numbers you accumulate on this
evaluation, the richer your experience of marital intimacy is likely to be. Don't forget to closely and openly
examine any significant disparities between your answers and your partner's.

Place an X before any areas where you and your
partner need to make constructive changes. Covenant
together to make those changes and be accountable to
each other on a regular basis to work for improvement.

ELEVEN

Why Can't I Say What I Want To Without Getting in Trouble?

Grace and Monty were on the verge of divorce.

"Monty withdraws from me," Grace said. "He crawls into his cave and hibernates until I go away."

"Is that how you respond when he withdraws?" I asked. "You go away? You ignore him?"

"Well," she paused, recalling past incidents, "that's what I do now. I just don't care anymore." I could hear it in her voice: she really did care. A lot.

"So," I said, "Monty withdraws, so you withdraw." I had just framed the situation as symmetrical: both sides withdraw.

"That's about right," said Grace. "But I didn't always withdraw. I used to try to drag him out of his cave and get him to open up. Back when I cared, I mean. I used to ask him what was wrong, why he was pulling away from me, why he was going into his silent mode." Here Grace described their former relationship as complementary rather than symmetrical: he withdrew, she pursued.

"How would Monty respond when you pursued him?" I asked.

"He withdrew even more. He'd get quieter."

I turned to Monty. "Is that true?"

"Well," he replied, hedging, "I wouldn't say I 'withdrew,' exactly." He didn't like the sound of the "withdrawal" frame; he chose his words carefully and reframed the situation in a softer and more favorable light.

"I'd say I like to be quiet and contemplative at certain times. If Grace can't just give me a little peace and quiet, then I have to pull away a bit. You know." He shrugged.

Grace rolled her eyes in an exaggerated, derisive way. "The way I see it," she said, "he's just moody. I really hate that. He used to get moody like that when we were dating, but I never bothered to confront it. I didn't realize how bad it could get. I didn't know what I was in for. I can't stand it when he pulls away like that."

Monty shot a glare in her direction. He obviously disapproved of the way she insisted on framing his behavior as "withdrawal," but he said nothing.

"Okay," I said. "One of you, tell me about the last time this 'quietness' of Monty's caused a problem. Monty? Grace? Who wants to start?"

"I'll start," Grace said quickly, almost eagerly. Monty bit his lip. "I remember when we had lunch at the restaurant with my sister," Grace continued. "I didn't think Monty conducted himself appropriately."

"How so?" I asked.

"He was withdrawn, sullen. Even my sister noticed it. When she and I left the table and went to the ladies' room, she said, 'What's wrong with Monty?'"

Monty muttered something.

I said, "What's that, Monty?"

"I said I wasn't withdrawn and I wasn't sullen," he said sullenly.

"Did you tell him you disapproved of his performance at lunch?" I asked Grace.

"Oh, yes! I told him!"

"Did she ever!" Monty added like a rifle shot.

Grace returned a stare that would bend steel.

"What happened then?" I asked.

"We had a long drive home," said Grace. "I tried to draw him out, but he wouldn't speak to me."

"You kept hammering at me," said Monty, "so I shut you out and went to Tahiti in my mind."

"Were you angry with her?" I asked.

Monty shrugged. "I didn't like the way she talked to me. The way she yelled at me. I don't have to take that. No man should have to put up with that."

"So you were angry," I said, putting my frame on his feelings to see if it fit.

"Okay, yeah," said Monty, buying my frame. "Sure, I was mad. Who wouldn't be? She was trying to manipulate me, boss me around, control me!"

"I wasn't either," Grace retorted acidly.

"Do you feel that way very often, Monty?" I asked. "Do you feel Grace tries to boss you or control you?"

"Yeah. At times."

"Like . . . ?" I prompted.

"Like the time she wanted me to get rid of my favorite shirt."

Grace launched, practically coming out of her chair.

"What?! What shirt? I never—"

"The blue one!" countered Monty. "The one with the alligator on it."

Grace spluttered, "I didn't tell you to get rid of—"

"Monty," I interjected, "you said Grace wanted you to get rid of that shirt. That word 'wanted' implies you didn't do what she wanted you to do. You still have the shirt, don't you?"

"I love that shirt," he answered defensively, not responding directly to my question, but close enough.

"When she asks something of you," I said, "you feel controlled. To break her control over you, you refuse to comply with what she wants. Am I right?"

"But I didn't tell him to get rid of that shirt," Grace interposed. "I just said it wasn't my favorite." It was clear that she felt that Monty was painting her as a "nag," and she didn't buy that frame.

"That's not what you said," Monty insisted. "You said, 'Monty, why do you always wear that ugly shirt?' That means you wanted me to get rid of it."

"Monty," I said, "you really feel that Grace was trying to control you."

"Exactly."

"Was there ever another time in your life," I continued, "when you felt other women were doing the same thing to you? Trying to control you? Trying to boss you around?"

The question seemed to catch him off guard. His eyebrows went up in surprise. "Well, yeah," he said. "I never thought of it that way before, but you're right. I once dated a girl who was trying to change me and control me all the time. She was always telling me to go here, to do this, to wear that."

"You dumped her?"

"You bet."

"Sounds like a part of you down inside is very sensitive to being controlled by a woman. Why do you think that is?"

"That's easy," he said. "My mother was really bossy. I love her, but I always resented the way she tried to control me."

"So, Monty, it seems to me that you've developed a sore spot in your personality that is very sensitive to this issue. You very much resent any suggestion or indication that a woman is trying to control you."

"Yeah, I guess you're right."

"So the question is, how can the three of us craft a solution to this problem? How can we find a pattern of communication that would enable Grace to register her preferences without your feeling that she is trying to control you?"

That was the big problem the three of us needed to solve together.

FROM DIFFERENT WORLDS

The issue that brought Grace and Monty to the brink of divorce was *communication*. Grace wanted to know, "Why can't I say what I want to without getting in trouble? Why, when I express my feelings, thoughts, and preferences, does Monty withdraw from me and punish me with his silence?"

Much of the trouble Grace and Monty experienced could be traced to simple biology: Grace was born female, Monty was born male. Men and women are different in many ways, including the way they think. This is a generalization, of course. People are individuals, and not all individuals fit neatly into box-shaped categories. But on the whole, as a result of both cultural conditioning and biological makeup, men tend to think like men and women tend to think like women. This is due, in part, to the fact that the brains of men and of women are actually wired differently.

For example, there is a structure in the brain called the corpus callosum. This small bundle of nerve fibers connects the right hemisphere of the cerebral cortex with the left hemisphere and allows the two halves of the brain to interact with each other. These two halves of the brain—which I have labeled "the storehouse brain" (right) and "the logical brain" (left)—have specific functions. Neurological researchers have found that the corpus callosum tends to be thicker in women than in men, which means that women have more nerve pathways connecting the two brain hemispheres. This may account for the fact that women tend to be more "whole-brained" in their thinking and emotional expression, while men tend to be more "left-brain dominant" in their thinking.

Language researchers have found that there are communication characteristics that are gender-related. Some of these communication characteristics are predominantly male, others are predominantly female. Women tend to be focused on feelings and relationships while men tend to be focused on information and tasks.

Take a simple component of communication—such as a question—and you will find that men and women use that component for fundamentally different purposes. Women tend to ask questions as a means of making connections, eliciting feelings, and fostering a relationship. Men tend to ask questions in order to obtain information and complete a task.

In a romantic relationship, these fundamentally different styles of communication inevitably come into conflict, resulting in misunderstanding and suspicion. In a real sense, men and women come from different worlds, as John Gray made clear in his book on understanding the opposite sex, *Men Are from Mars, Women Are from Venus*. Men and women truly are alien beings to each other, trying to communicate with each other across a deep gulf of biological and psychological difference. In order to live together in a relationship of love and mutual support, we have to find a way to communicate with each other and understand each other.

We enter into a relationship with a lot of faulty assumptions about communication. We think that because men and women use the same words, they should automatically understand each other. However, men and women actually use the same words to achieve different purposes.

Whether male or female, we tend to project our own needs, feelings, and thought patterns onto our partner. "You need what I need," we think. "Therefore I will give you what I want to receive." We fail to understand that what we want may not be what our partner wants. We project our insecurities onto our partner: "If you disagree with me, you must not love me." We fail to recognize our partner's need for individual space and boundaries: "If you really love me, you'll stay close to me all the time. If you want 'space' right now, then you must not love me." We ascribe magical power to this thing called "love"—including the power of mental telepathy: "If you really loved me, you'd know what I mean."

These faulty assumptions are at the root of an enormous amount of marital strife and pain. Somehow, we must find a way, as men and women, husbands and wives, to bridge the gender gap. We must find a way to understanding. In order for a marriage to be healthy, both partners must learn how to understand and communicate with each other's world.

MEN'S WORLD

How do men view and define themselves? Again, this is a generalization, but it is a general observation rooted in fact. Most men tend to see themselves as individuals in a hierarchical social order where they are either One-Up or One-Down.

How men view status: Status is very important to men. If you tell others what to do, you have a high status; if others tell you what to do, you have a low status. Having the respect of one's peers is very important to men's self-esteem.

How men view communication: Men process information more readily than they share feelings. They discuss problems in order to arrive at solutions. Men's sense of self is defined through his ability to get results.

How men view power: Men pride themselves on autonomy, efficiency, power, and competence. Men are empowered when they feel needed (for example, as providers or problem solvers).

What men fear most: A man's greatest fear is that he is not good enough and that he will fail. Fear often makes a man seem uncaring.

How men view relationships: Men tend to be more interested in objects and structures than in people and feelings. Men are goal-oriented and activity-oriented; they build relationships by engaging in activities. Men often view relationships in vertical, hierarchical terms: "Who is a rung above me on the ladder of life? Who is below me? Who is on the same rung with me?" Men often form friendships (particularly in the business and social worlds) based on who can best help them scale the ladder of life. Because of their consciousness of status and hierarchy, men are often uncomfortable in romantic relationships with women who are, in any sense, higher up the ladder than they are.

WOMEN'S WORLD

How do women view and define themselves? Once again, we generalize—but this is a useful and instructive generalization.

How women view status: Women see themselves as part of a network of connections and relationships. Consensus and intimacy are usually more important than status. Women generally seek to minimize differences and avoid superiority (because that would make others feel inferior). Women's sense of self is defined by their feelings and the quality of their relationships.

How women view communication: Women discuss problems in order to get close, not necessarily to arrive at solutions. Whereas men may feel affronted by the advice of others (especially a wife or another woman), women often see an offer of help and advice as a sign of caring.

How women view power: Women are empowered when they feel cherished and valued. They feel powerless when the most significant people in their lives seem to disregard or minimize the importance of their feelings.

What women fear most: Since the great desire of women is for relationships, the great fear of women is abandonment.

How women view relationships: In contrast to men, who build relationships through activities, women build relationships through being close, having conversations, sharing feelings, and revealing secrets. While men view relationships as vertical hierarchies, women view relationships as webs or networks, with themselves at the center. Women do not generally seek to climb higher than other people; they prefer to reach out and pull others into their orbit. They don't view friendships as a means to gain advantage in climbing higher in life, but as a network of caring, encouragement, and support. While men view relationships vertically, women view relationships laterally.

While men invest comparatively little time and mental/emotional energy in relationships, women are heavily invested in their relationships. They think about relationships and talk about relationships with friends. Women continually reflect on relationships (men generally pay attention to relationships only when something goes wrong or a painful problem or conflict arises). Women are attentive to "emotional dust bunnies" under the bed of their relationships, and they engage in periodic "emotional housecleaning."

WHEN WORLDS COLLIDE

Clearly, the female world and the male world are very different. When these worlds collide, both sides are often wounded and left bewildered as to exactly what happened. Why did we have that argument? Why did communication break down? Why doesn't my partner understand me? Why can't I understand my partner? If our confusion and pain come from our alienness to each other, then healing comes from learning to understand each other.

One common scenario is when a wife tries to help her husband by giving him advice. According to the rules of her world, when people offer help or advice, it means they care about you. She doesn't understand that by the rules of her husband's world, advice-giving suggests that someone thinks you are incompetent. It's an insult to a man's sense of status and self-esteem. Instead of feeling helped or cared for, he feels One-Down, controlled, or even humiliated. Husbands are especially likely to over react to their wives' advice if they have experienced critical, controlling parenting in childhood or if they saw their fathers being bossed by an overbearing mother.

A man, too, often gets into trouble by trying to be helpful. For example, Harry's wife Sabrina came home, frustrated and angry about her job. "Arrgh!" she fumed. "When I took that promotion to vice principal, I had no idea what I was getting into! We've got a hundred and fifty ESL kids and only one teacher to handle them. The health aide they sent us from the downtown office is clueless when it comes to first aid. Thirteen kids took wrong buses and had to be rounded up and brought back to school. And to top it all off, I had to call in a case worker on a child-protection case today! I just don't know if I'm going to make it!"

"Maybe you should go back to teaching," Harry offered helpfully.

Sabrina eyed him with shock and reproach. "What!" she retorted. "How can you say that! I *love* this job!"

"Well," Harry responded, trying to undo the damage he unwittingly did with his first suggestion, "maybe you should hire somebody to handle the overflow."

"There's no budget for more personnel!" Sabrina countered, her anger mounting. "Remember? You and about thirty thousand other idiots voted against the school bond!"

"You don't have to get nasty about it!" he growled defensively. "I was just trying to offer some helpful suggestions!"

"It might be helpful if you would just *listen* to me once in a while," Sabrina shot back. "You never listen to me!"

"I *was* listening to you!" Harry replied hotly. "That's why I was trying to help!"

"You weren't *listening*," she answered, fuming. "You were *talking!*"

"I was trying to help you solve your problems!"

"You always think you have the answer for everything, but you don't know diddly-squat about my problems!"

And so it went.

It all began when Sabrina began to pour out her troubles and Harry tried to solve them for her. Sabrina just wanted someone to listen to her tale of woe, someone to be a supportive friend and a sounding board. Information-oriented, task-oriented, problem-solving Harry thought she wanted someone to fix her problems for her. The result: frustration on both sides. Harry tried to be helpful, and he didn't have a clue as to where he went wrong.

When a woman is upset, tired, sad, or confused, she is usually not in the market for someone to come in and solve her problems for her. She just wants to be heard and understood. She wants emotional support. She wants to have her feelings validated, not discounted. To sum it all up, she really just wants a friend. When her husband takes the time to listen, to offer his empathy and his time, she feels loved and valued, and she is able to put her problems into a better perspective.

Another place where male and female worlds collide is in the use of words. Women tend to use words to express emotion, and they will often amplify the expression of their feelings by using higher-wattage words. When a woman says, "We *never* go out," or, "Why do you *always* forget to take out the garbage," her message is actually, "I feel very strongly about the fact that we don't go out often enough," or "I really want you to understand how upsetting it is that you often forget the garbage." She is not using "never" and "always" in a literal sense.

But men, being information-oriented rather than feelings-oriented, tend to jump on the fact that their wives have not accurately stated the facts. Eager to cancel out the criticism they hear in their wives' message, they seize upon the literal inaccuracy of the words "never" and "always." They counter with, "How can you say that? I took you out to dinner just three months ago!" or "I don't always forget! I remembered the garbage all by myself the Sunday before St. Swithin's Day, remember?"

Meanwhile, the woman feels she's not being heard. She thinks her feelings are being ignored. So how does she respond? She cranks up the emotional wattage. Her language becomes (from the male point of view) even more inaccurate.

Now we have a full-blown argument and neither side can even agree on the terms of the discussion. She is arguing her feelings. He is arguing the content of words. She feels her feelings are being disregarded and invalidated. He is trying to win the argument on debating points. In the end, no one wins. Everybody loses.

A DEAFENING SILENCE

The "silent treatment" is one of the oldest tricks in the book. It is one of the biggest challenges to marital communication. Both sides use the silent treatment, but men and women use silence in different ways and for different purposes.

Men sometimes withdraw from a conversation. They just stop responding. Sometimes they are mulling it over, processing information, and trying to come up with a response that will swat their wives' arguments right out of the ballpark. At other times, they use silence as a way to assert their control over a situation: "You want to have a conversation; I don't. Fine. I'm going to just sit here and read the paper as if you don't exist. Ha-ha, I win."

Whatever a man's reasons for using the silent treatment, a woman is likely to interpret it as a symbol of his lack of caring. Women value understanding, connection, empathy, and being cherished. Above all, they want to be heard and they want their feelings validated. Silence says, "I don't want to understand you or be connected to you. I have no empathy for your problems. I don't value you as a person. I couldn't care less about your stupid feelings. Go away and leave me alone."

There could hardly be a more destructive and insulting message than that! For many women, silence triggers her worst fear—the fear of abandonment. This is why so many women become desperate, almost panic-stricken, in their pursuit of a withdrawn husband.

Women tend to use the silent treatment in a different way. Often, a woman who has lapsed into silence and apparent withdrawal is not withdrawing at all. In fact, she may actually be trying to protect the relationship rather than inflict hurt on her husband. There are things she could say, things she wants to say, but she's afraid that if she says what's on her mind, it might be too damaging to her husband or to the relationship. So she bites her tongue.

Women also tend to go silent when they feel insecure in a situation. If a woman feels she can't compete with their husbands' debating skills (or his decibel level), she may go silent rather than look foolish. In any case, women are more likely to use silence as a defensive rather than an offensive weapon. They stop talking to protect the relationship, to protect themselves, and even to protect their husbands from their own anger.

When we know there is a desperate need for communication in the marriage relationship, silence can be deafening. It's important, then, that both partners have a strategy in place for responding to the "silent treatment."

The instinctive response is to charge right in and try to force a response. The first attempt may be sweet, kind, and patient: "Come on, honey. Talk about it. Tell me what's wrong. You'll feel better, you know you will." The second attempt seeks to probe for clues: "Is it something I said? Something I did? Something I didn't say?" With the third attempt, patience begins to wear thin: "Look, I'm trying to help. I really want to know what's going on, but you're not giving me anything to work with. I'm beginning to feel, well, a little frustrated."

By the fourth attempt, the gloves come off and we're at it, bare knuckles: "All right, you stupid jerk! That's the way you want it? Just sit there like petrified wood and see if I care! When you're ready to beg my forgiveness, you can find me at Starbucks!" *Slam!*

The above procedure is not recommended. Here's a more productive way to respond to the silent treatment:

1. If your partner withdraws in to silence, let him or her do so for a while. Give your partner some space. As much as possible, avoid showing disapproval. Be patient and accepting.
2. Avoid questioning your partner or trying to draw your partner out.
3. Avoid trying to solve your partner's problems by offering advice.
4. Get on with your life. Sure, it's hard not to think about the situation. One person's personal gloom has a tendency to settle over the whole house like a cloud. That can't fully be avoided, but as much as possible, try to carry on a normal routine. Do something to take your mind off your partner's silence. Take a walk or take the kids to the

zoo. Call a friend. Put on your favorite music. Do some gardening. Read a good book. Meditate and pray.

Don't allow your partner's moods to control your feelings. Your emotions do not have to rise or set with your partner's emotions. If you find that your partner's moods frequently dominate your emotions, then you need to establish healthier emotional boundaries. Counseling may help clarify these issues so that you can become less vulnerable to your partner's moods.

HOT TALK

Couples argue about all kinds of things: money (that's a big one), major decisions, minor decisions, discipline and child rearing, schedules and appointments, chores and responsibilities, in-laws, friends, and incredibly minor trivialities. Beneath the surface, however, there are usually only a few issues: fear of being controlled, fear of being abandoned, perceived lack of respect, and perceived lack of understanding. Many couples actually have the same argument over and over, but they don't realize it keeps appearing repackaged in a different surface issue each time.

The surface packaging is just camouflage for the big emotional symbol at the heart of it all: the sense that we are not being adequately loved and valued. The following paragraphs offer some examples of this.

She argues: "Sure! Stomp off into your den and slam the door! Run away from the problem! You just can't deal with a woman who has her own opinions and speaks her mind!" What she really feels: "Please don't withdraw from me and make me feel ignored. I do exist and I need your love."

He argues: "Why do you keep getting mad at me for such picky little things?" What he really feels (even though he may not realize it or be able to articulate it): "Why can't you accept me and love me just the way I am?"

She argues: "Go ahead, yell and pound the table, you big Neanderthal! Why don't you just haul me off and blacken my eyes! You're just itching to pop me one, aren't you?" What she really feels: "Your yelling and fist-pounding scares me and makes me feel insecure. I don't feel loved, valued, and cherished right now."

He argues: "Can't you stop telling me what to do and treating me like a kid?" What he really feels: "I need to be loved and respected as a competent man."

She argues: "How stupid can you be, forgetting our anniversary? What did you think that big red circle on the calendar was for?" What she really feels: "If our anniversary is unimportant to you, then you must not love me."

He argues: "Quit telling me how much you do around here! I do plenty! If it weren't for me, this household would fall apart!" What he really feels: "Why don't you love me and appreciate my contribution to the family?"

She argues: "Don't tell me I shouldn't feel this way! These are my feelings, not yours, and you have no right to tell me how to feel!" What she really feels: "Please don't tell me my emotions are not valid. Please love me and support me where I am right now."

Once we begin to see beneath the surface issue, we find a throbbing human heart, yearning to be loved. When we focus on the needs of that human heart rather than the surface issue, the argument begins to unravel. In order to communicate across the gulf that separates the world of men from the world of women, we must look beyond the surface and feed our partner's heart the one thing it hungers for: love.

Next chapter . . . sex!

TAKE ACTION
Questions of a Marriage

If you and your partner are answering these questions together, first write your answers down separately, then compare your answers—but remember to use covenant-love to deal with any disagreements! Use the information you gather from each other to better understand how each of you look at, and feel about, your love relationship.

1. In your marriage, who is more likely to withdraw or go silent, you or your partner?

   Why do you think you or your partner chooses silence rather than engagement and communication at those times?

   Is the silence itself a form of communication?

2. In this chapter, we discuss the fact that men and women use language in fundamentally different ways. Describe a recent event in your marriage which may have resulted from the different ways you and your partner use language. Is there an insight (or are there several insights) from this chapter that help you to put that event into perspective?

   How could that situation have been handled differently, with the help of an understanding of basic differences between male and female communication patterns?

3. Do you agree or disagree with the statement in this chapter that husbands and wives are "alien beings to each other, trying to communicate with each other across a deep gulf . . . [yet] forced to coexist in the same living space"?

   Why or why not?

   Is this image helpful to you in understanding why your partner does or says certain things?

   Why or why not?

4. What are some of the specific issues over which your world and your partner's worlds collide?

   After reading this chapter, are you able to see deeper symbolic and emotional issues which underlie the surface "packaging" of your marital conflict?

What are some of those deeper issues?

How can understanding these deeper issues enable you to manage your conflict more effectively in the future?

5. Does your partner's mood affect or control your emotions? Or are you able to separate your feelings from those of your partner?

When your partner is angry or unhappy for reasons that have nothing to do with you, what are some favorite things you can do to keep from getting overshadowed by your partner's emotional storm clouds? (Suggestions: Take a walk or take the kids to the zoo. Call a friend. Put on your favorite music. Do some gardening. Read a good book.)

6. Do you see the desire for love (your desire and your partner's) as being at the heart of most or all of your marital arguments?

How can your partner love you (or make you feel loved) in such a way that these arguments become less frequent and less intense?

How can you make your partner feel loved in such a way that these arguments become less frequent and less intense?

TWELVE

How Important Should Sex Be?

Franci closes her eyes and waits for it to be over. Her skin is like ice to Kyle's touch—hard and cold. Like so many times before, he senses no desire in her. Only anxiety. Even fear.

He tenses, all passion draining out of him.

"What's wrong?" he whispers into the darkness. The darkness makes no reply. "Franci? . . . Franci?" Kyle waits a long time, then he rolls away from her. He thinks he feels the trembling of her sobbing transmitted through the bed, but he's not sure. Should he be angry? Hurt? Should he talk to her? Leave her alone? Go out to the couch and fall asleep in front of the TV?

And there is a larger question that gnaws at his insides: Can he stay married to a woman who doesn't even want him in her bed?

HOW IMPORTANT IS SEX?

Studies show that roughly one out of five Americans have no sex life at all. Through their behavior (or lack of it), they are saying that sex is completely unimportant. Another ten percent of Americans suffer from uncontrollable sexual urges—that is, with sexual addictions. To them, sex overshadows everything else in their lives. The issue for those who want to have a healthy marriage is to strike the right balance and to make an appropriate place for passion in their relationship.

The good news, according to a Family Research Council study released in 1994, is that seventy-two percent of those who see sex as belonging exclusively within marriage report a high degree of sexual satisfaction—a much higher degree, in fact, than those who admit engaging in promiscuous or extramarital sex. The act of sex is not the be-all and end-all of marriage, but it is important, and seventy-two percent of faithfully married, sexually active Americans will tell you it's well worth the effort.

The sex act has a powerful, dynamic meaning in the marriage relationship. It symbolizes the sacred covenant-love relationship between a man and a woman. In the marriage ceremony, it is usually stated in various ways that "the two become one," and this statement is symbolized by such symbols as the ring ceremony or the cup of Holy Communion or two candles uniting to light a single flame. The act of sex is the physical symbol of this same spiritual truth. In this act, two human souls move from a state of isolation and aloneness into true, intimate connection with one another in the marriage relationship.

Women and men are paradoxically alike and unlike. They are similar enough to each other that they can share thoughts, feelings, hopes, and dreams, yet they are different enough that they are attractive, desirable, and mysterious to each other. The woman complements the man, completing what he lacks, and the man does the same for the woman. The sex act physically seals the covenant between the man and the woman, symbolizing the mutuality, intimacy, and exclusivity of their love, bonding their committed relationship, and showing them their need to live in dependence upon each other.

The sex act produces the most intense, concentrated pleasure in all of human experience, yet—amazingly!—pleasure is the most superficial benefit we derive from sex. In the sex act, the husband and wife express to each other that they have truly forsaken all others and that they totally, unreservedly open themselves to each other. Expressed within the safe, secure, private boundaries of marriage, the sex act is more than just a pleasurable biological drive. It is an emotional statement that a husband and wife make to each other: "I commit to you an aspect of my emotions, my soul, and my physical being that I share with no other human being on earth." In sex, we uncover our deepest, innermost selves and offer that selfhood to our partner as a precious gift.

Sex has a way of gathering up and focusing many of the other emotionally charged issues in a relationship. In the physical act of sex, a husband and a wife are completely vulnerable to each other. Their boundaries disappear and they enter each other. Trust is an essential aspect of a satisfying sexual relationship because both partners must trust each other in order to accept each other in a physical way. A trusting, satisfying sexual relationship is built on a foundation of a promise, a binding covenant. Marriage, the covenant relationship between a man and a woman, is a safe place where intimacy, vulnerability, and trust can grow.

Both partners must want sex. They don't have to want it at the same time or with equal intensity, but each, in his or her own way, must send the other the message, "I want you." In fact, wanting to be sexual, sensual, and affectionate may not always have a lot to do with intercourse. Men tend to be very "goal-oriented" in their love-making—with the goal, of course, being orgasm. Women have a lot to teach men about the other pleasurable and intimacy-building behaviors of sex—talking, holding, caressing, and exchanging non-verbal signals of affection.

In a healthy relationship, when one partner initiates sexual signals, the other responds appropriately. In love-making, it should be clear who is asking for what. Many people—particularly women—don't want to have intercourse all the time, but would like to be close, to be held, to be fondled. I've heard many women say in counseling, "I'd like to have him close, but every time I try to convey that to him, he takes it as an invitation for intercourse. That's not what I was asking for."

In the early stages of a marriage, temporary problems with sex are common and usually involve inexperience, inhibitions, or communication problems. But for many couples, sexual problems are a symptom of deeper distortions in the relationship. If left unresolved, sexual problems tend to crystallize. The sexual dimension is a crucial dimension of a marriage. Properly understood and approached with love and practical insight, sex can be an important tool for building long-lasting intimacy, satisfaction, and harmony in a marriage relationship.

YOUR SEXUAL EQUIPMENT

Most of us tend to think of sexual pleasure as something we experience in a few selected "erogenous zones" at strategically located points of our anatomy. Sometimes we forget that our most important sex organ is located right between our ears. All the sensory input that generates sexual arousal and pleasure—the sights, the sounds, the fragrances, the sensation of skin on skin, the feelings of warmth and motion—are all transmitted from the distant sensory points of the body to a single location: the brain.

The brain is where all of our sexual problems begin as well. Worries, anger, distractions, fears, memories, misconceptions—these are the obstructions that can block the pathway to sexual pleasure and satisfaction for both partners. Because the brains of men and women are wired differently, men and women experience sexual desire in different ways.

Men experience arousal primarily through imagery. A man can be visually stimulated to sexual arousal—but imagery doesn't have to be only visual. A sexually laden image can be formed in his mind by word pictures, by something he hears or reads that creates a sexual image in his mind, or by his own memories and imagination. A man "turns on" quickly, and he can generally achieve sexual release more quickly than a woman.

Men begin their sex life without a partner, through adolescent wet dreams and masturbation. Their first sexual experience tells them, "You can be aroused and experience orgasm all by yourself." Men must learn to be with a partner, to care for her needs, to allow her to be involved in his arousal and pleasure. Men need to learn that sex is interactive, not just a selfish grab for pleasure.

Unlike women, men are able to personally disengage themselves from their sex partner and to see a woman as an object, even as a possession. As a result, men sometimes get involved in unhealthy sexual patterns, becoming observers of a woman as an object (say, through pornography or using prostitutes) rather than caring for a woman's needs in a committed relationship. Men are also prone to reducing sex to a set of techniques instead of the uninhibited opening of the self in a sacred covenant-love relationship.

Women experience arousal primarily through communication. When a woman experiences a sense of security, intimacy, and emotional connection with her man, she is warmed and moved to open up the recesses of her being to him. Words of tenderness and caring are more important than images in arousing a woman.

Just as a woman is physically constructed to be joined with and penetrated, she also is emotionally designed with a desire to reveal her inner secrets to a man in an act of total vulnerability, openness, and reception. When she feels safe, loved, and accepted, her boundaries relax and she is not only willing but she actively desires to be physically, mentally, emotionally, and spiritually penetrated, because penetration represents connection, the ultimate closeness—the essence of being joined to another human being.

A SEXUAL PURSUIT

Nick had an unusual complaint about his wife, Darcy: "She's always after me for sex! She's always wearing these slinky, filmy things and putting her hands all over me, trying to coax me into bed!"

Darcy looked away as Nick spoke. She looked sullen and embarrassed. "Most men would be happy to have a wife who's affectionate," she muttered. "It's not like I'm unattractive or anything." Darcy had a point—she was very attractive.

Nick grimaced. "There's a difference between being affectionate and being oversexed!" he responded.

"There's such a thing as being undersexed, you know!" Darcy shot back.

With a little probing, I determined that Nick was not "undersexed." They had sexual relations about four to six times a week—but sometimes Nick just said no when Darcy pursued him. His libido simply wasn't up to Darcy's demands.

"How do you feel about your relationship with Nick," I said, addressing Darcy, "apart from the issue of sex?"

"I feel . . . underappreciated," she said. "Nick doesn't, well, *cherish* me like I want him to."

"What do you mean?"

"He takes me for granted. There's no romance in our lives. He doesn't treat me as special."

"When Nick agrees to have sex with you, do you feel special then? Does the sex satisfy your need to be cherished?"

She thought for several seconds, then admitted, "No, it doesn't."

I gave Nick an assignment: he was to initiate various acts of treating Darcy special—not with sex, but with kindness. Nick worked hard on his assignment for the next couple weeks. He called her from work, just to chat. He sent her notes and cards. He surprised her with a night out. Within days, the level of Darcy's sexual pursuits dropped to a level that matched Nick's own sex drive. Though she didn't consciously realize it, sex had never been the real issue in pursuit of Nick. She just wanted to know she was loved and accepted. Sex had become a metaphor of the emotional satisfaction she was lacking. Once Nick began to treat her as special, she ceased being "oversexed."

THE SEQUENCE OF SEX

Each partner is responsible to make sex comfortable and enjoyable for the other partner. Both partners in the relationship need to take responsibility for knowing each other's preferences and arousal patterns. The sex act takes place in a four-step sequence: arousal, passion, climax, and resolution.

Arousal begins in the emotions of one or both partners. The man may experience arousal quickly, almost instantaneously, with a single image, a kiss, or an embrace. The woman's experience of arousal may emerge slowly, almost imperceptibly, beginning as early as a morning hug in bed or a compliment over the breakfast table.

The slow building of a mood of desire may continue building with a caring phone call from work or an offer to help clear the table after dinner—an offer that symbolizes caring and connectedness. For a woman, the act of sex does not take place during a brief time in bed; it is a culmination of a network of acts, words, thoughts, and feelings that have accumulated throughout the day.

When a couple experiences sexual dysfunction at this point in the process of sexual intimacy—for example, if one partner consistently fails to experience arousal so that sex rarely or never takes place—the sexual problem is usually the result of emotional problems or conflicts embedded in the relationship, not a physical problem.

The second step is *passion.* The couple moves from the emotional phase to the physical phase of the sex act. Both the man and the woman experience a pink flush as the pulse quickens and blood pressure rises. The man experiences an erection of the penis and the woman experiences an erection of her nipples and clitoris, accompanied by the release of a lubricant from her vagina. He is ready to move into her and she is ready to be entered—but satisfying lovemaking is patient and slow; the couple need not progress immediately to intercourse at this time.

Sometimes a man does not fully understand the important role his wife's breasts and clitoris play in her sexual pleasure. His lack of attention to her need for physical stimulation—especially if she hesitates to communicate directly with him about her needs—often produces sexual dysfunction in marriage. Couples should use the passion stage as a time for exploring each other, caressing each other, enjoying each other, and communicating with each other—slowly, pleasantly moving toward the moment of climax.

Most women need some manual stroking of the clitoris in order to achieve orgasm. The man, whose passion tends to build more quickly than the woman's, may need to pace himself and match her rhythms so that the experience can be more mutually satisfying. The longer he delays his climax, the more intense it is likely to be.

Men who speed to intercourse and early climax often do so because of anxiety about their performance. A man may fear losing his erection, so he rushes toward orgasm. Counseling can often help reduce the anxiety level so that sex can be more mutually satisfying.

The third step is the *climax* or orgasm. At this stage, the man and the woman experience the overpowering and profound peak of the sexual experience. The man experiences the release of semen in an explosive outpouring of pleasure. The woman's orgasm is subtly different, usually longer lasting, involving powerful undulations of pleasure, like ocean waves. Even after the last wave has subsided, her body tingles with sensation and is pleasurably sensitive to being touched.

Despite the popular romantic mythology of books and films, most couples find simultaneous orgasm to be an elusive goal most of the time. From the standpoint of sexual satisfaction, it's not necessary that both partners climax at the same moment. In fact, it's not necessary that every sexual encounter result in orgasm for both partners; sometimes just holding and caressing can be enough, especially if one or both partners are just too tired to achieve climax. If couples feel the pressure to perform heroic feats of sexual prowess, the results can be "fake orgasms" that lead to sexual unhappiness, dishonesty, and a decline of intimacy in the relationship.

Physical problems that may interfere with the enjoyment of sex during the passion and climax stages include painful intercourse for the woman, and for the man, premature ejaculation or loss of erection. Sources of physical sexual dysfunction include fatigue, stress, drug or alcohol use, certain blood pressure medications (such as beta blockers), being overweight, hormone imbalances, or disease. A medical doctor should be consulted about such problems, because these problems can be medically treated.

Emotional problems that interfere with the sexual experience— anxiety, distractions, guilt, and so forth—can usually be resolved through counseling. Whether an experience of sexual dysfunction is physical or emotional in nature, clear communication between the marital partners is crucial. Sometimes, problems clear up when both partners convey to each other what kinds of sexual technique produce the greatest arousal and pleasure. If communication between partners does not solve the problem, a couple should not hesitate to take those problems to a medical or psychological professional for treatment.

The fourth step is *resolution.* Men and women experience this phase differently. Once a man reaches orgasm, you can "stick a fork in him—he's done." His sexual energy has been spent. But the woman is not done yet. She comes down from her climax more slowly and can achieve multiple orgasms, particularly if a state of emotional connection is maintained. During the resolution phase, both the man and the woman experience a warm sense of well-being that is conducive to hugging, tender words, and intimacy-building.

SEXUAL PROBLEMS AND HOW TO SOLVE THEM

Within the covenant-love relationship of marriage, both partners should feel free to engage in a wide variety of sexual techniques and behavior, so long as both partners agree and find it pleasurable. Sex should be experienced without guilt or undue inhibition between these two interconnected, interdependent human beings, husband and wife. The expression of physical and emotional passion is a beautiful and healthy human experience. An active, regular sex life is conducive to good emotional health and genuine intimacy. The joy and well-being that a good sex life produces is essential to the emotional health of a family.

Sexual dysfunction often occurs when one or both partners in a marriage do not have a healthy attitude toward sex. Many people enter marriage with a set of unhealthy attitudes toward sex as a result of taboos acquired in childhood. Some people, thinking that sex is sinful or dirty, become sexually dysfunctional because their conscience won't allow them to enjoy sex.

Others develop an attitude that the more sinful an act is, the more sexually exciting it is. These people often develop sexual addictions—that is, they get caught up in forms of sexual behavior that are not healthy (such addictions to pornography, phone sex, group sex, mate-swapping, or sadomasochism). The result of sexual addiction is guilt, shame, diminished self-esteem, and broken intimacy, often with such side effects as unwanted pregnancy and sexually transmitted disease.

Another source of sexual dysfunction is a history of sexual abuse. People who have experienced sexual abuse in childhood tend to experience some form of sexual dysfunction as adults. The sexual abuse of a child violates that child's boundaries and innermost being at a time when basic personality, emotional boundaries, and life long attitudes are being shaped. Abused children have endured the ultimate betrayal and are unable to feel safe so that they can relax their boundaries and become vulnerable in the sex act. There is no aspect of our being that is more intimate and personal than our sexuality, and the invasion of this dimension of ourselves produces scars that rarely heal without intervention through professional counseling.

Guilt is another factor in sexual problems. There are many issues that can haunt a person, producing guilt feelings that interfere with sexual enjoyment: sexual secrets, extramarital or premarital sexual experience, abortion, and past abuse (even though abuse victims are innocent, they often feel tremendous guilt long into adulthood). In order for a couple to experience a healthy sex life, old memories must be purged, old hurts must be forgiven, old losses must be grieved. It's often necessary for a couple to undergo therapy together in order to achieve these goals.

Not every sexual problem a couple experiences is a true dysfunction. Many problems are temporary and work themselves out. Some problems are related to cycles and seasons in a couple's relationship and changes in their level of intimacy. Sometimes, one or both partners tire of a sexual routine that no longer seems stimulating and exciting. Then, within a few weeks, the desire returns along with an interest in trying new techniques and forms of sexual expression. That's OK. It's just a rhythm that couples go through over the course of a life together.

The key to a satisfying sexual relationship is to focus not on sex, but on intimacy. Sex and intimacy are mutually reinforcing components of a healthy marriage. A mutually caring sex life helps to deepen the intellectual, emotional, and spiritual intimacy of a marriage. And genuine intimacy serves to heighten the passion of a marriage.

Many people, unfortunately, place such a high premium on the physical pleasures of sex that they neglect the emotional and spiritual pleasures of intimacy. Some, reaching a point where sex with the same partner no longer seems as exciting as before, decide that the romance is gone from the marriage. They become bored and they stray because they have missed the whole point of marriage.

Couples who make intimacy their aim discover that marital sex is an ever-changing, ever-deepening experience. Just because two people have sex doesn't mean they are truly intimate with each other. There is an insight in the language of the Bible that you may find helpful. The Bible uses two terms to describe the act of sex: to "lie with" and "to know." If a man "lies with" a woman in the Bible, it is usually an act of casual sex, such as sex with a prostitute, extramarital sex, rape or incest.

But when the Bible speaks of sex within a covenant-love relationship, it generally uses the term "to know," as in "Abraham knew his wife Sarah." It is an act that takes place within the safe, satisfying enclosure of promise, intimacy, and genuine love. To truly and fully *know* one's partner is a beautiful and satisfying experience.

The pleasures of sex don't diminish over time for a loving couple, because both partners are continually reaching for deeper levels of intimacy, connection, discovery, and understanding. Sexual desire finds its most profound and meaningful release in the context of a loving, mutual relationship with someone who is not merely a sex partner, but a soul mate for life.

In the next chapter, we will explore the question of leadership in the marriage.

TAKE ACTION
Questions of a Marriage

If you and your partner are answering these questions together, first write your answers down separately, then compare your answers— but remember to use covenant-love to deal with any disagreements! Use the information you gather from each other to better understand how each of you look at, and feel about, your love relationship.

1. Do you feel that you truly want to experience a satisfying sex life in your marriage? Why or why not?

2. Check any of the following statements that express a belief or attitude you have been holding about sex:

   • "The subject of S-E-X is too personal and embarrassing for me to talk about with my partner."
   • "The goal of sex is for both partners to experience simultaneous orgasm."
   • "Good sex must be a graceful, almost dance-like performance, like in the movies and romance novels."
   • "Each sexual episode in our marriage must lead to orgasm for both partners or it is a failure."
   • "A wife should do whatever her husband wants—even if she hates it and it makes her feel bad."
   • "A wife is sexually passive; it is not right for a woman to initiate sex."
   • "Men need sex more than women; women can do without sex."
   • "Men cannot be intimate or close. They must be manipulated so that a woman can get what she wants."
   • "A woman must use sex to control a man."
   • "No man can be trusted."
   • "Sex is for procreation, not for pleasure."
   • "It's my partner's fault I don't reach climax. I shouldn't have to talk about it. He or she should just know what I need and should do it."
   • "Sometimes you have to use sex as a threat or a reward to get what you want."
   • "I don't see anything wrong with having sex outside of marriage."

   After having read this chapter, what marital or emotional problems result from the attitude or attitudes that you checked?

3. When you experience a problem with sex, at what stage of the sex act do you tend to experience that problem?

• arousal
• passion
• climax
• resolution

4. When a problem gets in the way of your sexual satisfaction, what is usually the source of that problem?

• my partner
• my thoughts or emotions (such as guilt, anger, or worry)
• my attitudes about sex (such as "sex is sinful")
• a physical problem (fatigue, stress, medication, etc.)
• other _____

5. Do you feel you have unhealthy or unbiblical attitudes toward sex?

Where do you believe these attitudes came from?

Many unhealthy attitudes toward sex arise in childhood, either because of what we were taught or because no one took the time to teach us the truth about sex. The following checklist may give you a clue as to the source of some of your misconceptions about sex. Check any statements that apply to you:

• My parents' behavior toward each other was completely non-sexual and non-affectionate—I never saw them kiss, hug, or speak affectionately to each other.
• Sex was a taboo subject in our family—never discussed.
• I received no sexual information from my parents.
• I was taught in the home or in church that sex is a sin.
• My mother told me that sex is a wife's duty.
• My parents slept in separate beds or separate rooms.
• One of my parents had an extramarital affair or series of affairs and brought great hurt to our family.

- I was sexually abused by a parent or other adult when I was a child.

If you checked any of the above statements—and especially if you checked the last one—you should consider seeking help for your attitudes and issues from a professional counselor.

6. Consider making a "Romantic Covenant" with your partner, including any love-making wants, needs, or issues that are important to you and your partner. Some issues you may want to include are the following:

"We mutually agree to respect each other's desires and feelings in our sexual relationship."

"We agree to be frank and honest in discussing our needs and our sexual relationship."

"We agree to take the pressure off in our love-making—no more 'sexual goals' like simultaneous climax."

"We agree that sex is not to be used to get what we want from the other partner."

"We agree to ask for what we want, but not to criticize or belittle the other's wants or sexuality."

"We mutually pledge our caring, patience, and understanding, and promise not to make demands or inflict guilt into our romantic relationship."

"We mutually promise to be faithful and exclusive to each other in our sexual relationship; that we will not violate the boundaries of our relationship by taking our sexuality outside of marriage or even discussing our sexuality with others (except, if necessary, a professional counselor)."

THIRTEEN

Who Leads?

———————

Clark and Brandy came into my office for counseling. Clark was quiet and sullen. Brandy was frustrated to the point of fury. "For fifteen years, ever since we've been married," she said, "I've had the sole leadership role in the family. Clark never initiates anything. He's never spontaneous. He never has any ideas. He's a wimp! You've heard of Superman's alter ego, Clark Kent, mild-mannered reporter for *The Daily Planet*? That's my husband—Clark Kent! I'm sick of being married to Clark Kent. I want Superman!"

Clark sent a hostile glare in her direction but said nothing.

"Clark," I said, turning in his direction, "do you agree or disagree with Brandy's assessment?"

"Well," Clark began, "I guess I don't really initiate very much around our house. I don't get a chance! She's always telling me what to do before I get a chance to do it on my own. She's always saying, 'Be spontaneous! Be spontaneous!' Well, doesn't she see that the moment she tells me to be spontaneous, she makes it *impossible* for me to be spontaneous? Anything I do after that point will seem to be nothing more than my responding to her demands!"

Clark had just articulated a common leadership problem in marriage—the "Be Spontaneous" Paradox: How can anyone be "spontaneous" on command? The moment Brandy demanded that

Clark lead, she became the leader. The more she told him to lead, the more she paralyzed him as a leader.

But Brandy was also caught in a paradox of her own: If she didn't either lead or tell Clark to lead, *no one* would lead. Clark really was too passive in the relationship. Her problem: "How do I get Clark to lead without telling him to lead?" She was checkmated. If she waited for him to lead, she might wait forever. But when she led, she mentally and emotionally castrated her husband.

My task, then, was twofold: (1) I had to help Brandy learn new patterns of relating to Clark so that she could moderate her impulse to initiate and her impulse to berate her husband for not initiating; and (2) I had to encourage Clark to initiate action and demonstrate leadership at home.

Clark's first response when I encouraged him to initiate was to ask me, "What should I do?" In other words, he turned to me for leadership! I turned it right back on him: "Oh, no, Clark! If I tell you what to do, I'll just be replacing Brandy as the leader in your home. You have to assume that role. You have to do your own thinking, your own planning, and your own initiating. You must be the leader now, and Brandy has agreed that she's going to make an effort to step back and let you lead."

"But what if she doesn't step back?" he asked.

"And what if you don't step up?" I said. "You're both taking a risk, and you both need to be patient with each other, because you both need to relearn your roles. She's pledging to give you room to lead, and you are pledging to step up and lead. You're both going to make mistakes, and you're both going to learn from your mistakes. So take this opportunity to choose what needs to be done in your family, then initiate whatever action it takes to accomplish it."

Over the next few weeks, the three of us continued to meet together. It was a classic case of two steps forward, one step back. Old patterns died hard, and Clark found it difficult to become creative, confident, and assertive in his new role as leader. Brandy frequently had to be reminded to allow her husband to find his way in the new role.

During our sessions, I shared with Clark and Brandy the principles contained in this chapter. In time, Clark became—well, not

Superman exactly, but a man and a leader. Clark and Brandy became a more well-balanced, stable, and mutually supportive couple than Clark Kent and Lois Lane ever thought of being.

The leadership issue is a big one in most marriages. Who leads? Who follows? And when?

ROLES, NOT CONTROL

Most leadership problems arise when couples misunderstand what leadership is all about. Leadership is not a "power" issue. It's not about who "controls" or who is the "boss." It is an issue of roles. In some family matters, the husband may be more gifted to take the leadership role. In other matters, the wife may have a greater natural aptitude for leadership.

Authentic leadership does not derive from a strong will or a loud voice. Rather, it consists of the ability to initiate, direct, influence, and inspire others to follow. In a healthy relationship, leadership is reciprocal and shared. Sometimes one leads and the other follows, then they switch. The reins of leadership are passed from hand to hand. In less healthy marriages, the leadership roles tend to be complementary (one always leads, the other always follows) or symmetrical (both struggle for power or both withdraw). In a healthy relationship, both partners come to terms with the power issue. Neither partner feels threatened or diminished by accepting the role of follower from time to time.

Leadership can take the form of initiating sex, planning meals, earning money, budgeting the family finances, planning vacations, and so forth. In many areas of the marriage and family life, each partner can play to his or her personality strengths. The husband can lead in areas where his gifts, talents, and abilities are strongest, and the wife can lead in her areas of greatest strength. This way, instead of competing with each other, the partners complement each other.

Our natural human tendency is to look at the role of leadership as one of status and power, of being One-Up while everybody else is One-Down. In reality, leadership is a quality with many facets. A good leader must be a good manager, responsible for everything that goes on under his or her stewardship. Nothing should take place without the leader's awareness and approval. A good leader is also a good delegator, utilizing the abilities and skills of others rather than doing everything alone. A good leader is a visionary who can motivate others to implement a vision. A good leader doesn't intimidate; a good leader inspires, influences, and instructs.

Both the husband and wife should be leaders in the home. Both have equal status and equal worth. Both are worthy of honor and respect. Each has a different role, but both roles are leadership roles.

FITTING TWO LEADERSHIP ROLES TOGETHER

Because authentic leadership is servanthood, the person who "calls the shots" in any situation, whether in the office or at home, should do so with the humble attitude of a servant, not as a boss. To lead is to love in a self-sacrificing way. If one partner makes a family decision, he or she should base that decision on authentic love for the other partner and for the family. The leader should place the needs of the family ahead of his or her own need for prestige, fulfillment, ego, or pleasure.

Both partners have a happy duty to nourish each other, emotionally and spiritually. This means that both partners cherish and honor each other and build up each other. They should help each other to feel emotionally and physically secure. They should welcome each other's thoughts, ideas, and feelings. Leadership is ultimately about meeting the needs of people.

Leadership in a family is not supposed to be a matter of one partner being perpetually One-Up, the other One-Down. It's not healthy for marriage partners to occupy static roles: "me Tarzan, you Jane." Both the man and the woman are leaders in the home. There are different roles, different abilities, different tasks to be performed, but both partners are leaders. Both have equal status and value in the relationship.

Together, a man and woman who are able to lead in a relationship become an unbeatable team. There are many ways the responsibilities of a household can be divided up to maximize the gifts and strengths of both partners. In many marriages, the wife just happens to be handier with a checkbook and a calculator, so she handles the bill-paying and the family ledger. In some cases, the husband enjoys grocery shopping and cooking while the wife hates those chores—so he regularly carries out what was traditionally considered a "wifely" role. It's just a matter of putting each other's abilities to the most effective use.

The complementary nature of leadership between marriage partners is displayed in many ways. One partner may be an intuitive decision-maker, while the other is more methodical, pragmatic, and fact-based. By taking both approaches into account when making major decisions, the couple is able to make better decisions. One partner may be overly optimistic, while the other is more realistic and prone to consider worst-case scenarios. The realist can help to rein in the optimist's tendency to be over confident and overly trusting when taking on a challenge. One partner may be impulsive, while the other is a careful planner. One may be a risk-taker, the other a bit over cautious. Whatever their character traits, two people who share and apportion their leadership roles according to their strengths and deficits tend to balance each other, and to stabilize what might otherwise be a rocky boat.

In a healthy relationship, both partners are intimately involved in the decision-making process. Channels of communication are wide-open about such areas as money management and investment, major purchases, child rearing, relatives and in-laws, sex, and managing personality conflicts.

When children are involved, both parents should fully support each other in front of the children. Avoid doing anything that would undermine the respect your children should have for your partner. When the children are present, don't undercut your partner's leadership role or argue a parental decision your partner has made. If you have a disagreement about a parental decision your partner has made, discuss it in private.

LEADERSHIP PROBLEMS
AND SOLUTIONS

Initiative is the ability to define a situation, set a course, and influence people to move in that direction. Initiative is a prime ingredient of leadership. Many of the problems that surround the issue of leadership have to do with initiative—either too much initiative (which makes no allowance for the initiative of others), or not enough initiative. Problem areas involving leadership in marriage include complementary relationship patterns and symmetrical relationship patterns.

The word "complementary" can be used in both a positive sense and a negative sense. It is good for relationships to be "complementary" in the sense that the husband and wife use their strengths to complement each other and compensate for each other's weak areas. But it is not healthy for a relationship to be rigidly, consistently complementary in the sense that one partner does all the initiating and leading while the other partner always follows. Each partner should lead in the area of his or her strengths. At times, one should lead while the other follows, and then they should trade off.

Symmetrical relationships take one of two forms. In the One-Up/One-Up pattern, both partners try to initiate all the time, resulting in a constant head-butting contest between the husband and the wife. In the One-Down/One-Down pattern, both sides withdraw and wait for someone else to do the initiating. Neither pattern is healthy. In either case, both partners need to learn to share and apportion responsibility. Those who are consistently One-Down and withdrawn need to learn how to initiate and be assertive; those who are consistently One-Up need to learn to share, delegate, and trust the abilities and judgment of their partners.

The passive non-initiator tends to lack self-confidence. "I can't lead," this person says. "I can't initiate. The leadership role just doesn't work for me." Afraid that their partners will not follow, passive individuals settle for the role of a chronic follower. Often, they have learned to get what they want through passivity—by acting as if they are helpless or incompetent so that others will initiate and do for them.

"But," you might say, "what if I'm ready to lead in a certain area of our relationship but my spouse won't follow?" When followers won't follow, there is usually a reason—and frequently that reason is related to a lack of trust. In order to follow, a follower must believe that the leader is trustworthy and that the leader is working in the follower's best interests. Whether the issue is sex or finances or a major life change, the follower has to be able to say, "If I follow you, things will turn out all right. You will not lead me into a hurtful situation."

When a leader leads and the follower doesn't follow, there is a natural tendency for the leader to choose one of three unhealthy responses:

1. The leader withdraws and refuses to initiate.
2. The leader becomes belligerent and angry and attempts to *force* the follower to comply.
3. The leader turns to manipulation and hidden agendas, trying to *trick* the follower into following.

All of these responses are unhealthy and tend to undermine a trust relationship in the long run. A much healthier response is for the leader to openly communicate with the follower about the situation—not only trying to persuade the follower to follow, but listening attentively to the follower's reasons for holding back. Communication builds trust, and trust enables followers to follow so that leaders can lead.

Probably the biggest misconception people have is that leadership is about power. In fact, leadership is about *influence*. A leader is not defined as someone who has all the power. A leader is empowered by the followers and is powerless if no one follows.

A leader is a person who can inspire people to move together toward a common goal. The leader's job is to channel the power of the group in a productive direction. In a family, a leader is able to inspire the rest of the family members to carry out their roles and fulfill their functions in such a way that the family is as happy, well-organized, emotionally strong, spiritually strong, and mutually cooperative as possible.

Sometimes the man leads. Sometimes the woman leads. In a

healthy relationship, both partners trade and share, both lead and follow. But both love each other, seeking what is best for each other and for the family.

In the next chapter, we'll examine one of the toughest issues in a marriage relationship—the issue of conflict.

Questions of a Marriage

If you and your partner are answering these questions together, first write your answers down separately, then compare your answers—but remember to use covenant-love to deal with any disagreements! Use the information you gather from each other to better understand how each of you look at, and feel about, your love relationship.

1. List several areas where . . .
   - you lead on a consistent basis.
   - your partner leads on a consistent basis.
   - you and your partner take turns leading.

2. How would you describe the leadership relationship between you and your partner?
   - We compete with each other.
   - We complement each other.
   - Other _____.

   To what factors in your marriage relationship do you attribute the leadership relationship between you and your partner?

3. How does the level and kind of leadership you demonstrate in your family affect your self-esteem and sense of value in the family? (Explain with specific incidences why you answered as you did.)

   - My self-esteem and sense of being valued are diminished.

- My self-esteem and sense of being valued are increased.
- My self-esteem and sense of being valued are not affected.

4. How could you and your partner renegotiate and reapportion your leadership roles so that you would each better maximize your gifts and strengths? Name some specific changes you and your partner could make in your leadership roles in such areas as spirituality, child rearing, finances, sex, meal planning, chores, home maintenance, vacation planning, and so forth.

5. Here's a useful exercise for you and your partner to do in order to help you both to share leadership roles more equitably. First, divide up the days of the week with one partner taking odd days, the other taking even days. On your day, think of one small action that you can initiate (for example, selecting a restaurant for dinner tonight, a movie to go and see, or a game to play at home).

   Second, practice changing the way you communicate with your partner about decisions and needs. Communicate in a direct, decisive, first-person way. Instead of asking "Would you like to do X tonight?" state what you want: "I would like for us to do X tonight." Become aware of the difference between these two statements. The first is a question, stated in the second-person voice, from a passive point of view, putting all the responsibility for a decision on the other person. The second is a first-person statement, from an active point of view, taking personal responsibility for one's own wants.

FOURTEEN

How Do We Resolve Conflicts?

———————————

Darlene heard the crash and clatter from three rooms away. Dashing out of the kitchen, she heard Gary's heavy tread and quickened her steps, hoping to intercept him. Too late. Just as she reached the living room, she heard her husband's booming voice: "Kevin! Look at that lamp! What did I tell you about throwing that ball in the living room? Huh? Huh? Answer me! What did I tell you?!"

Darlene rounded the corner in time to see Gary towering like the Incredible Hulk over their seven-year-old son. Kevin seemed to have shrunk to half his size. His eyes were wide with fear.

"Gary!" Darlene said sharply, trying to find just the right note to get her husband's attention without angering him any further. "Gary, you're scaring him!"

"He should be scared," said Gary. "Look what he did!"

Darlene glanced at the lamp, one of a pair of end-table lamps, on the floor in pieces.

"I'm—I'm sorry!" Kevin stammered.

"Not half as sorry as you're gonna be!" Gary growled.

Darlene placed a hand on her husband's shoulder. "Gary," she said, "take a moment to cool down!"

Gary shrugged her hand off. "Stay out of this, Dar!"

That did it! Now Darlene was mad! Like a mother bear defending her cubs, she sprang into action. She latched onto her husband's shoulder with both hands and spun all 220 pounds of him around like he was made of straw.

"Kevin is *my* son," she said, "and no one tells me, 'Stay out of this, Dar,' when it concerns my baby! Now let's go in the bedroom and talk this over!"

Gary was about to speak, but Darlene turned to her son and added, "Kevin, go sit in your room until Daddy and I come back. Come on, Gary."

Without waiting for Gary to respond, Darlene turned and headed for the bedroom. It was a daring gambit—but it worked. With a quick backward glance, she saw that Gary was fuming, but following.

Once in the bedroom, Gary roared, "That's it, Dar! You have really crossed the line! You undercut my authority and made me out to be the heavy when I was doing my job as a father! He deliberately disobeyed me by throwing that football—"

"You don't have a clue what Kevin did or didn't do, Gary!" Darlene countered. "You weren't in the room when that lamp got broken, and you didn't ask Kevin what happened. You just started screaming at him!"

"I didn't need to ask him what happened!" Gary snarled. "That lamp didn't jump off the end table by itself! I tell you, that boy and his football—"

"Where was his football?" Darlene interrupted. "Did you see it?"

"It was on the floor someplace," Gary shrugged. "Who cares where the—"

"It was not!" Darlene responded firmly. "I looked in Kevin's bedroom when we came down the hall, and his football was sitting right on his bed! Face it, Gary, you were wrong! You heard a crash, and you went in there and scared the living daylights out of a little boy who idolizes you and wants to be a football star just like you were in college!"

"Oh, puh-leeze, Dar!" said Gary, his voice dripping with sarcasm. "That lamp got busted and Kevin was the only one within twenty feet of it when it happened. The kid's got some explaining to do!"

"So let him explain!" shouted Darlene. "The problem with you is you never listen! You just launch!"

"I'm sick and tired of—"

"Gary, I really couldn't care less what you're sick and tired of! You need to hear this and you're gonna hear it!"

And so it went for the next half hour. Meanwhile, little Kevin, sniffling in his room, could hear every angry, hurtful word, and he took all the blame and guilt for his mommy and daddy's fight onto himself. If he hadn't tried to be helpful by crawling under the end table to retrieve the TV remote control his father had accidentally dropped there, this whole mess never would have happened.

One of the most destructive forces in any human relationship is conflict. It divides marriage partners. It bruises the souls of adults and children. It creates painful memories and distorts the way people relate to each other. When conflict arises, devastating things are said by both sides, momentary anger sours into long-term grudges, and the cycle of conflict tends to spiral skyward. As in the case of Gary, Darlene, and Kevin, conflict usually results from a series of misunderstandings. Many marriages have been tragically—and needlessly—destroyed by conflict.

As hurtful as conflict can be, a family in which there is no conflict is often as unhealthy as the war-torn couple battling their way toward divorce court. Every once in a while, I encounter a husband and wife who proudly announce, "We haven't had an argument in thirty years of marriage!" I often wonder wheter this couple is being dishonest with me or with themselves. A marriage in which there is no conflict harbors a strong possibility that issues are being buried.

Conflict is inevitable in every living, breathing relationship— even in the best of relationships. Couples will always have differing tastes, personalities, and ideas, all of which will produce tension from time to time. Though conflict is painful, it does not have to be destructive. In fact, there *should* be dynamic, creative tension in a marriage. There *should* be differences of opinion that challenge both partners to learn, change, and grow. If you and your partner agreed on everything, you'd never learn from each other or grow through an exchange of opinions. An element of conflict can be a positive force in a healthy relationship.

The goal of healthy conflict is growth and resolution. In a well-managed conflict, both sides win, both partners grow closer in their understanding of each other, and important issues are addressed and resolved. Couples should not seek to eliminate all conflict, but to manage conflict in a healthy and constructive way whenever it arises.

Handled with love and mutual understanding, conflict can actually help couples experience a stronger relationship and deeper intimacy. Handled in an immature and selfish way, conflict produces only anger and frustration, leaving unresolved issues lurking below the surface, like the bulk of the iceberg that sank the Titanic.

THE RED ZONE AND THE BLUE ZONE

Conflict is often driven by change. But in the midst of conflict, we often fail to recognize that fact. As I have consulted with hundreds of couples over the years, I've heard many people label conflict in personal terms: "She's just being stubborn," or "He's so manipulative." Once we personalize conflict, we miss the opportunity to resolve it.

Personalized conflict is unsolvable because it shifts the conflict from an issue to a person. The moment we personalize a conflict, we stop focusing on problem solving and begin focusing on blame. By understanding the hidden emotional forces that triggered the conflict, we can make sound strategic decisions to resolve the problem.

There are essentially two types of conflict. I've found it helpful to label them "Red Zone conflict," which is focused on blaming the person, and "Blue Zone conflict," which is focused on solving the problem. Let's take a closer look at these two zones, starting with the Red Zone.

Red Zone conflict is personalized conflict. It is driven by our emotional reactions to another person. We couch it in highly charged personal terms. When we're in the throes of Red Zone conflict, we argue about our differences. But on an unconscious level, Red Zone conflict is rarely about our differences. Rather, it's focused on our similarities.

The Red Zone is about our own emotional issues and emotional baggage from the past—usually very similar to the issues and baggage the other person has. When I work with couples, I often see that the intensity of the conflict is much greater than the issue deserves. For example, I may see a couple locked in combat over something as trivial as a broken drinking glass ("I've told him a thousand times not to overload the dishwasher!") or a bird-splat on the windshield ("I told her not to park the new car under that tree!"). When people become enraged over trivial surface issues, they're operating in the Red Zone.

Beginning in childhood, you began to draw an unconscious mental and emotional map of your life. As we saw earlier, we keep our mental maps in our unconscious storehouse brain, and we consult these maps continuously on our journey through the territory of relationships. Our maps are based on our experiences, perceptions, and conclusions about reality and relationships. We tend to think that our map is an accurate representation of reality, but our map is actually an *interpretation* of reality—and often a *distorted* interpretation at that. The more distorted our mental maps, the more distorted and unhealthy our behavior and relationships will be.

Imagine trying to take a trip somewhere using a badly drawn, grossly inaccurate road map as your guide. You'll get lost for sure. The same is true when you try to navigate your marriage relationship while using a distorted mental map as your guide. Is it any wonder that couples often get hopelessly lost in conflict and misunderstanding?

The most serious distortions in our mental maps usually occur during childhood. These distortions are often inflicted on us by the significant people in our early lives—parents, siblings, extended family members, teachers, or others in our early life who abused, molested, neglected, overprotected, smothered, or otherwise inflicted emotional hurt on us. While unconsciously drawing our map of reality in childhood, we made various notes on our mental map: "Contact with Mom is painful; avoid her as much as possible," or

"Stepdad is dangerous when drunk; the moment he starts drinking, hide!"

Your mental map becomes your guide to life and relationships. It explains where your life is going and what it all means. The map in your storehouse brain shapes your unconscious attitudes and the ways in which you respond to people and situations.

Depending on the kinds of experiences and parenting we've had, our mental maps tend to fall into one of four categories. Those categories are: Survival ("The world is dangerous, and I must be very careful in order to survive"); Acceptance ("People don't like me because I am unacceptable as a person"); Control ("I must remain in complete control at all times; I must never let anyone else control me"); and Competence ("People think I'm stupid and incompetent; I must constantly prove them wrong").

You have at least one of these four mental maps in your storehouse brain right now. As you experience life and interact with other people, you interpret the experiences and people in your life in terms of the mental symbols on that map.

Let's say that your map is Acceptance. From your earliest years, you have felt that people judge you and reject you as unacceptable. Perhaps when you were a child, your parents' love for you was a conditional love. They only seemed to approve of you and accept you if you got the best grades, if you were the best little dancer or Little League player, and so forth. Whenever you disappointed or displeased your parents, they communicated that you were unacceptable and unloved. This made you feel insecure and hungry for the approval of others.

Decades later, you're an adult. Even though you aren't consciously aware of it, you still interpret every experience of your life according to the map of Acceptance in your storehouse brain. You go to the department store and try to get the attention of a salesperson, but she ignores you. So without even consciously examining the situation, you assume, "The salesperson hates me because I'm unacceptable. I've always been unacceptable, even when I was a child." You go home and fix dinner, and your marriage partner puts ketchup on the meatloaf. You think, "My partner thinks I'm a terrible cook and the food I make is unacceptable. I've always been unacceptable, even as a child."

The reality, of course, is that the salesperson's hearing aid needs a new battery and your partner has always liked ketchup on meatloaf, but those explanations don't even occur to you. Why? Because they don't fit your mental map of reality. You unconsciously screen out facts and interpretations that don't fit the map, while giving inordinate weight to every impression (no matter how far-fetched) that seems to fit the map.

The result: everything that happens to you serves to reinforce your mental map of reality and to make it grow more and more distorted over time. Your map may have little or nothing to do with the way people actually relate to you and view you, but you are convinced that your flawed, defective mental map is absolutely true. That map is the core of your Red Zone issue. When conflict erupts between you and your partner, the conflict is unconsciously patterned to fit the mental map you keep in your storehouse brain.

This is why trivial issues in our lives—the broken drinking glass or the bird-splat on the windshield—can suddenly take on epic proportions. In a moment of conflict and angry emotion, that trivial issue can symbolize the entire map of your life.

Because of a mental map of Survival, Acceptance, Control, or Competence in your storehouse brain, that trivial issue is no longer trivial. It now represents a threat to the very core of your being. It screams at you, "She's threatening your survival, your very existence!," "He's saying that you're unacceptable as a person, just like you've been told all your life!," "She's trying to control you; you're losing control of the situation!," or "You know what he really means—he's saying you're stupid and incompetent!" That is what conflict in the Red Zone is all about: seemingly minor issues loom large because they symbolize the map of your whole life.

THE FOUR MAPS OF THE RED ZONE

Now let's look at the Red Zone issues—your mental maps—and see how these issues cause conflicts to become intensified out of all proportion to reality. Note that each of these issues has a positive side and a negative side. It's the negative side that fuels Red Zone conflict.

Let's begin by examining each of the four maps of conflict in the Red Zone. The first map is Survival. People whose mental map is Survival tend to come from the most disorganized families. Their rule of life was: "Survive, don't make waves, don't trust anyone else, rely only on yourself." Parents don't parent much in these families; instead, they tend to abuse or neglect their kids. Children in these families learn from an early age that if they are to survive their perilous childhood, they'll have to do it on their own. No one is going to help them or rescue them.

People whose map of reality is "Can I survive?" tend to be extremely competent at what they do, because they learned to fend for themselves at an early age. This high level of competence is the positive side of this map.

Unfortunately, these people often lack a sense of nurturing and wholeness. They tend to feel that something is missing or incomplete in themselves, and that feeling serves to shape their symbolic Red Zone issues. They blame themselves and even hate themselves for the way they were treated in childhood. They are haunted by a sense that if they had just been better people, they would not have gotten the rough treatment they received growing up.

Trust is a major issue in the lives of people whose map is Survival. In viewing people and relationships, they tell themselves, "I don't think this situation is safe. I don't think I can trust you. I don't think you'll be there for me." Abandonment goes hand-in-hand with this distrustful outlook on life: "Everyone I ever cared about has abandoned me. I know you'll leave me, too. It's my fault. I'm not worthy of your love."

The second map is acceptance. Acceptance means approval, favor, recognition, and endorsement. People whose map is that they are unacceptable are usually focused outward toward others, have a genuine concern for others, and tend to monitor others for even the smallest clues of acceptance or rejection. These people seek to build feelings of peace and harmony within families and organizations. This ability to focus on the feelings of others is the positive side of people whose mental map is Acceptance.

The destructive side of the Acceptance map, the side that fuels Red Zone conflict, is the unconscious attitude that says, "I must be acceptable to everybody. Being rejected leads to abandonment and rejection, and rejection is a form of death." These people often become overly compliant and self-effacing. They will endure anything, go along with anything, and submit to any indignity or mistreatment if only people will not reject them. That is why so many people who are hungry for acceptance end up in abusive and destructive relationships.

The third map is control. Control includes mastery, initiation, and responsibility. Those whose map is Control are the very people who drive much of the economic and social activity in our world. They are the movers and shakers in our businesses, organizations, churches, military, and government. They find what needs to be done, and they either do it or lead others to do it. Among their ranks are some of the most accomplished leaders in our society. That's the positive side of this map.

Red Zone issues develop, however, when Control-oriented people feel vulnerable ("Someone is trying to control me!") or when they feel they must control every situation and every person around them. They interpret all experiences according to a mental map that says, "I must be in control at all times! Being a follower means I'm not in control. I must never let other people control me—in fact, I can't even let other people get close to me. If I do, they'll try to control me."

The fourth map is Competence. The mental map of Competence includes such concepts as ability, expertise, mastery, and skill. People focused on competence usually attend the best universities and reach for lofty goals. They have very high expectations of themselves and usually reach them. That's the positive side of this mental map.

Unfortunately, people whose map is Competence frequently feel that they are never competent enough, no matter how high their achievements. They work hard to achieve the highest levels but somehow never feel as though they've quite made it. They inwardly berate themselves for the smallest mistakes. They keep working and building impressive résumés, hoping to find a sense of approval from others and a sense of "I made it!" from themselves. For these people, love is based on performance. Because they never quite perform up to their own impossibly high standards, they never feel worthy of being loved.

The table below summarizes the positive and negative sides of the four maps.

Map: SURVIVAL

Self-Description: "I must take care of myself. The world is full of peril, so I must enjoy the moment."

Positive Side: These people have traits of competence, self-reliance, and responsibility.

Negative Side: These people lack the ability to trust others and tend to be wary and troubled in relationships. They have little interest in anything but what is of practical benefit. They become angry and panicky (Red Zone) whenever they feel their survival has been threatened.

Map: ACCEPTANCE

Self-Description: "I will do anything to be loved and accepted by others. I am a people-pleaser."

Positive Side: These people have a heart for serving others and are very attentive to the needs and feelings of other people.

Negative Side: These people are overly compliant and self-effacing. They tend to be rescuers. They become angry and carry personal grudges (Red Zone) whenever they feel they have been rejected.

Map: CONTROL

Self-Description: "The world is a threatening place, and the only way I can feel safe is if I can control every situation and the people around me."

Positive Side: These people tend to have strong leadership qualities. They are vigilant, highly organized, and have high expectations of themselves.

Negative Side: These people often wall themselves off emotionally. They do not let others get too close to them.

They can be overly controlling toward others—bossy, directive, demanding, rigid, and nit-picking. They impose perfectionist demands on others. They become anxious and angry (Red Zone) whenever anyone or anything threatens their control.

Map: COMPETENCE

Self-Description: "I am loved only on the basis of my performance. My performance is never good enough, so I never feel worthy of being loved."

Positive Side: These people tend to be high achievers. If you are a leader, you want these people on your team, because they will work hard to achieve a great performance.

Negative Side: They are never satisfied with their achievements. They have a hard time receiving from other people. They impose perfectionist demands on themselves. They are defensive and easily angered (Red Zone) whenever they perceive that their competence has been questioned.

THE EMOTIONAL DIMENSION

The first key to resolving conflict in a relationship is to understand ourselves and the hidden forces that rumble around inside of us, affecting virtually every area of our lives. We need to understand why we see ourselves the way we do, why we feel and behave the way we do, and why we make the choices we make. Each of us, without exception, has a dominant Red Zone issue: Survival, Acceptance, Control, or Competence. That Red Zone issue rules our emotions and triggers our responses to people and situations.

Surrounding our Red Zone issues are the emotions that erupt within us in the various situations and conflicts we experience. Emotions are constantly surging through us, though we are not always aware of our emotions. Why do we have feelings that we aren't aware of? How is it possible that we have emotions we don't know we have?

In part, it's because we've been taught from an early age that some of our feelings are unacceptable. They are still there, under the surface, but we have pushed them away from our awareness. Those emotions only break in upon our conscious awareness as they increase in intensity.

The table below shows how our emotions grow from slight to moderate to intense to extreme magnitude:

Emotion: SAD

Slightly Sad: Disappointed or Wistful
Moderately Sad: Dejected or Despondent
Intensely Sad: Sorrowful or Mournful
Extremely Sad: Desolated or Anguished

Emotion: BAD (Guilt)

Slightly Bad: Regretful or Sheepish
Moderately Bad: Repentant or Contrite
Intensely Bad: Remorseful or Reprehensible
Extremely Bad: Self-Hating or Self-Flagellating

Emotion: MAD

Slightly Mad: Frustrated or Annoyed
Moderately Mad: Resentful or Indignant
Intensely Mad: Bitter or Wrathful
Extremely Mad: Raging or Furious

Emotion: GLAD

Slightly Glad: Cheerful or Contented
Moderately Glad: Glad or Delighted
Intensely Glad: Elated or Exhilarated
Extremely Glad: Blissful or Ecstatic

Emotion: FEARFUL

Slightly Fearful: Uneasy or Worried
Moderately Fearful: Anxious or Frightened
Intensely Fearful: Dreading or Apprehensive
Extremely Fearful: Terrified or Panicked

Emotion: AVERSION

Slightly Aversive: Dislike or Disrespect
Moderately Aversive: Repugnance or Disdain
Intensely Aversive: Contempt or Disgust
Extremely Aversive: Abhorrence or Loathing

Adapted from: *Words for Our Feelings* by Dan Jones (Mandala Publishing, 1992).

How do Red Zone issues relate to emotions? Red Zone issues exist close to the throbbing core of your identity. The line between your unconscious Red Zone issues and your hidden emotions becomes increasingly difficult to draw. Why? Because your issues are infused with emotion. If someone does or says something that touches on that Red Zone issue (Survival, Acceptance, Control, Competence), then all the emotions that surround that issue immediately spring up from within, and you didn't even realize those emotions were there!

If your Red Zone issue is Survival, for example, you see the world as dangerous, you see people as unpredictable and unreliable, and you lack the ability to trust others. You are wary and troubled in relationships.

The feelings associated with the Red Zone issue of Survival are fear, pain, and anger. Until you are able to purge those destructive emotions, you will always have an underlying sense of mistrust in relationships. You will interpret the things people say and do according to your Survival map. You will view every relationship as threatening, every contact with other people as a potential menace, and every word someone says to you as a possible attempt at intimidation.

Your continuous filtering of reality through the map of Survival only reinforces what you already believe to be true: people and relationships are threatening. Convinced that the world is dangerous, you look for a threat in every encounter, every relationship, and you *find* it, whether it is really there or not. As you treat people with wariness and distrust, they soon become wary and distrustful around you—and your filter of reality becomes a self-fulfilling prophecy.

We constantly create the relational environment we inhabit. By viewing people and situations according to our Red Zone maps, we actually create a cycle of Red Zone conflict with the most important people in our lives.

YOUR EMOTIONAL "SMOKE DETECTOR"

Have you ever noticed how your emotional intensity rises and falls during the day? You may not show it outwardly, and the people around you may not be aware of it, but it's true. Your ill-tempered boss approaches and your stomach clenches with anxiety, even fear. You glance at the birthday card your preschooler made for you with crayons and finger-paints, and you suddenly feel all warm and gooshy inside. You think about that speech you have to give next week, and your blood pressure rises and you feel tightness in your chest.

There is emotional activity going on inside you all the time. It surges deep within you, below the surface of your awareness. When your emotional intensity reaches such a pitch that you notice your emotions, your internal warning system is activated. This warning system acts like a smoke detector, alerting you to danger.

It doesn't mean that you are in *physical* danger, of course. But the emotional part of your brain alerts you to dangers both real and imagined. This is where your map comes in. Many of the symbols of your map were drawn during your childhood, at a time when many aspects of life seemed imposing, threatening, and dangerous.

When you were a child, you might have been raised by abusive or neglectful caregivers. On a day-to-day basis, you feared for your very survival. Or you might have been raised by caregivers who made you feel that you might be rejected or abandoned if you disappointed them in any way; in this way, you grew up starved for acceptance and approval.

You might have grown up with a negative message continually hammered into your soul: "Why can't you do anything right?" So you grew up obsessed with the need to prove your own competence. You might have grown up with caregivers who ruled your life, who made all of your decisions for you. Growing up with little, if any, control over your life, you became obsessed with the need to control.

Now you are an adult. In your conscious mind, you know that parents and other caregivers can no longer hurt you, abandon you, reject you, or control you. The adult part of your brain knows that these old experiences are in the past and should no longer rule your life. But there is a hidden emotional part of our brains that can't tell the past from the present, the real from the imagined. That's where our emotional "smoke detector" is located. That's where our childhood memories are stored, and where the map of our life is etched—the map we impose on all of our experiences, the map we use to shape the meaning of our lives.

The hidden emotional centers of our brain, acting like a smoke detector, activate old feelings when stimulated by situations that are superficially similar to our mental maps. The emotional part of the brain does not check with the rational, logical part of the brain to get an adult perspective. It simply "sounds off" (like a smoke detector) with a loud, blaring, emotional response. Instantly, you find yourself in the emotion-charged Red Zone of conflict. You are angry out of all proportion to some trivial matter. Why? Because it's no longer about the trivial matter. It's about your entire childhood, about all the hurt and fear that your emotional brain still remembers.

For example, Clay and Angie were discussing how to redecorate their house. "We need to choose four of our favorite colors," Angie said, "and use them throughout the house. That will give the entire house a theme. In the living room, we'll let one color dominate, then use half as much of the next color, and then just accent with the third and fourth colors. In the dining room and bedrooms, we'll vary the proportions, and in the den—"

"You're not going to change my den," Clay interrupted.

"Clay," Angie said, her anger flaring, "it's not *your* den, it's *our* den! And it's part of *our* house! We have to keep a theme flowing throughout the house!"

"You can have your stupid theme in every room but the den!"

Clay said, his blood pressure surging.

"My 'stupid theme'!" Angie said, her expression trembling between hurt and rage.

"And another thing," Clay added. "It *is* my den! That's where I go to relax and get away from it all. You hardly ever go there, unless it's to nag at me!"

From there, the "discussion" escalated into an hour-long battle replete with accusations, counter-accusations, insults, name-calling, and door-slamming. The silent "cold war" that followed lasted over a week. Why did Clay and Angie become so quickly embroiled in an all-out marital conflict over a color scheme and a den? The reasons became clear in counseling, as Clay and Angie looked at their own childhood histories and discovered their hidden maps of reality.

Clay's Red Zone issue was Control. He had lost his father when he was ten, and he had been dominated by an over protective mother who never let him make his own decisions. He felt he had no control over anything in his life, not even his own bedroom. His mother kept his room spotless for him, tossed out any of his possessions that she disapproved of, and wouldn't let him decorate his walls with his school awards and souvenirs. As Clay grew older, his mom tried to choose his girlfriends for him and even maneuvered him into attending the university she picked out for him.

Decades later, when Angie came to him and started laying out her plans for the entire house, a hidden emotional part of him became that controlled little boy again. Suddenly, he felt the fresh grief of losing his father (which symbolized the fact that life was unpredictable and uncontrollable; Clay had no say over the fact that people could simply disappear from his life). He remembered the hurt of having his mother controlling every aspect of his life.

Though he was an adult, his wife symbolically stepped into the role of his controlling mother. She was going to control "his room"—the den—and he would have no say over it. The same rage, resentment, and fear he had felt as a child suddenly surged to the surface, exploding in Red Zone anger that was completely out of proportion to the adult issue he was discussing with his wife, Angie.

Angie's Red Zone issue was Competence. "I grew up being constantly berated by my mother," she revealed in counseling, "because

I couldn't do anything right. She'd yell at me when I couldn't make my bed the right way or when I didn't clean every last dust bunny under my bed. She used to tell me that I would never be able to keep a husband when I grew up because I couldn't clean a house to save my life.

"I tried and tried to live up to her standards, but nothing I did was ever good enough. She even made up a catchy little song about 'Angie's little empty head,' and she'd sing it to me whenever she got frustrated with me. Mom's been dead for ten years, but I can still hear her voice in my head, telling me, 'How can you be so stupid? Can't you do anything right?'

"Today I have a career, and people tell me how talented and competent I am at my job—yet every morning when I wake up, I have this terrible feeling: 'What if I make a mistake? What if I screw up and get fired?' I mean, logically I know I'm good at what I do. But there's some part of me that is just scared to death that I'm really going to blow it. Most mornings, I don't even want to get out of bed. I'm so afraid that what my mother always told me is true: I'm hopelessly incompetent."

Why did Angie get so angry with Clay over the remodeling project? "When he made that remark about my 'stupid' color theme," Angie said, "I just became furious. There's something about that word 'stupid'—whenever I hear it, it's like I feel my mother standing over me, calling me 'stupid' or singing that horrible song about my 'empty little head.' I felt that Clay was belittling my ideas about the remodeling project. It made me feel completely incompetent. It made me feel like I was twelve years old, being told by my mother that I would never hold onto a husband because I couldn't make a bed or clean a floor. I felt like a stupid, incompetent little child."

Though neither of them was aware of it at the time, both Clay and Angie were experiencing strong Red Zone emotions that were rooted in childhood experiences and family stories. The map of Clay's life was, "I must not allow anyone to control me." The map of Angie's life was, "I must not allow anyone to make me feel stupid and incompetent." Like blaring smoke detectors, the emotional portions of their brains sounded alarms of danger: "Clay, you're being controlled again!" and "Angie, your husband is calling you stupid and incompetent!"

Whenever you become disproportionately, intensely angry with your partner and you wonder, "Why am I so intense about this?", you are in the Red Zone. Your anger is being fueled by old issues—a map of your life that was drawn in childhood. The present situation—the broken drinking glass or the bird-splat on the windshield—is merely the trigger that activated your emotional "smoke detector" and set off the alarm. When you are engaged in Red Zone conflict, you are re-fighting the struggles and fears of your childhood.

The next thing we need to understand about conflict in the Red Zone is that when two people are locked in combat, they are *at the same place* emotionally. In other words, if you and I are locked in combat, and I want to know what you are feeling inside, all I have to do is reach down into my own feelings and check my emotional state. What I'm feeling is what you are feeling. If I'm feeling disrespected and belittled, *so are you.* If I am feeling anxious and panicked, *so are you.*

People in conflict never seem to grasp this basic truth. In the midst of the battle, both sides assume that the other partner is in some other place emotionally, but it just isn't so. We tend to think that conflict is just about anger, but conflict always involves a complex array of emotions, such a fear, panic, shame, and guilt, and whatever we are feeling, the other person is feeling, too. As the Greek philosopher Aristotle once said, "Anyone can become angry—that's easy. But to be angry with the right person, to the right degree, at the right time, for the right purpose, and in the right way—this is not easy."

So how can we resolve our conflicts and restore peace, love, caring, and mutual support to the relationship? We do this by moving from the Red Zone to the Blue Zone.

THE BLUE ZONE

We have just seen that the Red Zone represents personalized conflict involving unresolved emotional issues. By contrast, the Blue Zone is conflict revolving exclusively around issues. The intensely personal and emotional elements have been removed from the conflict so that we can focus logically and constructively on the issues by monitoring the process.

You will never eliminate conflict from your relationship. Emotionally healthy couples experience conflict, but they adopt strategies to keep their conflicts out of the Red Zone and safely in the Blue Zone. When couples keep their conflict in the Blue Zone and out of the Red Zone, they lower the level of anger, anxiety, and fear. Emotion recedes and reason comes to the fore. Problems are resolved fairly and intelligently.

Conflict creates change and change creates conflict. When conflict takes place in the Red Zone, the partners are like opponents in a boxing ring. But when conflict takes place in the Blue Zone, the partners are like a couple in a dance. They are working together as partners, cooperating with each other to resolve a problem, not battling each other or seeking to hurt each other.

In a healthy relationship, both partners articulate their own points of view. They disagree, they negotiate, and they achieve resolution. Both partners stay in the present when discussing issues. They avoid the temptation to dredge up old issues and old wounds from the past. Both partners keep the lines of communication open despite the temptation to withdraw or close down. By monitoring and resolving minor problems before they become major issues, couples keep emotional pressures from building to explosive levels.

Normal, everyday conflicts are like minor earthquakes. Geologists and seismologists tell us that little 3.0 earthquakes serve a valuable function—relieving pressure and stress along fault lines in the earth. There are places in California (where I lived for a few years—happily, I'm safely back in Virginia!) where the land along fault lines is actually bulging upward with unrelieved pressure. When there are no small quakes for long periods of time to reduce the pressure, scientists get nervous. That's why they're predicting that The Big One—an 8.0 or more—is just waiting to happen.

Marriages are like that. Many couples never learn how to express their needs or negotiate their expectations. They go along with their partners, never disagreeing, never engaging in conflict—but they are profoundly unhappy in their relationship. Pressures are building. There are no little 3.0 conflicts in the relationship, and everything looks oh-so-civilized and serene—but The Big One is coming!

That's why couples need to manage conflict by keeping it safely in the Blue Zone. A series of small, well-managed Blue Zone conflicts can help keep big, destructive Red Zone blowups from destroying a relationship.

HEALTHY COUPLES THINK "WIN/WIN"

People tend to adopt one of a number of postures in times of conflict. The following are some typical postures:

- *Accommodation.* One partner instantly yields to the other's desires or demands—a one-down posture.
- *Avoidance.* One or both partners respond to conflict by withdrawing or avoiding the other—again, a One-Down posture.
- *Smoothing.* One partner tries to conciliate and "make nice." This could be done by backing down (One-Down) or by patronizing the other person (One-Up).
- *Forcing.* A very unhealthy posture, which works against intimacy. This One-Up posture uses intimidation and threats to win.
- *Persuasion.* One partner tries to convince the other to change his or her position. Persuasion usually involves both partners adopting postures of equality and both being willing to listen and reconsider their views.
- *Bargaining.* This posture can be a healthy way of reaching agreement. It involves exchanging concessions until both sides are satisfied with the agreement.

Bargaining and persuasion are healthy "Win/Win" postures for dealing with conflict. (The term "Win/Win" means that a solution is found in which there are no losers—both sides win.) Other postures, such as accommodation, avoidance, smoothing, and forcing, discount the legitimate feelings and desires of either oneself or one's partner.

Healthy couples continually think "Win/Win." They understand that conflict can serve a positive role in a healthy marriage. The purpose of conflict is not to make one partner a winner and the other a loser, but to create understanding between both partners regarding issues and emotions. When couples focus on listening to each other, understanding each other, and managing and resolving their conflicts instead of winning arguments, they create a strong foundation for healthy, satisfying marital intimacy.

POINTS TO REMEMBER ABOUT CONFLICT

With insight and understanding, we can make conflict work for the marriage instead of against it. This next part will discuss some insights that may help you to work through the conflict in your marriage.

One insight that may help is that conflict is painful. Disagreement is unpleasant. Arguments make our stomachs hurt, but not all pain is destructive pain. Like the pain of surgery or dentistry or strenuous exercise, some things that hurt are good for us. Conflict brings pain, but it also brings about meaningful dialogue, an exchange of feelings, and an exchange of ideas. When conflict is viewed as an opportunity for creating deeper understanding, it becomes a tool for intimacy instead of a weapon of division.

Another good insight is that conflict is risky. Anger can get out of hand—which is why so many people avoid conflict at all costs. But the most important aspects of life are usually the most risky. If we dare to manage our conflicts with understanding and love, those conflicts can actually lead us deeper into our most important relationships.

Some other advice that may help is that conflict doesn't always lead to consensus. For example, my wife, Marcy, and I disagree on several issues, and we know that we will never agree on them. That's

OK. Fortunately, these issues are not disagreements over basic values. They are in the realm of secondary issues, such as "At what age should a child be allowed to see a PG-13 movie?" Every once in a while, we drag out one of these issues, hash it out until we remember that this is an issue we will never agree on. Then we put it back on the shelf until next time.

Knowing that conflicts are made up of gradations may also help. It's important to recognize low-level disagreements and petty annoyances for what they are. Some people seem to only have an ON/OFF switch when it comes to conflict—no channel selector, no volume control. If you find out that your marriage partner has given your recently paroled brother-in-law permission to set up his meth lab in your basement, you certainly have reason to be upset. But if you fly into a screaming rage because your wife left her pantyhose hanging in the bathroom or your husband left his golf clubs in the living room, then you lack a sense of proportion where anger is concerned. It's important to recognize the gradations in the magnitude of issues, and to develop a capacity for disagreeing without going ballistic on every little issue.

The last insight is that in any conflict, there is usually more going on beneath the surface than above the surface. What you *think* you are arguing about is usually not what you are *really* arguing about. There are often deep Red Zone issues lurking in the shadows. You may think you are arguing about the socks on the floor or the missed appointment or the thoughtless remark, but in most cases you are really struggling over such questions as: Am I loved? Am I respected? Will I be abandoned? Am I being controlled? Am I being emotionally smothered?

Ongoing arguments we have today are simply extensions of Red Zone conflicts of the past, including conflicts that go back all the way to childhood. Because these conflicts are about "me," not about issues, they are by definition unresolvable. You cannot solve your childhood hurts and fears by arguing with your marriage partner.

So it is helpful, when conflict arises, to emotionally step back from the situation and ask yourself, "What am I really angry about? What is my partner angry about? What Red Zone issue do I need to deal with? How can we both get our real wants and needs met so that this cycle of conflict can be broken?"

A certain amount of emotional distance is useful in resolving conflict. As we have already seen, two people often get locked into a mode of conflict I call "Stuck/Fighting." Both partners are hostile to each other while at the same time dependent on each other. Each says, "I can't live with you, I can't live without you." Conflict is used to maintain both distance and contact—simultaneously.

Only when two people are able to move from the Red Zone (Stuck/Fighting) to the Blue Zone (Unstuck) can both partners see each other clearly. Only in the Blue Zone do issues come into focus so they can be reasonably resolved.

HEALTHY MANAGEMENT OF CONFLICT

Some people approach marriage as if it were the Alamo: "I'd rather die than surrender!" They don't look at the issues as a problem to be solved but as a cause to be defended to the death. In times of conflict, we need to seek practical solutions and avoid taking emotion-charged "last stands." The following section gives practical steps you can take to reduce the level of conflict in your relationship without sacrificing your core beliefs or your selfhood.

The first step is to anticipate danger. Both partners have a right to feel safe in the relationship. You shouldn't have to walk on eggshells around your spouse. Even so, you both know that there are certain issues, certain behaviors, certain remarks that tend to produce conflict in the marriage—so why venture unnecessarily into those areas? Avoid provoking each other. Focus on building each other up and making each other feel secure in the relationship. Watch for warning signs that conflict and tension may be building in the marriage, and take action to defuse it.

The second step is to act promptly. When you see the early warning signs of Red Zone conflict, act immediately to intercept the situation before it grows into all-out war. If appropriate, apologize.

Remember, you don't have to be "in the wrong" to apologize. You can say, "I didn't mean any harm, but I know you were hurt by what I inadvertently did or said, so I want you to know I'm sorry. I never meant to hurt you."

Next, be willing to give up the lesser to gain the greater. What do couples always seem to fight over? Trivial issues. The problem is that those trivial issues symbolically represent big Red Zone conflicts in our unconscious minds. Those trivial issues include: purchases and possessions; off-hand remarks; decisions about parenting and setting rules; household chores; in-laws; who's to blame for making the family late; and on and on.

The truth is that very few of the conflicts couples bring into my office are of the "my spouse wants to run for President and I don't want to live in the District of Columbia" variety. They are not the big life-altering decisions. Most of the conflicts I see are of the "how should we agree to squeeze the toothpaste tube" variety. If we would be willing to let go of these trivial issues, we would make great gains in the much larger issue of a happy and healthy relationship.

Lastly, look for alternatives to conflict. There are many ways to avoid or resolve conflict besides arguing in the Red Zone. Constructive Blue Zone alternatives include:

- *Compromise*—each partner gets part (but not all) of what he or she wants.
- *Counseling or arbitration*—for truly serious conflicts, a pastor, counselor, or therapist can be helpful in clarifying communication and leading both partners to a mutually caring and loving resolution.
- *Prayer*—both partners can pray together about the problem, asking God to give guidance, wisdom, and willing hearts to both partners as they seek a solution.
- *Unconditional love*—both partners should communicate to each other, "I am absolutely and unconditionally committed to loving you and seeking what is best for you. I care far more about you and your feelings than I care about any issue. Though we disagree, my love for you transcends any disagreement we may have."

- *Mutual forgiveness*—in any conflict, there are usually wrongful words or actions on both sides, and these should be mutually confessed and mutually forgiven. Avoid keeping score and nursing grudges. Avoid an attitude that says, "You were more wrong than I was, so I have a right to stay mad."
- *Time out*—if one or both partners feels too much Red Zone anger to carry on a productive Blue Zone discussion, then both should agree to take a time out and come back together at another time. Whenever possible, both partners should agree on a set time to come together in the Blue Zone and discuss the matter.
- *Agree to disagree*—sometimes, an agreeable solution is simply not possible. At those times, agree that you cannot agree, and that it's OK to leave it at that. Agree that you will simply not bring the matter up again.

Conflict is inevitable, but it doesn't have to drive a wedge into the relationship. Properly managed, conflict can actually become an opportunity for two people to bond more closely and discover deeper levels of love and intimacy.

In the next chapter, we will explore the wonderful world of in-laws.

TAKE ACTION
Questions of a Marriage

If you and your partner are answering these questions together, first write your answers down separately, then compare your answers—but remember to use covenant-love to deal with any disagreements! Use the information you gather from each other to better understand how each of you look at, and feel about, your love relationship.

1. What is your usual response to conflict?
   - I avoid conflict at all costs.
   - I think a little conflict is healthy in a relationship.

- What conflict?
- I believe in getting things out in the open and talking them through to resolution.
- When disagreements arise, I need a little time to settle down and collect my thoughts.
- I thrive on conflict.
- Other _____

2. How do you and your partner usually deal with conflict?

- It's a declaration of war and all-out hostilities.
- We both try the best we can, but conflict is still very difficult for us to resolve.
- I try, but my partner doesn't seem to care how I feel.
- We do a pretty decent job of managing conflict and caring for each other's feelings.
- We bury feelings and deny issues.
- We never have conflict.
- Other _____

3. Describe your most painful episode of conflict during the past week or two.

   Why was it so painful?

   What was the surface issue that you argued about?

   Now that you think about it, was there a deeper, Red Zone issue involved on your side? What was it?

   - acceptance
   - competence
   - control
   - survival

Do you think there was a deeper, Red Zone issue on your partner's side? What do you think it was?

- acceptance
- competence
- control
- survival

How could that episode have been handled better by your
partner?

How could you have managed your own behavior
better?

Suggest some covenants between you and your partner that could help keep conflict from getting out of
hand.

4. What is the biggest problem you have in dealing with
your own feelings of anger?

What is the biggest problem you have in dealing
with your partner's anger?

What are some steps you and your partner can take
to enable you both to better manage anger in your
times of conflict?

Also, if either you or your partner has a major problem with anger that is out of control, you should serious-
ly consider obtaining counseling to enable you to better
manage your anger.

FIFTEEN

What About My In-Laws?

<hr />

"I'm not going," said Carlos.

"What do you mean?" asked Silvia.

"Just what I said. You can visit your parents without me. I'm staying home."

"But what do I tell them? Am I supposed to say you're sick or what?"

"Tell them the truth. Tell them I can't stand being around them."

"Carlos!"

"Look, Silvia, they're your parents, you've *got* to love them. But what do I ever get from them? Your father criticizes me all the time, and your mother calls me a failure because she doesn't like what I do for a living. Your brother, who's thirty years old and still living at home, is always giving me advice on what I should invest in or what kind of car I should drive."

"But Carlos—"

"And remember what your mother did last time we were over there? She tried to fix you up with your old boyfriend! As if you weren't even married! As if your husband weren't standing right there in the room when she said it!"

"She just said that John is getting a divorce and—"

"And what an item you two were and remember how you and John almost got married and isn't he going to make some girl quite a catch someday and—"

"OK, OK, Momma was a little out of line, but—"

"A *lot* out of line," said Carlos.

"Okay, a lot out of line," Silvia agreed, frowning. "I've tried to talk to her. Everything from hints to direct confrontation. Nothing fazes my mother."

"Exactly my point," said Carlos. "She's not going to change, so why should I keep exposing myself to your mother's hatred? Honestly, Silvia, I don't understand how such a wonderful person as you could come from a family of—"

"Don't say it!"

"All right, I won't. But my mind's made up. I'm not going. If your mother wants to fix you up with John, fine, but I'm not going to stand around and act pleasant while she's doing it. You're my wife and I'm your husband, and if your parents can't accept that after seven years, that's their problem. I'm staying home and that's that."

What should Carlos do? Does he have a moral obligation to maintain a relationship with people who continually treat him as if he were invisible or, worse, an unfit husband for their daughter? Does he have a responsibility to be nice to the people who treat him like dirt?

NO LAUGHING MATTER

In-laws have provided surefire jokes for stand-up comics since the beginning of time. But for many married people, the subject of in-laws isn't funny. In-law problems frequently drive wedges of conflict and hurt between marriage partners. One common problem is unexamined attitudes and assumptions held over from the family of origin. These old mindsets—which I call "baggage"—may include beliefs, habits, expectations, traditions, and values that have been absorbed from the parents throughout childhood and adolescence.

For example, Jack just naturally assumed that it's OK in all families for family members to clip their toenails in the living room and leave the clippings in the carpet—after all, that's why God invented Hoover vacuum cleaners. His parents always did it, he always did it. It didn't even occur to him to clip his toenails over a wastebasket, in the bathroom, in private, as his wife, Cindi, always did. But the first time she came into the living room and saw one of Jack's toenails go flying off into the deep plush pile of her brand-new carpet, she let out a scream that could be heard for blocks.

To have a healthy marriage, couples need to continually "un-pack" their "baggage." They need to sort through all the attitudes and assumptions they have unthinkingly absorbed from their family of origin. They need to mutually agree on which pieces of "baggage" are worth keeping and which should be discarded. Unfortunately, many couples never go through the baggage-sorting process. They just naturally assume they were raised the right way—and that their spouse's habits and attitudes are "weird" or "wrong" or "silly."

Another problem is marriage partners who have made an incomplete break with their families of origin. Often, one partner in the marriage continues to feel a greater allegiance to his or her parents than to the spouse. Sometimes, even though the husband and wife sincerely want to be loyal to each other, their parents make demands on their loyalties that cause them to side with the parents against the spouse.

For example, there are intrusive, insulting, or controlling in-laws. A parent-in-law who thinks it's OK to interfere in your marriage at any time, for any reason, can be a painful cross to bear and a dangerous bear to cross! I've counseled couple after couple who tell of being tormented by bullying, meddling, or sharp-tongued in-laws. I've seen couples pushed to the brink of divorce by such controlling personalities.

There are helpful strategies for dealing with problem in-laws. One strategy is to recognize that you are an adult. You do not have to be intimidated or bullied by a parent or parent-in-law. You are free to ignore the advice or criticism of others, including the people who raised you or who raised your partner.

You could also discuss in-law problems honestly with your partner. State clearly and firmly that you expect your partner to align himself or herself with you. Explain that you need to have your partner's cooperation in heading off the in-law's controlling or meddling behavior.

The last strategy is to declare your independence respectfully, but firmly and clearly. You don't have to get into a shouting match with your in-laws; in fact, it's much better if you don't. When an in-law tries to interfere with some area of your life, state your case simply, calmly, and confidently: "That is an area of privacy, and I choose not to discuss it with anyone else." Don't get drawn into an argument; just close the subject. If the in-law persists, restate your position: "As I said before, I choose not to discuss it." If the in-law still pursues, then stop responding. There is nothing anyone can do or say to move you if you remain silent. Eventually, the in-law will tire of the game and recognize that you are invulnerable to attempts to attack or control you.

In some very extreme cases, an in-law will be so difficult, so intrusive, and so obnoxious that the marriage relationship itself is threatened. In the case of Carlos and Silvia at the beginning of this chapter, we saw a situation that approached this extreme. Carlos had tried to reach out to his in-laws, but doing so had only gotten his hand bitten. Silvia's parents continually barraged him and Silvia with criticism, interference, and comparisons to Silvia's old boyfriends. Silvia had tried hinting and even tried confronting her mother directly, but the woman refused to accept Carlos.

In response, Carlos made a conscious decision to avoid contact with his parents-in-law. Was he right to do so? His wife, Silvia, didn't think so. That's why Carlos and Silvia brought this issue into my office for resolution. "I think Carlos should turn the other cheek," Silvia explained. "I know it's hard, but he should try to ignore and forgive the things my family says."

"But do I have to spend time with her parents in order to forgive them?" Carlos asked me. "Do I have to keep subjecting myself to their insults?"

"Let me ask you something, Carlos," I replied. "How do you feel about Silvia's parents? Are you bitter? Do you resent them?"

"Well," he said, his brow furrowing, "I have to be honest—I really don't like these people. I mean, who would, if that's the way they treat you? But I don't hate them. I don't want to hurt them. I just want them to stop hurting me. And I figure the best way to keep them from hurting me is to stay out of their way."

"Have you tried to confront them about the way they treat you?" I asked.

"Sure I have," said Carlos. "So has Silvia. These people are just going to be the way they are, and I've accepted that. But I don't hold a grudge against them."

"Silvia," I said, "does Carlos ever complain about your parents? Does he gripe about them to other people? Have you ever heard him say something that would injure their reputation?"

"No," she said. "In fact, I'm always amazed at how positively he talks about my parents in front of other people. I think he does that out of love for me, and I'm grateful for that. I just wish he would go with me when I visit them. They're my family, just like Carlos is my family. I like to have all my family together sometimes—even if they don't get along together."

"It seems to me," I observed, "that Carlos has done a good job of responding to this situation in a healthy way. He doesn't try to get even with your parents and he doesn't hold a grudge; he just wants to remove himself from a painful situation. I don't believe Carlos is duty-bound to maintain a relationship with people who continually attack him and insult him. I think Carlos is responding to the best of his ability, with forgiveness and understanding. What do you think, Silvia?"

"I think," she said, "you're both right. I was just hoping we could pull our family together."

"Maybe you can someday," I said. "The next time you go to your parents' house, you could tell your parents how much their behavior has hurt Carlos and you. Point out to them that if they truly love you, they'll accept and respect the man you married. Maybe, in time, they'll come around. The decision by Carlos to withdraw from them may be the catalyst for change."

CREATING AND MAINTAINING A SAFETY ZONE

In every marriage, there are adjustments and accommodations to be made in relating to our partner's parents: annoying habits, different styles of relating and ways of doing things, unwelcome intrusions, differences in values and beliefs, friction, conflict, or emotional outbursts.

Our goal is to make these adjustments and come to a place of mutual acceptance. We may have to work through some issues with our in-laws while letting other issues go in order to keep the peace. Ultimately, if all goes well, we'll come to a place where we have established a mutual zone of inclusion and acceptance, along with a set of commonly agreed-upon and recognized boundaries.

Every couple should be able to say, "Here are the boundaries. Inside this boundary line is our zone of privacy and safety. This is who we are as a couple, and no one else, not even parents, is allowed in without an invitation. Over here, outside of this boundary line, is our zone of inclusion and acceptance. That zone defines who we are as an extended family, a community of parents, siblings, in-laws, and so forth."

It's not healthy for a couple to dig a moat around their relationship, completely closing out parents (unless the parents are destructive or abusive). But neither is it healthy for a couple to have a drawbridge down that parents and other extended-family members can use any time of the day or night to intrude into the couple's safety zone.

When everyone in the larger family understands where the boundary lines are—and when everyone respects those boundaries—then that extended family becomes a rich and rewarding network of connections and relationships. In-laws can often become loving resources and repositories of emotional support and spiritual strength, helping couples to experience security and stability.

Sure, difficult issues will arise from time to time, even in the healthiest of extended families. Conflicts will erupt now and then—a certain level of conflict is normal and manageable. The goal is to create the kind of caring, mutually supportive atmosphere between couples and their parents, grandparents, and siblings, so that love can overcome any problem that arises.

One of the best ways to ensure that we are building healthy extended-family relationships and setting healthy boundaries is to continually re-evaluate our relationships in terms of what I call "The

Hierarchy of Priorities." This hierarchy, based on the tenets of the Jewish and Christian tradition and scriptures, represents a healthy order of priorities for our loyalties and emotional attachments:

The Hierarchy of Priorities

1. God
2. Marriage Partner
3. Children
4. Family of Origin (Parents and Siblings)
5. Neighbors (Fellow Human Beings)

If you believe in God, then you probably know that your first duty is to love God above all else. Deuteronomy 6:5 tells us, "Love the Lord your God with all your heart and with all your soul and with all your strength." After God, we are to love others according to a hierarchy of priorities. After your relationship with God comes your relationship with your marriage partner, followed by your relationship with your children, and then your relationship with your parents, your partner's parents, your siblings, and other family members.

It's important to understand, however, that this hierarchy of loyalties needs to be applied with care and understanding. It would be a mistake to say, "Well, since my loyalty to God is number one, then I have to give all my time to the church. Unfortunately, that leaves no time for my family's needs."

The fact that our relationship with God is number one doesn't mean every other relationship means nothing. We have to prioritize time and energy for all of these relationships—but we have to make sure we place them in the proper order. A healthy relationship with God will enable us to have healthier relationships in every other arena of our lives.

It's a balancing act because we all have so many relationships to attend to in so many areas of our lives that it is easy to neglect some of our priority relationships. It's crucial that we invest our greatest human loyalties in our marriage—not in parents, children, or any other human relationship. The marriage relationship is our primary human allegiance. When that is healthy, every other relationship will naturally fall into place. A healthy relationship between Mom and Dad is the best of all possible worlds for a child. An unhealthy marriage tends to distort all of our other relationships.

The boundary around the zone of marital privacy and safety must be maintained and guarded. All intrusions into that safety zone—including parental intrusions, no matter how well-intentioned—must be fended off for the good of the marriage. As in the traditional words of the marriage ceremony, both partners in the marriage need to leave father and mother and, forsaking all others, cleave only to each other.

Most in-laws are treasured members of a couple's extended family, contributing love, support, friendship, and experienced counsel when the husband and wife want and need it. Some in-laws, however, contribute only chaos and turmoil. But even our problem in-laws can be endured if they are taught to recognize and respect the boundaries of a marriage relationship.

In the next chapter, we'll look at some of the special issues that come with blended families.

TAKE ACTION
Questions of a Marriage

If you and your partner are answering these questions together, first write your answers down separately, then compare your answers—but remember to use covenant-love to deal with any disagreements! Use the information you gather from each other to better understand how each of you look at, and feel about, your love relationship.

1. Think back over your marriage. What is some of the "baggage" from your family of origin that you have already unpacked?

   What kinds of "baggage" do you wish your partner would unpack and discard?

   Ask your partner what kind of "baggage" he or she would like you to unpack.

2. Do you feel your marriage is a safety zone, free from intrusions by in-laws and others? Or is it a war zone, under enemy attack? Or somewhere in between? Circle a place on the scale of 1 to 10 below to indicate your answer:

      1 . . 2 . . 3 . . 4 . . 5 . . 6 . . 7 . . 8 . . 9 . . 10

War zone   Safety zone

3. What is the biggest problem or issue you currently have with your in-laws?

Does your partner align with you and support you or do you feel your partner maintains an allegiance to your family of origin and against you?

What steps could your partner take to alleviate this problem or issue you have with your in-laws?

Compare notes with your partner and make a covenant together to be more supportive of each other in dealing with in-law problems.

4. Take another look at "The Hierarchy of Priorities" below.

The Hierarchy of Priorities

Do you have your loyalties and priorities in a healthy, biblical order or does your own "Hierarchy" need some work?

Be brutally honest with yourself: In the blanks below, list your priorities in the order in which they actually occur in your life.

Priority 1: My relationship with _____.
Priority 2: My relationship with _____.
Priority 3: My relationship with _____.
Priority 4: My relationship with _____.
Priority 5: My relationship with _____.
Priority 6: My relationship with _____.

SIXTEEN

What
About
Stepfamilies?

━━━━━━━━━◆━━━━━━━━━◆━━━━━━━━━

"Sure," Howard said into the phone. "Uh-huh. . .Yeah, I know. . .
No, it's no problem. I'll be right over." He hung up the phone,
turned, and almost collided with his wife. She glared at him, hands
on hips, blocking his path. Howard's heart leaped into his throat
and stuck there like a sideways watermelon.

"Who was on the phone, Howard?" asked Janice, her voice hard-
edged with suspicion.

"Well, uhhhh—" Howard's eyes darted guiltily.

"It was The Sponge, wasn't it?" That was Janice's term for Howard's ex-wife, Emily. In the four years he'd been married to Janice, he'd never heard Janice use Emily's name. It was always The
Sponge—or worse.

"Emily needs help," Howard nervously explained. "She's got a
foot of water standing in the sink, her gardener didn't show up,
the front lawn's a foot high, and she's got a dozen twelve-year-olds
showing up in three hours for a birthday party."

Janice's eyes burned like twin nuclear meltdowns. "*Whose* birthday party?"

Howard gulped hard. "Little Dwayne's."

"Little Dwayne is her boyfriend's son! Let Big Dwayne unclog her drain and mow her lawn for Little Dwayne's birthday party!"

"But Big Dwayne is picking up the cake and the party favors. Emily really needs—"

"Howard!" Janice yelled right in his face. "I've been asking you to take care of our lawn and our shower drain and our broken fence and our broken screen door for six months! There are three children in this house—my two daughters and the baby we made together—and they don't get enough of your time. I'm your wife, and I hardly ever see you! But let The Sponge call you up—a woman you haven't been married to for six years, a woman with a boyfriend of her own, a woman who already soaks up half of every dollar you make—and you're Johnny-on-the-spot! Get this straight, Howard. I'm a wife. She's an ex. If you don't want me to be an ex as well, then call her up right now and tell her you can't come."

Howard gulped. "I can't do that! I promised!"

"Call her back and un-promise."

"No way!"

"Fine," said Janice. "I'll do it." She picked up the phone.

"What are you doing?" Howard made a grab for the phone, but Janice yanked it away.

"Hello?" she said. "Guess who? . . . That's right. . . . No, Howard can't come over today—or any other day."

"Gimme that!" Howard lunged and grabbed the phone. "Em? It's me. . . . No, Janice is just clowning around. I'll be right there!" He threw the phone to the floor and stomped it under his heel.

"Are you crazy?" shouted Janice. "You just destroyed our telephone!"

"Don't you *ever* do a thing like that again!" Howard snarled, then headed for the door.

Two hours later, Howard returned home, tired and sweaty from fixing his ex-wife's sink and mowing her lawn. Janice and the children were gone. There was no note.

BLENDED OR ALL MIXED-UP?

What was Howard's problem? He was divorced and remarried, a stepfather and a father, with full responsibility for his new "blended" family. His wife and the children in his own new family needed him, yet his ex-wife continued to make demands on his time. He had no responsibility to his ex, yet he continued to do things for her that he couldn't find time for in his own household. Why did he feel duty-bound to accede to all the demands of a family he was no longer part of?

The biggest reason: *guilt.* He felt responsible for the breakup of his first marriage, so he continued to allow his ex-wife to enter his life in ways that were totally inappropriate. Unable to set healthy boundaries between his former family and his current family, Howard had brought himself to the brink of another divorce.

As one newly initiated stepfather once put it, "Now I know why they call it a 'blended family.' I feel like someone put us all in a Waring blender and pushed the button marked *liquefy!*" The term "blended family" is really a misnomer. When divorced people come together and try to build new families, the result is rarely what you would think of as a nice, smooth, homogenized "blend." Instead, what you frequently have is a lot of people living together, trying to build relationships, and getting all mixed up.

A better term, perhaps, than "blend*ed* families" is "blend*ing* families," since this term suggests that the people in this family are engaged in an ongoing process of coming together. Blending families have specific issues to be faced—very different issues from the issues in "first families." When blending family issues are not addressed head-on, with care, commitment, and love, the result is enormous pain for the couple and for the children involved. Sometimes these tensions can pull a marriage apart.

We have already talked about the chronological stages of marriage. In blending families, however, the normal stages of chronological progression do not march logically from one stage to the next. In fact, the stages may get shuffled like cards in a poker deck. For instance, if a man in his forties with two college-age children marries a woman in her early thirties with a small child, you have a man and woman at two different developmental stages, dealing with different sets of parenting issues.

There are big adjustments to make whenever two people get married even for the first time. But in a remarriage, the number of adjustments multiplies and the size of the adjustments magnify.

The lines of relationships in blending families tend to get tangled. There are many losses and changes in every relationship that must be dealt with on an individual basis. Both partners must negotiate and balance a multitude of additional relationships at the same time, including:

- relationships with birth children
- relationships with ex-spouses
- relationships with new in-laws
- relationships with ex-in-laws
- relationships with stepchildren

Partners have to manage expectations from previous families, such as when their stepchildren critique their actions: "That's not the way we did it when Mom and Dad were together!"

BLENDING IN THE REAL WORLD

Many couples who are blending their families together get into trouble because of their expectations. We have an entire generation of adults who were raised on an entertaining but misleading television show, *The Brady Bunch*. In this show, a man with three sons marries a woman with three daughters. Sure, they have their ups and downs and just enough stepsibling conflict to build a half-hour script around. But nowhere in this show do you find the intense dynamics that take place in real blending families.

On this show, the daughters embrace the new stepfather and call him Daddy. The boys stick up for the girls and the girls befriend the boys. It's wonderful, but rarely does that stuff ever happens in real life. Out here in the real world where life is something that happens to you day after day and there are no commercial breaks, no reruns, and few of those tidy Hollywood happy endings, the children usually resent their new stepfather as an intruder and a threat. The stepsiblings often hate each other and battle each other for turf. The children want their real parents to get back together again and often spend much of their time thinking up ways to sabotage the new marriage. To top it all off, the stepfather often blows in and announces, "Okay, I'm your Dad now, and you've gotta call me Dad and do what I say," to which the children respond, "Yeah, right!"

Stepmothers have a rough time of it, too. They have to adjust to children who resent them for replacing their real mom. They face especially stiff resistance from stepdaughters, who often try to compete with them for Dad's attention and affection. Expectations tend to be higher on the stepmother (who's supposed to be the primary manager of house and children—even if she is employed outside the home) than on Dad (who tends to be viewed as essentially a breadwinner). Stepmothers are expected to come in and be Mom, with all the responsibilities that go with the job.

Many stepparents get tripped up by paradoxical expectations. A stepfather, for example, often finds himself presiding as the male authority figure in a household where he is, in many ways, viewed as the outsider. Mom has been taking care of her children all by herself for months or years. Yes, she has wanted a man around the house to help her, but she was managing by herself. Now she has to share responsibility, check decisions with another person, negotiate roles, and give up autonomy.

When she married, she told her new husband she wanted him to have an active role in the parenting of her children. She wanted the children to respect his authority. But something strange happened the moment he actually assumed that role and began to discipline the children: Suddenly, Mom's whole demeanor changed. She became a momma bear protecting her cubs, and he became the big bad wolf! This is just one example of many of the conflicting, paradoxical loyalties that have to be sorted out in a blending family.

REDEFINING "FAMILY"

In the new marriage arrangement, Dad has his children, Mom has hers, but Dad's children are probably living elsewhere and he only gets to see them every other weekend. In fact, his children may be living with a stepfather, which introduces another layer of issues. Children feel disloyal to their biological dad if they show any friendliness to the stepfather, yet they feel disloyal to Mom if they don't. Therefore, the children feel a lot of inner conflict.

Children live in one parent's house, spend holidays and weekends in the other house, and they're in, they're out, bouncing from house to house like Ping-Pong balls. What is the concept of family these children are learning? It might be three people this week, ten people the next week.

In a first marriage, a young couple has months or years in which to bond and build a relationship. They can get through the settling-in phase, make their adjustments, fight their battles, make up, and get to know each other without a lot of prying little eyes checking on their every movement.

However, couples in blending families don't have that luxury. They don't live in a safe, private enclosure; they live in a fish bowl—and some of those little fish can be piranhas! Partners in a blending family are thrust into family life with a bunch of strangers. They are rubbing elbows with children, competing for the bathroom, struggling to maintain privacy, struggling to build intimacy, jostling and jockeying for respect and control under chaotic conditions. Then, on top of all these problems, this couple might have to deal with the chaos of an intrusive or vindictive ex-spouse.

A civil and amicable divorce can help to ensure the success of a remarriage; a bitter and destructive divorce can make remarriage a living hell. When two divorced parents love their children enough to separate on good terms, they are able to support each other's house rules, support each other's authority, and avoid tearing each other down in front of the children. The success of a blending family often hinges on whether the ex-spouses are committed to being decent and supportive or bent on destruction.

THE DEVELOPMENT OF A BLENDING FAMILY

A blending family develops in a different way and through different stages than a first family. These differences can be clearly observed as early as courtship.

When two previously married people come together in a dating relationship, there is usually a sense of awkwardness that exceeds even the awkwardness of adolescence. For most previously married people, "dating" is ancient and dimly remembered history. Both sides are a little rusty at the rituals and rites of courtship.

Looking back over my own life, I realize that I've literally never had a single life. Marcy and I got married right out of college. I wouldn't know where to go or what to do if I were single. If anything happened to our marriage at this point in my life, I would have to ask myself, "How is a man my age supposed to act when he's dating? Should he behave like a teenager? Call a woman up, take her to the movies, hold hands, and act ginky all the time?"

That's a real problem for a lot of people who find themselves back in the courtship phase after years of marriage. They feel awkward in a situation they haven't experienced in many years. (That's one reason I hang on to Marcy so tightly!)

When people find themselves single again, they frequently make mistakes in reading situations and potential partners. At an unconscious level, they are eager, even panicky, to restore that old, familiar situation: a husband, a wife, two to three children, a house with a white picket fence. This obsessive desire to restore the family unit often drives people to view life, people, and relationships through rose-colored lenses. They see a potential mate not as who he or she really is, but as a symbol of caring and nurturing. *Aha!* they think. *This time I've finally found the person who can support me, meet my needs, and make me feel whole again.*

As a result of this filtering and the unconscious craving to restore the familiarity of a family unit, many recently divorced or bereaved people tend to jump into new relationships with both feet. The courtship phase becomes intense and serious—very fast. A couple of single-again people can become suddenly, intensely, powerfully "Stuck" on each other. In their passionate attraction, they become blind to the fact that they need time to truly get to know each other.

In many cases, they hear that biological clock ticking away or they feel a bit of mid-life panic. They think, "Life is passing me by!" Both partners are likely to make a mistake in choosing a second (or third or fourth) partner. They are also likely to be very needy, having come through the pain of loss or divorce, and they clutch at anything or anyone who can make the pain go away. If anyone suggests they should go slower, these people will likely reply, "I'm old enough to know what I want, and we're happy, so butt out!"

I've seen it again and again while doing premarital evaluations and counseling. I'll have couples take a written psychiatric evaluation, and when I got the evaluation back, it's clear that these people see each other through a romantic haze. They are marrying into the very same problems and issues that caused their divorce a few months or years earlier. The same old problems come at them again—only worse. *And they have no clue.* I can wave red flags, shoot off warning flares, shout at them with a bullhorn, and they won't hear me. "We're in love!" they say. "This is the real thing at last!"

This is not to say that all—or even most—remarriages are doomed from the start. But experience shows that remarriages fail at an alarming rate.

Another serious complication that arises when people contemplate remarriage involves children. One or both partners usually have them, and children get very uneasy when they see their parents dating. In fact, it's not unusual to see children behaving with hostility toward the "intruding" partner. The children involved may be in grade school or adolescence, or they may even be grown up and living away from home. Children of any age usually resent their parents bringing a "stranger" into the existing family system. And from a child's point of view, a new stepfather or stepmother is nothing more than an intruder and a stranger.

Once a couple enters into remarriage, they find themselves facing an array of difficult and complex tasks. One such task is establishing and maintaining boundaries. Remarried couples are thrown into the paradox of trying to establish safe perimeters around their new relationship while being forced to maintain a lot of contact with children and adults from the old relationship. Time must be carefully scheduled for relationship-building with one's partner and with each individual child. During this time, the couple must set rules to guarantee that their own privacy is respected, as well as the privacy of the children. Every individual in the family should have his or her own personal space and boundaries.

Another task is establishing intimacy in the family fish bowl.

Once the honeymoon is over, it's really over. The new couple comes home to a house full of children and relationship issues. Somehow they must continue to build relational closeness with each other despite the chaos and competing demands of family life. They must make the most of the limited opportunities for privacy and marital togetherness.

Establishing new family traditions is another complex task remarried couples face. Both partners will want to blend elements from their own family histories to create new family traditions for celebrating holidays and birthdays, creating memories, and so forth. Traditions help to create a sense of identity and security as a new family unit. Children need to be allowed to maintain some old traditions from the previous family unit (providing security and continuity) while building new traditions that say, "This is who we are as a family today."

A final task is monitoring and recalibrating expectations. Those in the family who are living with—or disillusioned over—their Brady Bunch fantasies need to be brought along and allowed to realize that family love and mutual acceptance take time and require adjustments. One of the tasks of parenting in a blending family is to help all members in the family express their feelings and adjust to change.

STEPPARENTHOOD

Both adults and children in a blending family are prone to unrealistic expectations. You can't jump into a situation and make the children like you. Relationships have to emerge and grow at their own gradual pace. Many stepparents want to immediately become firm, respected disciplinarians, or they want to take long, happy walks in the park, hand-in-hand with their stepchildren, or they want to spend happy hours helping their stepchildren with their homework. In the overwhelming majority of cases, the step-children are just not ready for that.

In time, with patience and perseverance, you can probably build a relationship with your stepchild, but don't force it or rush it. The key to success in the step-parent role is to take your time and keep your cool. Expect to be tested. The only way to pass the test is by showing these children (who resent your very existence in their home) that you love them unconditionally and that you are tough enough and patient enough to go the distance.

In a blending family, children are always coming and going. They spend weekends, holidays, summers, and other times with their "other family." So it's important to maintain clear expectations and rules for children who aren't there all the time.

If the couple decides to conceive additional children of their own, they need to explain to the step-children what is happening. Children need to be able to ask questions and express feelings. Parents and stepparents need to supply answers for questions children are either afraid to ask or cannot articulate. For example, parents and stepparents need to reassure the existing children that a new baby doesn't mean anyone is being replaced. No matter how many there are in the family, there's always enough love to go around.

PRACTICAL KEYS
TO BLENDING A FAMILY

The following section offers some practical suggestions for helping everyone in the family make adjustments toward a healthy, balanced blending family.

One suggestion is to resolve major issues before marriage. The issues that need to be discussed and resolved in advance include rules, discipline, boundaries, roles, and so forth. In as many areas as possible, try to create clear understandings going in. As a parent and stepparent, agree in advance on house rules and discipline styles. When you are in front of the children, support each other 100 percent. If you have disagreements with your spouse on parenting issues, settle them in private. Don't let the children think they can drive a wedge between you and your partner. If they can, they will.

Another suggestion is to make the marriage your first priority.

Place a higher priority on the marriage relationship than on relationships with children. The best thing your children and step children can possibly experience, especially if they have been through a marital breakup before, is to see what a good, functional, strong marriage looks like. Schedule time to be alone with your partner on a regular, weekly basis, deepening and strengthening your marriage relationship.

Starting fresh in a neutral location can also help your family make adjustments. If you can, start your new life together in a neutral location—not his house or her house, but a new house, a fresh new start. Everyone in the new family system needs to recognize that this is not the old setting, with the old roles and old rules. This is a new adventure, and we're all starting out fresh.

It may also help to take time to negotiate family roles. Have family meetings in which all members participate, express feelings, ask questions, and share ideas. Make sure no one is left out and that every member is able to wrestle openly, and without being criticized, with the question, "Where do I fit in to this new system?" Stepparents should lay the cards on the table and ask their children, "How would you like me to relate to you? How do I fit in? What kind of step-parenting would you like me to do?" Children should be invited to voice their questions: "Have the rules changed? How do I relate to my stepparent? Who do I obey?" These issues should be faced openly, not left hanging and unresolved.

Another suggestion is to accept conflict and crises as opportunities for relationship building. Remember that intimacy is built not only during the warm-fuzzy times, but also during the crunch times in a relationship. Family conflicts can actually become opportunities for bonding to one another if those conflicts are faced with honesty, courage, and love. Times of conflict force family members to unpack their feelings and "get real" with each other.

You could also give everyone a chance to blend. Each family member will move toward acceptance of the new system at his or her own pace. The new system will seem a little artificial and "weird" to some family members who cling to the memories of their "real family," the first family that no longer exists. What many family members miss most about the old family was the sense of security and validation it provided. In time, everyone will learn to feel secure and validated in the new family system. It just takes time.

Encouraging honest, open family communication can also help family members adjust. Avoid showing shock, surprise, or anger when someone raises a question. Validate all feelings, even if you disagree with what is being expressed: "I certainly understand why you'd feel that way. We're all going through a lot of changes in this new situation."

A final suggestion is to learn all you can about the issues and problems of blending families. All couples, no matter how well matched they seem to be, can benefit from counseling, and this is especially true for couples going into second or third marriages. Seek a counselor who has experience working with blended families. For more information and resources, use Google to search for the National Stepfamily Resource Center website.

Even though *The Brady Bunch* is largely a myth, a blending family is for real. With hard work, honesty, love, and patience, you and your new family truly can achieve a dream—the dream of becoming "one big happy family."

In the next chapter, we will show that it is possible to survive the toughest crisis a marriage can undergo: the crisis of marital infidelity.

TAKE ACTION
Questions of a Marriage

If you and your partner are answering these questions together, first write your answers down separately, then compare your answers—but remember to use covenant-love to deal with any disagreements! Use the information you gather from each other to better understand how each of you look at, and feel about, your love relationship.

1. What is the biggest challenge facing you in your new marriage?

On a scale of 1 to 10 (below), how much support do you receive from your partner in managing or resolving this challenge?

1..2..3..4..5..6..7..8..9..10
No support / A fair amount / Total support

What could your partner do to help you to better resolve or manage this challenge in your remarriage?

2. If you were divorced:

On a scale of 1 to 10 (below), how civil was your divorce?

1..2..3..4..5..6..7..8..9..10

| It's a wonder anyone survived | So-so | We parted as best friends |

What steps could you take to ease tensions with your ex so that his or her remarriage and your remarriage could function more smoothly and effectively?

3. What stage of emotional development is your marriage in?

- Stage 1: Stuck (or Stuck/Fighting.)
- Stage 2: Unstuck
- Stage 3: I-ness
- Stage 4: We-ness

Are you and your partner at the same stage together? Why or why not? Explain your answer.

What blended family issues are currently impeding the progress and emotional growth of your marriage? (Explain your answer.)

- lack of privacy (intrusions of children)
- lack of boundaries (intrusions of exes and others)
- deliberate or unconscious sabotage of the relationship by children or others

- confusion over roles
- family conflict
- conflict over parenting styles
- unrealistic expectations
- other _____

4. Take another look at "The Hierarchy of Priorities" from chapter fifteen:

The Hierarchy of Priorities

It's very easy, under the best of circumstances, for couples to reshuffle these priorities in very unhealthy ways. For example, many parents and stepparents see the hurts of their children resulting from bereavement or divorce, and they feel very guilty. The children are demanding and needy, and the parents or stepparents feel very guilty, so the result is that the children often are placed at the top of the list of priorities. Exes, parents, and in-laws put their demands into the mix, and before you know it, the needs of the marriage—such as the needs for intimacy and boundaries—get shoved to the back seat. It is at this point that many second marriages fail.

Be honest with yourself. In the blanks below, list your priorities in the order in which they actually occur in your life.

Priority 1: My relationship with _____.
Priority 2: My relationship with _____.
Priority 3: My relationship with _____.
Priority 4: My relationship with _____.
Priority 5: My relationship with _____.
Priority 6: My relationship with _____.

Now, list three specific steps you will take, beginning this week, to put your priorities in their proper, healthy, functional order—God first, then your marriage, then children, and so forth. Ask a trusted friend to hold you accountable for taking these steps.

5. List at least six activities in the spaces below that you and your partner could do to get away from the house and the kids for a few hours to build some intimacy. Covenant with your partner to do at least two of them per month for the next three months.

(1)_____.
(2)_____.
(3)_____.
(4)_____.
(5)_____.
(6)_____.
(7)_____.
(8)_____.
(9)_____.

SEVENTEEN

Why Did My Partner Have an Affair?

⬦ ⸺⸺⸺⸺⸺⸺⸺⸺⸺⸺⸺ ⬦

"Why, Stan?" asked Debi, staring at her husband through red-rimmed eyes. "Why did you do it?"

Stan looked away and shrugged. "I told you—I don't know. People do things without knowing why."

"It wasn't as if I wasn't available to you. It wasn't like your needs weren't being met. Half the time, I pursued you for sex! It can't be that you needed someone to talk to. I was always saying, 'Stan, you can tell me anything. I want you to share deeply with me.'"

"Yes, Debi, you always said that."

"And you said, 'I'm all right.' You were always closed to me, Stan."

"Look, Debi, affairs just happen, you know? I didn't get involved in this—" Stan paused, groping for the right euphemism. "this *situation* because you are somehow not adequate as a wife. It's not as if I needed to go elsewhere to get better sex or to find a better listener or anything. It just happened, that's all, so stop looking for reasons. Sometimes there just aren't any reasons."

Stan really believed what he said. He was genuinely convinced that adultery occurs for no reason at all. But he was wrong. Every time a marriage partner strays from the marriage bed, there are reasons. The reasons may be hidden, tangled, confused, and even contradictory, but there are always reasons.

Infidelity deals a massive, traumatic shock to a marriage. But the wound of infidelity can be healed—if we can uncover and treat the root causes of the affair.

THE NATURE OF BETRAYAL

What is infidelity?

Some people would say that infidelity occurs only when there has been "actual intercourse" (usually defined as coitus or vaginal sex). Of course, that leaves a lot of territory open to interpretation and self-deluding denial. Does this mean that kissing and intimately touching someone other than your partner is not infidelity? Does it mean that oral sex "doesn't count"? What about a homosexual or lesbian affair? Or a hand up the skirt or down the blouse of an ex-wife, a co-worker, or an old girlfriend? Is flirting okay? What about lunch and sexy talk with someone from the office? What about "phone sex" or "Internet sex"?

A lot of people play mind games with themselves and their partners, pretending that if they engage in this or that behavior, then it "doesn't count" as infidelity. I would suggest to you that *infidelity* consists of any sexually related act you keep secret from your partner or which your partner would view as betrayal.

Infidelity is behavior that breaks the promise and breaches the trust of marriage. Since promise-keeping and trust are essential ingredients of marital intimacy, infidelity attacks the very essence of a marriage bond. Infidelity drives a wedge of dishonesty, secrecy, and distrust into the very heart and soul of a marriage.

There are many common myths about infidelity, and when couples come to me for counseling about one partner's infidelity, the offending partner usually articulates one or more of these myths during the first session. One such myth is, "Affairs are good for a marriage. A little fun on the side keeps you from getting bored at home." Fact: You really think so? Then let's reframe this statement and see if it still makes sense: "Lies, secrecy, and betrayal are good ways to build intimacy and togetherness in a marriage." While it's true that marriages can and do become dull, it is a myth that marriage has to be dull or that faithful monogamy is to blame. It's intimacy—not infidelity—that makes marriage exciting.

Another myth is, "Well, it's all out in the open now—I guess divorce is the only option." Fact: In roughly half the infidelity cases I've worked with, both partners have found ways to use the discovery of infidelity as a wakeup call. In time, after trust has been rebuilt, the discovery of infidelity can often serve as a springboard to a stronger relationship. Obviously, it's wiser and healthier to strengthen the relationship *before* one partner strays; a strong marriage relationship is the best way to prevent infidelity from happening.

"It's my partner's fault I did this" is also a myth. The offended partner often owns this point of view as well: "It's my fault. If I had been a better partner, my spouse wouldn't have had to go outside of the marriage for a sexual relationship." Fact: We are all responsible for our own actions. No one else makes us jump into the wrong bed. In order for a relationship to be healed, the person who committed the infidelity must take personal responsibility for his or her actions. The offender must stop making excuses and blaming others for what he or she did.

The next myth is, "This affair must mean all the love has gone out of our marriage." Fact: While affairs are frequently a warning sign of deeper problems in the marriage, they usually do not signal that "the love has gone." This myth is based on a fundamental misconception about love. The notion that "love" is a magical feeling that strikes two people like a bolt out of the blue, then disappears without explanation, is romanticized nonsense. It's a silly, simplistic, "high school" way of looking at love.

The reality is that covenant-love is a decision—a tough, no-nonsense commitment to seeking the best for your partner and doing the hard work of making a relationship work. Feelings of attraction and desire may ebb and flow, and there is a lot that two people can do to rekindle those feelings when they have begun to subside. But *love*—genuine, committed, covenant-love—is always a choice that both partners can make.

The last myth is, "Everybody does it. All my friends have had affairs. Why shouldn't I?" Fact: Despite what you see in TV shows and *Playboy* magazine, everybody's not "doing it." For the past several decades, statistics and surveys have consistently shown our society to be mostly monogamous. According to those surveys, roughly half of all husbands and roughly a third of all wives have been unfaithful, and even those statistics are misleading.

Many of the affairs included in the survey were one-time, never-repeated episodes—not "lifestyle choices" as the "everybody does it" comment would indicate. Also, many who reported having extramarital affairs did so only after the marriage was clearly dying of other causes and was headed for separation or divorce. Marriages that are otherwise intact show much lower rates of infidelity than the average. In contrast to the myth that "everybody does it," faithfulness is actually the norm.

Let's get rid of the myths. Let's accept the truth about infidelity as our starting point, and then we can begin rebuilding a damaged relationship and make it whole and strong again. The truth about infidelity is:

- Affairs are deceptive and destructive, and endanger the very existence of a marriage.
- Marriages *can* survive infidelity, but it's not easy.
- While an affair involves sex, most affairs take place for reasons having little or nothing to do with sex.
- Infidelity is not normal; it is a disorder in the relationship and needs to be treated and healed.

WHY AFFAIRS HAPPEN

Back to Stan and Debi.

They came to me after Debi discovered that Stan had been having an affair with a woman Debi knew only slightly. The woman's name was Celeste. Debi was doubly surprised by Stan's choice: Celeste seemed like such a plain, uninteresting woman. Why did he get involved with her?

Stan and Celeste had apparently become close while working

together on a church committee. The affair had lasted four months and ended when Debi overheard Stan's side of a phone conversation with his lover, then checked his cell phone and found incriminating text messages. The discovery of her husband's adultery came as a shattering revelation to Debi, and for a while she strongly considered leaving him.

Prior to this discovery, Debi had pursued her husband for affection, sex, and intimacy. She had literally *begged* him to discuss "deeply" (one of her favorite words) all of his feelings and thoughts. Stan, however, was emotionally closed to her and continually stated that everything was all right.

"So why, if everything was 'all right,'" asked Debi, "did you go to bed with another woman? Did you think Celeste was sexier than me? Was she better in bed? Do you think she's prettier, smarter, what?"

"Don't be ridiculous," Stan responded. "I wasn't in love with her. You know Celeste, and you know she's not even in your league. She was just . . . there."

Debi was desolated. "It makes no sense."

Stan had to agree. It made no sense to him either. Later, it would all make sense.

Why do affairs happen? Frequently, even those who are involved in infidelity don't understand what drives their behavior. There are many reasons marriage partners stray (some affairs may involve two or more of these factors, and the two partners in an affair may enter into the adulterous act for very different reasons).

One reason that marriage partners stray is unplanned passion. A man or woman may unexpectedly encounter a situation of temptation. He or she may be the target of another person's scheme of seduction. Or unexpected circumstances may simply throw two people together in a sexually volatile state. This does not excuse either person from responsibility to "just say no" when sexual temptation arises. To say that an incident of infidelity was "unplanned" or "accidental" is not to say it was inevitable. Both participants are responsible. Both have the power to choose to do the right thing.

After an initial unplanned incident, a participant often experiences enormous guilt and anxiety. He or she has violated a sacred trust, and many people react by feeling remorseful and promising themselves and God never to do it again. They blame themselves— and rightly so. The anxiety they feel usually focuses on the fear of exposure, and all the losses that might result from that exposure. There is usually a tinge of anxiety about other possible consequences, such as a sexually transmitted disease or an unwanted pregnancy. In some cases, a participant in an unplanned incident of adultery may find that he or she likes it and wants it to continue, and this will create conflict within that person. He or she will feel excitement and anticipation about future sexual encounters along with strong feelings of guilt and anxiety about getting caught.

Addiction is another reason why affairs happen. Some people become obsessive about engaging in infidelity, as if extramarital sex were an addictive drug. A single "hit" of this "drug" may cause the "user" to become "hooked" on a pattern of promiscuity. The sex addict typically engages in a variety of sexual behaviors. These behaviors include compulsive use of pornography (including print, video, or Internet porn), voyeurism, compulsive masturbation, exhibitionism (exposing oneself), engaging in anonymous or high-risk sex acts, and phone or Internet sex. Sex addicts tend to depersonalize their sex partners, viewing them as bodies (or even body parts) rather than as human beings with souls and feelings.

Most sex addicts are men, although there are certainly female sex addicts. Sex addicts generally have no conscience about violating the intimacy of their marriage relationships because they fear genuine intimacy. They don't want to be truly known in the depths of their being, nor do they want to truly know another human being, nor do they want to be "cured" of a pattern of behavior that they find pleasurable. Sex is their drug. It's a substitute for genuine human contact and for contact with God.

Another possible reason for an affair is relationship addiction. Just as most sex addicts are men, most relationship addicts are women. Relationship addicts like to fantasize about life as if it were a Harlequin romance novel. They are in love with love—idealized romantic love. Their drug is not sex, but passion—lush, crescendoing, romantic emotion that carries the relationship addict away on strains of violin music. They always believe that "this moment will last forever" and this relationship (whichever relationship it happens to be at the time) is finally "the love of a lifetime."

Relationship addicts go from partner to partner, not so much because they are sexually promiscuous but because they always believe that the next encounter will be with Prince Charming. The "perfect match" is the sex-addicted man and the relationship-addicted woman. They are a symbiotic couple: she feeds his lust and he feeds her romantic fantasies while exploiting her sexually. When it's over, the relationship addict is left with guilt, regret, self-directed anger, and a sense of being used. These feelings last until the next time the violins begin to play.

Revenge can also cause affairs. An affair is sometimes used as a way of getting even with one's marriage partner for some perceived insult or injury. It is sometimes used to get even for a past act of infidelity by the partner. Revenge affairs often take place near the end of a marriage that is clearly on the rocks, sealing the fate of a relationship that might otherwise have been salvageable if either partner had tried to save it.

Another cause is midlife crisis. Many affairs happen when one or the other partner reaches a point of dissatisfaction with the marriage, a career, and life in general. He or she feels life is passing by too quickly and many of life's more exciting experiences have still not been tasted. A "grab for the gusto" mentality sets in, supercharged by the fear that "maybe I'm losing my virility" or "maybe I'm losing my attractiveness." In an effort to prove he or she "still has what it takes" and to reduce the anxieties of this transitional stage in life, the individual initiates an affair.

Midlife is an extremely dangerous time for a person to suddenly decide, "I think I'll have an affair." Experience shows that the vast majority of divorces among couples married twenty-five years or more are the result of infidelity. Decades of accumulated trust, happy memories, family relationships, and the respect of one's children can all be tossed away for the sake of a casual, meaningless (and often unpleasant) sexual encounter. If you see yourself drifting in this direction, you will save yourself and your family a lot of agony if you stop the affair before it begins.

Dysfunctional marital arrangements can also lead to affairs.

Sometimes one spouse turns a blind eye to the other spouse's serial infidelities. In some cases, one partner doesn't like sex while the other has normal drives. A person who has no sex drive needs therapy to heal the emotional issues that hinder the normal enjoyment of his or her sexuality. In all too many cases, the sexless partner—to avoid being bothered by the other partner's needs—allows (or even sends) the other partner outside the marriage to get those needs met.

In other arrangements, both partners behave sexually toward each other, but one turns to extramarital sex either because of a sexual addiction or to maintain emotional distance from the spouse (fear of intimacy). The non-adulterous partner allows the other partner's behavior for fear of losing that partner, because he or she also desires emotional distance, or has bought the partner's claim that "some people just have a high-powered sex drive, and a monogamous relationship isn't enough to satisfy."

Frequently these arrangements are made in silence; both sides know what's going on, but neither side talks about it—a case of mutual denial. But sometimes these arrangements are actually arrived at through discussion and negotiation. The two partners may work out a verbal arrangement between them whereby one (or both) partners may carry on affairs, often with certain conditions thrown in ("never bring a woman into our house" or "you can have a one-night stand on a business trip, but never in town where someone we know might see you").

Those who enter into such arrangements—either silently or by agreement—fail to understand how destructive such behavior can be. The risk of one partner bringing back a disease to the marriage bed is only a small part of the danger of these arrangements. The greater harm comes from the psychological and spiritual damage of maintaining a marriage relationship with damaged intimacy, indeterminate boundaries, and the repression of normal feelings of anger, anxiety, and jealousy.

For other couples, the reason for having an affair is unfulfilled expectations. Couples enter into marriage with both spoken and unspoken expectations. In fact, most people are not fully aware of all the expectations they harbor regarding marriage and their partners. If these expectations go unsatisfied, the relationship begins to deteriorate and the unsatisfied partner may choose to go outside the marriage to seek satisfaction. These unfulfilled expectations are usually not of a sexual nature. The unfaithful partner may just want someone to listen, someone who will offer emotional acceptance and affirmation.

Attention-getting is another cause of affairs. Some partners, feeling ignored, may use an affair as a way to get "noticed." In such cases, the goal (whether conscious or unconscious) is exposure, not secrecy. The unfaithful partner will usually find ways to leave clues and hints so that the affair will be "accidentally" discovered by the other partner.

Other times, simply looking for excitement can lead to affairs. Some partners get bored with each other or with their lives and simply go looking for excitement—not just the excitement of sex, but the excitement of living dangerously and risking getting caught. Some people who feel a lack of sexual desire, or who have a sexually unavailable partner, seek excitement outside the marriage. Sometimes a person who has trouble becoming aroused in marital sex finds that the danger of extramarital sex, along with the adventure of experiencing sex with a new partner, stimulates greater arousal and sexual excitement. In counseling, these individuals can often be helped to see that sex is clean and good, and wholesome sex is the best sex of all.

Some affairs are strictly business, or utilitarian affairs. People sometimes allow themselves to be sexually used in order to gain a job, a promotion, or some other favor. Properly viewed, most utilitarian affairs are really nothing more than a form of prostitution. In some cases, sexual favors are extorted from another person, as when a boss sexually harasses an employee because he has the power over her career and her paycheck. Though individuals who find themselves in such situations still have the power to say "no" to harassment, those who say "yes" should be viewed more as victims than as perpetrators.

Finally, a reason for affairs results in exit affairs. Sometimes, when a partner makes a decision to leave the marriage, he or she will initiate an affair. An exit affair may be a premature "shopping trip" for a new partner, or it may be a way of announcing to one's partner (and even oneself), "This marriage is over. I'm taking my sexuality elsewhere." For people who have difficulty verbalizing feelings and confronting issues, having an affair—then allowing the other partner to find out about it—is sometimes used in place of face-to-face communication.

People have affairs for all kinds of reasons, and none of those reasons are particularly logical or healthy. There were reasons why Stan cheated on his wife Debi, even though Stan himself couldn't articulate what those reasons were. It took a lot of digging and probing in therapy before he and Debi were able to understand what had taken place in and outside of their marriage.

HOW TO RESPOND TO INFIDELITY

A couple times in counseling, Debi suggested a frame for Stan's behavior as "the midlife crazies." Each time she raised that phrase, Stan rejected it. He liked to picture himself as a careful, logical thinker. He didn't do anything that was "crazy." As our sessions unfolded, however, it became clear that Stan—who denied having any problems or anxieties, who practically denied having emotions at all—had been carrying a great emotional burden even before the affair.

Stan was a worrier, and he tended to "own" all the problems and issues in the home—that is, he felt personally responsible for everything that happened in the family. He had always been reasonably but not spectacularly successful in his sales career, but the bad economy had put his industry in a slump. As a result, he was chronically anxious about finances, though he never confided his concerns to Debi. He also worried about conflict between Debi and their adolescent daughter and about Debi's apparent emotional neediness.

In counseling, Debi had said, "Half the time, I pursued you for sex! It can't be that you needed someone to talk to. I was always saying, 'Stan, you can tell me anything. I want you to share deeply with me.'" Stan interpreted that statement as an expression of neediness and desperation on Debi's part. On top of all the pressure and worry Stan felt, Debi's urging that he open up emotionally felt like just one more pressure. While Debi thought she was helping Stan to unburden himself, Stan perceived it as Debi pressuring him to meet *her* emotional need for connection.

"Debi seems unhappy," Stan said, "and she's always after me to give her a lot of sharing and conversation that I just can't deliver. I have a lot of pressure in my career, and then I come home and Debi just loads on more pressure. I just can't handle it. Here I am, in my late forties, my business life is tanking. Meanwhile my friends are bragging about the smart investments they made and how they're taking early retirement. One of them bought a golf villa on Marco Island. And here I am, just getting by."

As we talked, it became clear that Stan was unhappy with his career and his family life, feeling inadequate as a husband and worrying a great deal about his virility and his own mortality. He had been thinking about all the experiences that had passed him by in life—including the experience of "sowing some wild oats" (he and Debi had married young, and both were virgins on their wedding night). He'd begun to wonder what sex with another partner might be like. Stan didn't realize it, but he was actually going through the typical thoughts and feelings of a "midlife crisis."

One day, after a church committee meeting, Celeste asked Stan for a ride home. During the drive, she talked about how difficult her life had been since her husband died of cancer two years before. Stan felt tongue-tied and awkward, wishing he could think of something to say that might be helpful and supportive. As she was getting out of the car, however, Celeste thanked him for being "a good listener."

Stan drove home that day with a strange, indefinable feeling inside. Somehow, without really knowing what he had done, he'd managed to be emotionally supportive to a woman—something he had not been able to do for his own wife. He went home and, in response to Debi's questioning, told her a few superficial details about the committee meeting. He did not mention driving Celeste home.

Two weeks later, he attended another committee meeting and again gave Celeste a lift home. Again she talked about her unhappy life. She made one comment that stuck in Stan's mind: "It's so hard getting into that big empty bed every night." It was a statement that seemed to step across an unspoken boundary—ever so slightly. In Stan's mind, it sounded almost like—well, like an invitation. Those words continued to roll around in Stan's mind for days.

Two weeks later, there was another meeting and another ride home. This time, Stan stood by her front door for a few minutes, listening to Celeste's problems, and she invited him in for coffee.

He said, "No, thanks, I really ought to be getting home." But instead of leaving, he kept talking and listening another few minutes. He knew Debi wasn't really expecting him for a while—the meeting had ended early. When Celeste invited him in a second time, he accepted. But he never did get that cup of coffee.

When Debi accidentally discovered the affair, she suffered a shock much like that of bereavement. She entered the five-stage grief process that everyone experiences with the loss of a loved one:

- denial
- anger
- bargaining
- depression
- acceptance

When she first overheard her husband talking to Celeste on the phone about their relationship, her initial reaction was denial. Not her husband! Surely, she had misinterpreted what he was saying! Even when she sifted through his incriminating text messages, and even after she confronted him and he admitted the affair, all she could say to herself was, "This can't be happening! Stan would never do this to me!"

Then she became angry. Enraged, in fact. Interspersed with her bouts of anger were bouts of bargaining—bargaining with Stan ("What can I do to make sure you never do this again?") and bargaining with God ("Please, God, make this all go away! Can't it be like it was before?").

By the time Debi and Stan came in for counseling, she was deep in depression and a long way from acceptance. Her mood was a black aura of mingled sadness, hopelessness, and anger turned outward toward Stan and God, and anger turned inward: "What did I do to cause this? How could I have been so stupid?"

How should a couple respond when an affair takes place? Infidelity doesn't have to destroy a marriage. In fact, the honesty and caring required to save a marriage can actually cause a relationship to emerge stronger. The restoration of the relationship depends on both partners making emotionally healthy, loving choices in the aftermath of the infidelity. Trust has been broken and can only be rebuilt by patient effort, honesty, and love. Here is how both partners should respond:

If you are the offending partner, confess the affair to your spouse. "But," you may say, "my spouse doesn't know. Wouldn't it be better for me to quietly end the affair, make sure it never happens again, and not say anything to hurt my spouse?" No. That's not only cowardly but it's bad for the marriage. You build a healthy marriage on intimacy and honesty—not secrets and lies.

"But," you may say, "my partner might divorce me! What about the damage to my children if my marriage is destroyed?" The welfare of your kids is something you should have considered before the affair. Now that the affair has taken place, there's a real risk of "collateral damage"—damage to your spouse, to your kids, and to other people who trusted you and looked up to you.

In the long run, the best way to make sure that the other people in your life are never harmed in this way again is by confessing the affair to your partner and taking firm steps to keep it from happening again. As long as the affair remains a secret, the risk that you will be unfaithful again remains high. The only way to have a healthy relationship is to seek the deepest possible level of intimacy. You can never experience intimacy with another person by keeping secrets.

Revealing the affair is risky, but intimacy is always risky. You willingly took the risk of having an affair and breaking the intimacy of your most important relationship. Now it's time to demonstrate the character and courage to take the risk that provides the only hope of restoring the intimacy you have broken. It's time to stop being selfish, dishonest, and cowardly in your relationship. Take a risk for true intimacy.

An affair is usually symptomatic of deeper problems in the

relationship that need to be unpacked, addressed, and resolved. If you fail to honestly confront the core problems in your marriage, you will probably find that, despite your good intentions, the infidelity will not stop. Either you'll end up going back to the affair or you'll become involved in a different affair. The issues that led you into the wrong bed are still there, waiting for you at home, unresolved and unhealed.

Face the problem. Face the truth. Face your spouse and settle the matter.

I advise that you confess to your spouse in the presence of a counselor. Marriage counseling is almost an absolute necessity. Avoid making excuses, using euphemisms, or minimizing the seriousness of your conduct. Above all, avoid blaming anyone but yourself for your actions. Admit it that you are responsible—not your spouse, not the other person in the affair. It's time to own your own actions and ask your spouse for mercy and forgiveness. Nothing less than repentance and contrition will do.

Expect your partner to be angry and hurt. Expect tears and shouting. Expect probing questions about issues you'd rather not discuss. Expect questions such as, "Was she sexier than me?" or "What kind of sex acts did you do with him?"

Be honest. Be humble. Accept every accusation and indictment without defending yourself. Don't retaliate. Don't counter-accuse. Don't do anything but accept responsibility for your actions.

If you are the wounded partner and your spouse is confessing to you, then hear your spouse out. Avoid acting or speaking rashly. Seek help from a counselor. Make sure you obtain answers from your spouse to the following questions:

- Is the affair still going on?
- Are you going to immediately end the affair?
- Are you willing to be honest and open with me in working through the reasons why this happened?
- What is the significance of this affair to you? Was it a casual fling or is it a romantic entanglement?
- What decisions have you made about our marriage?
- How do you think the children will be affected by these decisions?

As you talk with your spouse, carefully monitor your own thinking. Expect to experience strong emotions and distorted perceptions. Thoughts will occur to you that may fill you with panic, pain, dread, despair, hopelessness, or rage. You'll be barraged by such thoughts as, "I'll never be happy again," "My entire marriage has been a lie," or "God can never untangle the mess my life has become." The crisis will eventually pass. Yes, this is a horrible moment in your life—one of the worst you have ever experienced—but you will come through it.

If you are the wounded partner and you have just discovered your partner is having an affair, try to remain calm. You may want to get the help and insight of a counselor before confronting your spouse. But make no mistake: you must confront your spouse about his or her infidelity.

When confronted, your partner may: (1) deny the affair; (2) admit the affair, but defend himself or herself; (3) admit the affair, but blame you; (4) admit the affair, but blame someone else; (5) refuse to talk about it; or (6) admit everything and beg for forgiveness. There are several important pointers to remember. Once such pointer is that if your partner becomes defensive or—worse—offensive, refuse to accept blame or shame for your partner's affair. This was his or her choice, and you are not to blame for your partner's infidelity.

Another pointer is that if the affair is ongoing, make it clear to your partner that *it ends now*—instantly. You may want to insist that your partner get on the phone in your presence and end it on the spot. Don't accept a plea that, "I need some time to get out of this." If your partner doesn't want to lose you, he or she should be willing never to see or speak to the other person again, period. Force your partner to make a choice, and don't compromise.

Express your hurt and anger, but avoid doing so in a destructive or violent way is another pointer. Express the fact that you want something positive to come out of this—a closer relationship, not greater distance. Remember, the safer your partner feels, the more likely he or she will be open and truthful with you. If your partner feels threatened, there's a temptation to "edit" the truth as a self-protective measure.

Feel free to express curiosity or questions you have about the affair. Intimacy has been broken by your partner's lies and secrecy. You have a right to some information. But avoid asking for gory details ("What specific positions and sex acts did you engage in?"); these details are not necessary, and they will fill your mind with images that will make it harder for you to forgive and move on.

Another pointer is to let your marriage partner explain and apologize. Understand that you probably see everything—including your marriage relationship—more clearly than your partner, whose perceptions are still in the haze of unreality that is a part of being unfaithful. Right now, you probably hold most of the decision-making power regarding the fate of your marriage. Resist the temptation to punish or exact revenge. Resist the temptation to inflict rejection or shame. Don't threaten a "revenge affair" of your own.

Above all, pray. Ask God for wisdom, peace of mind, serenity, and a spirit of love and forgiveness so that the marriage can be healed.

As a special word of caution for if you find that your partner has been involved in a series of affairs or multiple affairs at the same time, you should realize that your partner is extremely self-centered and not a likely candidate for repentance and permanent change. If your partner is inclined to multiple affairs, he or she is probably very good at conning other people—including you. Such individuals are bad risks. Don't attempt to deal with a multiple-adulterous partner by yourself. You need the help of a counselor who understands the unique psychological dynamics of these individuals.

Normally, I would avoid suggesting divorce if you are willing to work to restore the marriage. Serial adulterers and sex addicts are a category unto themselves. Staying married to a person who is virtually incapable of being truthful, faithful, and monogamous can be a soul-destroying experience.

REPAIRING THE RELATIONSHIP

As you and your partner work through the process of restoring the relationship, allow emotions to flow freely. There will be many strong, painful feelings. They will subside for a while, and then come on with full force at later times. Expect ups and downs.

Take inventory of your relationship together. Ask yourselves some questions and answer them honestly. "How did we get to this place?" "Are we finally being fully honest with each other, or are we still holding back?" "Are there secrets that still need to be uncovered, feelings that still need to be expressed?" "Where is God in our relationship now?"

Avoid blaming each other. Both partners should take responsibility for their own actions and their own neglect of the relationship, but the offending partner should remember that no one else is to blame for an act of infidelity. One partner may have to own the fact that he became too busy with his career or that she allowed communication and intimacy to deteriorate, but that does not excuse an affair.

Trust will need to be rebuilt—patiently, piece by piece. An offending partner may say, "You're just going to have to trust me when I say it will never happen again." But that's nonsense. Trust is not a light switch you can click on. Trust is built up slowly over years of experience and can be destroyed by a few hours of illicit pleasure.

Trust is a commodity that is spread out over the various compartments of one's relationship. There is sexual trust, emotional trust, and financial trust. If your partner discovers you have been lavishing gifts and favors on the person you had an affair with, don't expect your partner to trust you with the credit cards for a while. If you made your liaisons during business trips, expect your partner to check in on you frequently and unexpectedly when you're away. If your affair grew out of a friendship with someone at work or at church, expect your partner to demand that you sever all opposite-sex friendships.

You'll need to make many life changes in order to rebuild the trust that you have broken. It's not that your partner is trying to punish you; these are just the natural consequences of infidelity. If you want to rebuild your marriage, be prepared to accept those consequences.

You can, however, negotiate solutions to some of these problems of broken trust—solutions that will, over the long haul, enable you to rebuild trust and intimacy in your marriage. For example, your partner may say to you, "After what you did on that trip to Chicago, I can't allow you to take business trips anymore."

A positive response might be: "I understand how you feel, but my job requires me to travel. So let's find a way for me to put you at ease and help you to know that you can trust me when I'm gone. I'll give you my itinerary so you'll know when I'm in business meetings and when I'm on my own. When I'm not in meetings, I'll be in my hotel room. Any time you want to check on me, call my room and I'll be there. I won't even leave for meals—I'll get room service instead. Every moment of my free time, I'll be in my room, accountable to you. If I feel tempted in any way, I'll call you and we'll talk about it."

Throughout the restoration time—which will be a matter of years, not weeks or months—concentrate on building the relationship through specific activities. One activity might be to renew your mutual caring and kindness. Plan to do acts of caring for each other so that you can experience again the feelings of affection and support you felt for each other before the affair. Set aside a weekly night for these caring acts, and make specific requests of each other: "Take me out to dinner tonight." "Give me a back rub in front of the fireplace before we go to bed." "Do the dishes and put the kids to bed for me tonight."

You could also remember the good times. Get out picture albums or the wedding videos. Share positive memories and rebuild the emotional ties that once bound you so intimately together. Relax together and let those old feelings come flooding back.

Talking about things you never talked about before is a good activity to do together to build the relationship. Share childhood memories. Share feelings you've kept hidden and secret. Share fears and hopes. Don't avoid the subject of the affair, but purge the emotions on an ongoing basis. Don't let bad feelings or angry thoughts build up inside. Let emotions and thoughts flow between you.

Mutually commit yourselves to total, uncompromising honesty. No more lies, no more secrets, not even in the littlest matters. Become transparent to each other. Nothing rebuilds trust and intimacy like truth.

Face sexual issues squarely. Expect to have problems with sex for a while, since the act of sex between you and your partner will inevitably arouse mental images of the affair. Be patient with each other. If sexual dysfunction becomes persistent, seek professional counseling.

Forgiving again and again is another important activity to help rebuild the relationship. A hurt like this can't be forgiven once and for all. Memories and emotions will continue to recur, and anger will unexpectedly come back, red-hot and stinging, even months or years after you thought you were finally healed. Remember that forgiving doesn't mean forgetting or condoning, nor does it mean you don't hold your partner accountable. Forgiveness and accountability go hand in hand.

Adultery is a violation of your relationship, but you are choosing to release your partner from condemnation for the wrongdoing. For your own sake, as much as for your partner's, you are going to let go of anger and bitterness, and you are going to get on with your life and your relationship.

You could also symbolize a renewed commitment. Consider making a meaningful gesture or ceremony to mark a new beginning in your relationship together—a renewal of your wedding vows, a new ring ceremony, a second honeymoon, a communion service. Mark the event with photos, and hang the photos on the wall of your home. As you forgive, make sure you never forget the new beginning of your love and intimacy together.

Monitor the emotional needs of your children. Your children may not be aware of the infidelity, but even your youngest child will sense something wrong in the family. Be aware of your children's feelings during and after the crisis. They are likely to experience insecurity, fear, anger, sadness, distrust, and so forth.

Grown-ups often fail to realize that children often feel as betrayed or unloved by an unfaithful parent as the betrayed partner feels. Young children and teenagers become more susceptible to depression, suicidal impulses, and regressive behavior (thumb-sucking, bed-wetting, rebellion, night terrors, petty crimes, running away, vandalism, and arson).

If you don't feel motivated to reconcile with your partner,

consider your children. The crisis you're going through will have a profound effect on their attitudes about men, women, marriage, honesty, and infidelity. Before this crisis, they lived in a comfortable, secure world of trust and family unity; their world may now be fractured and distorted, but it can still be mended if you are willing to do what it takes to heal the family.

Experience shows that children of adulterous marriages are much more likely to become adulterers themselves. They see the dishonesty, secrecy, lack of intimacy, and lack of self-control of their parents, and they sometimes emulate those patterns. Looking at their two parents, they see one parent who is wounded, sad, hurt, ignored, disregarded, and treated as unimportant. They see the adulterous parent as one who breaks promises, deceives, acts irresponsibly, and potentially as one who behaves badly and gets away with it. Which parent do you think the child will choose to identify with?

Some children, particularly those who have experienced extreme emotional pain and humiliation as a result of a parent's infidelity, react against the unfaithful parent and grow up to be extremely moral and faithful. But all too many children grow up to adopt the self-centered ways of the irresponsible parent.

How much should children be told about the infidelity? They should not be burdened with information or emotional content that is beyond their years or emotional development. If they have been exposed to some of the conflict between their parents, they should be reassured that both parents are working on a problem between them, that the problem will be solved, and that none of the conflict is the fault of the children. If the child is upset, the parents should pray with the child and reassure the child of their love.

Finally, start over with each other. Don't try to restore the old relationship. Focus on building a new relationship on a foundation of total openness, vulnerability, availability, and intimacy.

That's the caring, courageous choice Stan and Debi made. It was a long journey, and their journey is still continuing. They had painful issues to unpack, a lot of tears to shed, and a lot of secrets to uncover. It was hard for Debi to learn to forgive and to trust again. It was hard for Stan to be open about his feelings and his deepest thoughts. But in the process, these two people discovered depths to their relationship that they never realized could exist before.

"I'm not thankful for the act of infidelity that brought us to this point," Debi says today. "It still hurts too much to think about it. But I'm thankful for everything that has happened since. For the first time since we said our marriage vows, Stan and I are really together, and I'll always be thankful for that."

What about you? The act of infidelity was a break in your relationship. You have the option of turning this crisis into an opportunity to build something new and lasting in place of the old, broken relationship. A marriage that has been restored, rebuilt, and transformed is well worth the effort it takes to rebuild it.

In the next and final chapter, we will bring all the questions, answers, and themes of this book together and show how these concepts work together in the exciting adventure of the marriage relationship.

TAKE ACTION
Questions of a Marriage

If you and your partner are answering these questions together, first write your answers down separately, then compare your answers—but remember to use covenant-love to deal with any disagreements! Use the information you gather from each other to better understand how each of you look at, and feel about, your love relationship.

1. What do you consider infidelity? Rate the following acts as "faithful" or "unfaithful":

   My partner makes a business call at the office of an old boyfriend or girlfriend.
   Faithful ☐ **Unfaithful** ☐

   My partner gives a hug and a kiss to several opposite-sex co-workers at an office party.
   Faithful ☐ **Unfaithful** ☐

My partner makes an appreciative, almost flirtatious comment about my best friend's appearance in my presence.

Faithful ☐ **Unfaithful** ☐

My partner makes an appreciative, almost flirtatious comment about my best friend's appearance when I'm *not* present.

Faithful ☐ **Unfaithful** ☐

My partner goes dancing with someone he's introduced to while on a business trip. Nothing else happens.

Faithful ☐ **Unfaithful** ☐

My partner watches a sex-laden R-rated movie starring his or her favorite sexy film star one night after I go to bed; he or she doesn't tell me about the movie.

Faithful ☐ **Unfaithful** ☐

My partner meets an "old flame" for coffee and reminiscing after work. Afterwards, they shake hands, say, "It was really good to see you again," and parts company.

Faithful ☐ **Unfaithful** ☐

My partner makes a business call on a prospective client in the client's home. The client "comes on" to my partner, an obvious attempt at seduction, and my partner exits the situation, but does not tell me about it afterwards.

Faithful ☐ **Unfaithful** ☐

My partner has a secret opposite-sex friend. They have been meeting for years—not for sex, just to talk, sometimes holding hands or hugging. But it's not really an affair; it's more of a friendship. My partner does not discuss it with me.

Faithful ☐ Unfaithful ☐

My partner insists on a one-week separate vacation every year. I don't know what takes place on those vacations. My partner says, "Everyone's entitled to just a week away a year, no questions asked."

Faithful ☐ Unfaithful ☐

My partner talks to an old boyfriend or girlfriend once a week on the phone. This person lives five states away, and my partner hasn't seen this person in ten years.

Faithful ☐ Unfaithful ☐

My partner flirts with almost every opposite-sex person he or she meets. My partner says it's just his or her personality: "I'm outgoing and fun-loving—that's all."

Faithful ☐ Unfaithful ☐

While I'm out of town, my partner accompanies an opposite-sex friend to dinner and a concert. Nothing else happens.

Faithful ☐ Unfaithful ☐

My partner makes a business call on a prospective client in the client's home. The client "comes on" to my partner. My partner sees that this person is needy and lonely. To push this person away would make him or her feel hurt and rejected, so my partner engages in sex—not so much an act of passion, but really an act of mercy, kindness, even politeness. At least, that's how my partner later explains it to me when confessing.

Faithful ☐ Unfaithful ☐

My partner and I have a huge fight. My partner storms out of the house and drives away. The next day, my partner comes home and remorsefully confesses to having had a "quickie" revenge affair with someone he or she met in a bar. It was a meaningless act, only intended to get back at me for the argument, and it will never happen again.

Faithful ☐ **Unfaithful** ☐

My partner, who is bisexual, occasionally engages in sex acts with same-sex partners. My partner explains that this is not infidelity and I should not be jealous, because these are not "affairs" with opposite-sex partners.

Faithful ☐ **Unfaithful** ☐

My partner engages in sexual touching and fondling with another person, but does not engage in actual intercourse. It only happens once.

Faithful ☐ **Unfaithful** ☐

My partner has been exchanging annual Christmas letters with an old flame for the past fifteen years.

Faithful ☐ **Unfaithful** ☐

After you have rated these statements, have your partner rate these statements. Then compare your answers. How does your partner's attitude on infidelity compare with yours? Does your partner draw different boundary lines than you? On statements where your answers differ, discuss why each of you responded as you did.

2. Do you have two standards of faithfulness and fidelity—one for yourself and one for your partner?

After doing the "faithful/unfaithful" exercise (number one, above) and comparing your responses with those of your partner, do you see areas where your standards need to change and become more consistent? Explain your answer.

In view of the insights you have gained from this exercise, are there changes you need to make in your lifestyle or behavior? Explain your answer.

3. Do sexual or romantic thoughts interfere with your ability to effectively perform your career, club, church, or household duties?

Do you think about sex more than you would like to? Are there aspects of your sexual behavior that are beyond your power to control?

Do you feel empty or ashamed after experiencing sexual fantasies or sexual activity? Do you use sexual thoughts or sexual activity to avoid certain feelings or problems in your life?

Is there an opposite-sex person in your life, other than your partner, who makes you feel special, and who you are unwilling or unable to tell your partner about?

Does your sexual behavior cause you to violate your conscience, ethical principles, or beliefs? Does your sexual behavior cause you to risk your job, your health, or your financial security?

Do you "channel-surf" TV or flip through reading material in search of sexually stimulating partnerrial? Do you seek out sexually stimulating partnerrial in stores, video shops, cable TV, or via your computer?

Has an important relationship in your life ever been endangered, damaged, broken, or compromised as a result of your sexual behavior outside of that relationship?

If your answer to any of the above questions is "Yes," then you are probably either involved in or at risk for an affair. You should strongly consider obtaining professional counseling to resolve the issues which are placing your marriage relationship at risk.

4. Do you trust your partner? Why or why not?

Does your partner trust you? Why or why not?

5. Think of three secrets about yourself that you have never shared with your partner. What effect do you think these

secrets have on your level of marital intimacy?

Would you be willing to share those secrets with your partner at this time? Why or why not?

How do you think your partner would respond if you shared them?

If your partner shared these exact same secrets about him- or herself with you, how would you respond? Would you still love your partner?

Having answered the last question, do you now feel more safe and comfortable about sharing your secrets with your partner so that intimacy can be enhanced?

6. On a scale of 1 to 10 (below), rate the level of intimacy that exists between you and your partner:

1 . . 2 . . 3 . . 4 . . 5 . . 6 . . 7 . . 8 . . 9 . . 10

| We are totally | We are completely |
| closed to each other | transparent to each other |

What steps could you and your partner take right now to become more open, vulnerable, and intimate with each other?

EIGHTEEN

Where Do We Go From Here?

NASA's space shuttle is the most complex machine ever constructed. In order for a space shuttle to safely perform its job, every interlocking system and subsystem of the shuttle—from its three powerful main engines to its high-tech zero-gravity toilets—must function as designed. Most importantly, each system must function cooperatively with all the other systems. If one system fails—even a seemingly minor one—disaster can result.

That's what happened on January 28, 1986, when the space shuttle *Challenger* leaped off the launchpad and clawed its way into the chilly Florida sky. What no one knew was that a simple piece of space technology—a circular rubber seal—had become brittle in the freezing temperatures of the pre-dawn morning. The heat of the solid rocket booster caused the brittle rubber seal to rupture, allowing blowtorch-like gases to escape, firing straight into the thin hull of the huge main fuel tank. Just 73 seconds into its flight, that blowtorch burned through the tank wall, igniting the fuel in the tank. The space shuttle exploded about nine miles above the ground, killing seven astronauts and shutting down the entire US space program for two years.

The government commission investigating the disaster

determined that many warnings from engineers had gone unheeded, that quality-control measures had gone slack, and that communication between various parts of NASA had broken down. As a result, the decision to launch the shuttle on a freezing-cold morning, when the rubber seals were dangerously brittle, was flawed.

A marriage is much like a space shuttle. The relationship between a husband and a wife is incredibly complex, and many of the systems and subsystems of that relationship must interlock and mesh together or major breakdowns can occur. Warning signs must be heeded and problems must be corrected. Quality-control is a must in such areas as intimacy, boundaries, trust, expectations, and sexuality. Communication channels must be open, clear, and free of distortion. Leadership roles must be carefully apportioned and conflict must be managed.

If all these systems are not working correctly and are not functioning together, if a marriage becomes brittle at the pressure points, or if important warning signs are ignored, the entire relationship can blow sky-high.

So how do we do it? How do we juggle all the complexities of a marriage and keep it aloft? How do we successfully mesh all the components, systems, and subsystems of a marriage so that a relationship can truly soar?

It all starts with love.

THE "MAIN ENGINE" OF MARRIAGE

Love is the "main engine" of a marriage. It's the driving force that propels a marriage, but the love we're talking about isn't passion, romance, or sexual attraction. It's not the transitory, "now-you-feel-it, now-you-don't" emotion we find in popular books, movies, and TV shows. Authentic love isn't a feeling at all. It's a commitment, a decision of the will. It is "covenant-love," rooted in loyalty and faithfulness to a promise.

Over time, a marriage is exposed to many forces that strain the relationship. There are both external stresses and internal conflicts. As we saw in chapter 2, romantic love (*eros*) and friendship love (*phileo*) are not strong enough to withstand those forces. Romantic love and friendship love only last as long as the person you love is lovable. But in marriage, you can expect to encounter many situations where your partner is not going to be very lovable at all. (And believe it or not, there are times when you're not so lovable yourself.)

When things temporarily turn not-so-lovable, many people throw in the towel and dash to the divorce court. They mistakenly conclude that "the love is gone," so they pull the eject lever and bail out. This is an immature response. If these people had a mature understanding of covenant-love (*agape*), rooted in a promise, their marriage could hold together through the crisis. Eventually, both partners would become lovable again; they would grow emotionally, spiritually, and relationally through the crisis; and their bond of intimacy would become all the stronger.

This is why I say that love is the "main engine" of the marriage—covenant-love, based in a commitment of the will—keeps the relationship moving higher, toward more intense levels of intimacy. Once two people learn to authentically love each other, they discover depths of love that other less patient, less mature couples never even imagine.

THE "HEAT SHIELD" OF MARRIAGE

The space shuttle is covered with a heat shield of protective ceramic tiles. These tiles shed the heat of re-entry and protect the crew from destructive outside forces. The crucial importance of the space shuttle heat shield was tragically underscored on February 1, 2003, when the space shuttle *Columbia* was destroyed during re-entry after a scientific mission in orbit. All seven crewmembers perished in the disaster.

The cause of the disaster was that on takeoff, sixteen days earlier, a chunk of insulating foam had broken off the main fuel tank of the shuttle, striking the ceramic heat shield tiles on the left wing of the shuttle, breaking the tiles. During re-entry, white-hot gases burned through the breach in the tiles, vaporizing the aluminum skin of the shuttle's wing. Within minutes, the intense heat caused the entire spacecraft to disintegrate. From the ground, observers saw the space shuttle break into dozens of white trails of flaming debris. A small breach in the heat shield resulted in death, destruction, and failure.

Every healthy marriage has a "heat shield"—a series of protective buffers in a marriage that we call "boundaries." Our boundaries draw clear, healthy zones of protection around the relationship. Healthy couples do not allow parents, in-laws, friends, acquaintances, and others to invade that zone. An emotionally healthy couple is made up of two people who have left their respective families and have established clear physical and emotional zones that are out of bounds to others.

Sexual boundaries protect a marriage from the "heat" of infidelity. When both partners understand that certain behaviors and certain people are clearly out-of-bounds, the marriage is protected against the risk of sexual intrusion.

Healthy couples also maintain internal boundaries to draw clear, healthy distinctions within the relationship—boundaries between one partner and the other. It is our separateness that allows us to fully enter into a close and permanent bond with another person. Though the goal of a healthy marriage is intimacy—an emotional, intellectual, and spiritual bonding so intense it borders on fusion—each partner must also maintain his or her own identity and individuality.

Boundaries keep some things out while keeping other things in. The boundaries around the relationship shield both partners from the destructive "heat" of the world, of parents and siblings, and of all other forces that attempt to intrude on the relationship. Boundaries within the relationship protect each partner from taking too much "heat" from each other. A husband and wife must be able to say to each other, "This is who I am as opposed to you. These are my thoughts, my feelings, my desires, my goals."

Boundaries—the "heat shields" of marriage—are a critical component of the relational system. With strong, secure boundaries, the vehicle of marriage can soar. Without this "heat shield" in place, a couple can burn up in the atmosphere of stress, conflict, and infidelity.

THE "LIFE SUPPORT SYSTEM" OF MARRIAGE

Astronauts have to breathe. A space shuttle without a life support system is not going to get very far. In a marriage, the "life support system" is something we call trust. Both partners need to know that it is safe to "breathe" in the relationship—that it's safe to be intimate, open, and vulnerable with each other.

Individuals whose ability to trust was damaged in childhood may have issues and emotions which need to be examined through counseling. Old wounds must be flushed out and dealt with so they can no longer hinder the present relationship. The partner who is haunted by fears of engulfment or abandonment must come to a place where it's emotionally safe to experience genuine intimacy within the protective enclosure of love, boundaries, and mutual trust. In order for trust to grow, both partners should commit themselves to:

- a reaffirmation of their wedding vows
- a lifestyle of total honesty
- making and keeping promises
- giving and receiving trust

The commitment of a promise is foundational to trust in a marriage. Like the oxygen supply in a spacecraft, a promise guarantees that the things we depend on for our survival will be there when we need them. A promise looks to the future and overcomes the unpredictability of tomorrow, enabling us to feel secure so that trust can grow. When we make and keep promises, we declare ourselves to be reliable and unchanging, even in the face of changing circumstances and unpredictable events. As we generate trust in the relationship, we remove fear and anxiety so that the relationship becomes strong, healthy, and durable.

The "life support system" of trust makes life possible in a marriage and is one more system in the marriage that makes it possible for the relationship to move upward and onward.

THE "MISSION" OF MARRIAGE

When a space shuttle launches, it follows a "mission profile." The entire flight has been planned to achieve certain goals and expectations.

Marriage, too, has a "mission profile." Both partners in the relationship have their goals and expectations. Some are conscious, spoken expectations. But many of the expectations we have of our partners are unspoken expectations, such as "If he loved me, he'd just know what kind of love making I want," or "After twenty years of marriage, I shouldn't have to tell her what makes me mad. I'll just sulk until she figures it out."

Unspoken expectations are dangerous. The "mission profile" of a marriage—both his expectations and her expectations—should be brought out into the open and negotiated verbally and clearly. An emotionally healthy couple continually seeks to bring hidden expectations out of hiding. This is done by setting aside regular time for discussing issues and communicating openly about mutual expectations, and practicing good listening habits; listening receptively rather than defensively. Good listeners seek creative ways to meet the emotional needs the other person expresses. Poor listeners seek to evade or deflect those needs. This is also done by using "I" statements when expressing needs: "I need more time to myself," not, "You need to go away and leave me alone." Writing out a mutually negotiated "Contract of Expectations" expressing such matters as mutual faithfulness and support, spiritual expectations, emotional expectations, sexual expectations, and practical expectations (chores, children, finances, and so forth) is another way to bring out hidden expectations.

When we go through the process of actually articulating and negotiating our expectations, we begin to see that some of those expectations are not realistic or reasonable. Because of this, we discard some expectations, modify others, and attempt to mesh our expectations with those of our partner. This keeps our "mission" on course, flying straight and true on a stable flight plan.

THE "GUIDANCE SYSTEM" OF MARRIAGE

Like the guidance system of a spacecraft, our human brains collect, analyze, and sort data and enable us to use that information to stay on course and respond to emergencies and new situations. As we have seen, the brain can be viewed as consisting of three main divisions:

1. The Survival Brain (made up of the brain stem and the limbic system, centered beneath the cerebral cortex)
2. The Storehouse Brain (the right hemisphere of the cerebral cortex)
3. The Logical Brain (the left hemisphere of the cerebral cortex)

Each division of the brain plays a unique and crucial role in marriage communication and relationships. When our mental "computer" is "programmed" with accurate perceptions and information, we tend to respond appropriately in various situations, and our relationships stay on course. But there is that pesky "GIGO principle" that often gets in the way of our relationships: "Garbage In, Garbage Out." If the "programming" of our brains is flawed, then our responses to various situations in marriage will also be flawed.

What is our "programming"? It is what I call the maps, symbols, filters, frames, and postures that we have accumulated in our storehouse brain. These powerful symbolic images, which are stored at a level below our conscious awareness, cause old emotional issues, old hurts, and old struggles to resurface again and again in our relationships. They create distorted impressions of our marriage partners and generate suspicion and wariness that can damage trust and inhibit intimacy.

Our mental maps tell us how to respond in various situations. That's fine as long as our map is accurate. But if our mental map of reality is distorted, it will lead us off course. We may think we know what our partner is thinking and what his or her motives are, but our map could be inaccurate. The less accurate our map, the more likely we are to get lost in our relationships.

Our maps tend to magnify isolated actions and incidents into powerful, emotional symbols. If your partner absent-mindedly turns his or her back on you while you're speaking, it probably only means that he or she was momentarily distracted. But if your mental map is that turning away equals disrespect and hostility, then your partner's moment of distraction will be magnified into a symbol of rejection. Over time, your mental maps can harden into deep misconceptions. Instead of seeing the reality of your partner, you may begin to see only a stereotype, a caricature you have built up in your minds.

When couples begin to relate to each other on the basis of stereotypes and false impressions, the entire relationship becomes distorted. Each partner takes on a posture toward the other—either One-Up or One-Down. There are several actions you should do in order to make sure that the "guidance system" of your marriage is functioning properly and giving you realistic information on which to base your decisions and responses. One such action is to seek to understand the workings of your unconscious, symbolic *mind*. For example, if you become angry over something your spouse says, ask yourself, "Is my anger proportional to what my spouse actually said? Am I overreacting? And if I am overreacting, why? What is my map of this situation? How am I filtering and framing it? What symbols does this situation provoke within me? What posture am I assuming? What posture is my partner assuming?"

Another action to take is to take an emotional "reality check." Before responding to your spouse, pause to get in touch with your feelings and understand what has triggered those emotions. A pastor, counselor, or therapist can often be helpful in enabling you to better understand the reality of your marriage relationship.

You can also recognize that your partner also has maps, symbols, filters, frames, and postures. Your partner may not be so much in conflict with the real you as with a mental symbol or caricature of you. By recognizing this possibility, you will be better able to avoid actions and words that contribute to your partner's misperceptions, and you can underscore those actions and words that communicate love, caring, and understanding.

Accept the fact that you and your partner both have unresolved feelings and issues from childhood. If those issues are serious and difficult for the two of you to resolve between yourselves, consider seeking counseling.

Finally, make a commitment to grow in genuine intimacy and understanding of your partner. Make a decision to set aside any mental or symbolic caricatures of your spouse. Listen and try to understand your partner as if you are getting to know him or her for the first time. Be attentive to the things your partner says and does that *contradict* your mental image of him or her. Those details are clues to the reality of your partner—a reality that you may have been missing and misunderstanding for years.

THE "COMMUNICATION SYSTEM" OF MARRIAGE

A successful space flight depends on good communication. So does a successful marriage. A space shuttle needs to remain in constant contact with Mission Control in Houston. Astronauts need to be able to communicate effectively and clearly with each other. Marriage partners also need to remain in constant communication.

We need to be aware of how communication styles vary between men and women and from individual to individual. Women and men come from different worlds, and they communicate in very different ways. The same words may mean different things to each partner and may be used to accomplish different purposes.

Clear communication is also crucial in the negotiation and apportioning of leadership roles in the relationship. Leadership is not a matter of "Who controls?" but "Who serves—and how?" Leadership in marriage should be reciprocal and can take the form of initiating sex, planning meals, earning money, budgeting the family finances, planning vacations, and so forth. In many areas of marriage and family life, each partner can play to his or her strengths. The husband can lead in areas where his gifts, talents, and abilities are strongest, and the wife can lead in her areas of greatest strength. Instead of competing with each other, marriage partners should complement each other.

Clear communication is also crucial in the realm of conflict management. Conflict is inevitable in the best of relationships. In fact, a certain level of dynamic, creative tension should be welcomed in a healthy relationship so that both partners will be challenged to learn, change, and grow. When we deal with conflict in the healthy and mutually caring realm of the Blue Zone, when our focus is on solving the problem instead of winning the war, then conflict leads to understanding and deeper intimacy. But conflict that takes place on the battlefield of the Red Zone can often destroy a relationship.

In a healthy marriage, both partners learn to disagree, negotiate, and achieve resolution. Each partner stays in the present while discussing the issues and avoids the temptation to dredge up old issues and old wounds for use as ammunition. By continually monitoring and resolving communication problems while they are small, healthy couples keep emotional pressures from becoming explosive and destructive.

In times of conflict, healthy couples think Win/Win. They seek each other's benefit while avoiding the doormat role. Instead of approaching every issue from an "I win, you lose" stance, they seek solutions to conflict that make everybody a winner.

MISSION ACCOMPLISHED!

Every space shot has a set of goals, and the success of that journey can be measured by how close it comes to achieving its goals. We tend to forget that marriage has a goal, too. We assume that marriage is just about two people coming together, making life less lonely, and hopefully staying together for life. But there's more to a good marriage than that.

A healthy marriage has a sense of direction. In a healthy marriage, there is always someplace new to go, some new adventure to experience, some new uncharted territory to explore. The goal is not more money or more status or a bigger car or a new house. The goal of a healthy marriage is intimacy, and the success of a marriage can be measured by how intimately connected the marriage partners become.

Intimacy is the intersection at which two human souls connect. Intimacy in all its facets—emotional, intellectual, aesthetic, sexual, creative, and spiritual—is the fulfillment of the purpose of marriage. When you reach that intense level of intimacy with your partner, you can say, "Mission accomplished!"

Intimacy takes place in an atmosphere of safety (trust) and honesty (vulnerability). A sense of safety and trust is created by covenant-love, by promises made and kept. When you and your partner both feel safe and free to be honest and vulnerable, then you can share aspects of yourselves that you could never share with any other human being on earth. The deeper you move into intimacy with each other, the more you truly know each other. That is your goal—to know and be known as fully as any two people on earth can know each other.

Now you can see how all of these different systems of marriage mesh and support one another, enhance one another, and enable a marriage to truly soar toward the goal of intimacy. Covenant-love enables us to care for each other, meet each other's needs, work together, forgive each other, and keep promises. When promises are made and kept, we build trust. Trust makes us feel safe. Boundaries enable us to feel protected. A sense of safety and protection enables us to be honest and vulnerable. With clear communication and careful Blue Zone conflict management, we are able to see and hear each other more clearly. We are able to understand the depths of each other's feelings.

When all of these components work together, supporting and amplifying each other, they produce the one thing that marriage is preeminently about: *intimacy*. That's our mission. That's the destination of a spiritually, emotionally, relationally healthy couple.

How long have you been married? A year? Ten years? Twenty? Fifty? No matter how many years you have known this person at your side, there are mysteries to be explored. There are depths of intimacy ahead of you and your partner that neither of you has yet imagined. That is your mission: to explore new worlds of intimacy, to discover new depths of understanding, and to boldly go where no married couple has ever gone before.

So take off on this adventure together. Be truthful and trustworthy in everything. Maintain that zone of safety around your marriage. Stay within that zone, revel in the joy of fully knowing and loving another wonderful human being. Go deeper into intimacy and into the soul of the one you love.

Godspeed you both on your journey.

TAKE ACTION
Questions of a Marriage

If you and your partner are answering these questions together, first write your answers down separately, then compare your answers—but remember to use covenant-love to deal with any disagreements! Use the information you gather from each other to better understand how each of you look at, and feel about, your love relationship.

1. On a scale of 1 to 10 (below), where are you on your mission toward intimacy with your partner?

   1..2..3..4..5..6..7..8..9..10

   Sitting·on the launching pad   Mission accomplished

   What one action will you commit to this week to help build intimacy with your partner?

2. On a scale of 1 to 10 (below), how satisfied are you with the level of committed covenant love you demonstrate toward your partner?

   1..2..3..4..5..6..7..8..9..10

   Very dissatisfied / Somewhat satisfied / Very satisfied

3. On a scale of 1 to 10 (below), how satisfied are you with the level of committed covenant-love your partner

demonstrates toward you?

1 . . 2 . . 3 . . 4 . . 5 . . 6 . . 7 . . 8 . . 9 . . 10
Very dissatisfied / Somewhat satisfied / Very satisfied

4. How would you describe the present state of the boundaries between you and your partner?

1 . . 2 . . 3 . . 4 . . 5 . . 6 . . 7 . . 8 . . 9 . . 10
No boundaries   Just right   Too much separation
(Enmeshed)   (Balanced)   (Isolation)

5. On a scale of 1 to 10 (below), how satisfied are you with the security and appropriate boundaries around your marriage, separating your marriage from intrusion the outside world (including parents and in-laws)?

1 . . 2 . . 3 . . 4 . . 5 . . 6 . . 7 . . 8 . . 9 . . 10
Very dissatisfied / Somewhat satisfied / Very satisfied

6. On a scale of 1 to 10 (below), how satisfied are you with the way and extent to which your partner meets your needs?

1 . . 2 . . 3 . . 4 . . 5 . . 6 . . 7 . . 8 . . 9 . . 10
Very dissatisfied / Somewhat satisfied / Very satisfied

7. On a scale of 1 to 10 (below), how satisfied are you with the level of trust that exists between you and your partner?

1 . . 2 . . 3 . . 4 . . 5 . . 6 . . 7 . . 8 . . 9 . . 10
Very dissatisfied / Somewhat satisfied / Very satisfied

8. On a scale of 1 to 10 (below), how satisfied are you with the amount, openness, and clarity of communication between you and your partner?

1 . . 2 . . 3 . . 4 . . 5 . . 6 . . 7 . . 8 . . 9 . . 10
Very dissatisfied / Somewhat satisfied / Very satisfied

9. On a scale of 1 to 10 (below), how satisfied are you with the frequency, quality, and mutuality of sexual expression between you and your partner?

1 . . 2 . . 3 . . 4 . . 5 . . 6 . . 7 . . 8 . . 9 . . 10

Very dissatisfied / Somewhat satisfied / Very satisfied

10. On a scale of 1 to 10 (below), how satisfied are you with the way leadership roles are negotiated and apportioned in your marriage?

1 . . 2 . . 3 . . 4 . . 5 . . 6 . . 7 . . 8 . . 9 . . 10

Very dissatisfied / Somewhat satisfied / Very satisfied

11. What is the biggest roadblock to intimacy you face in your marriage?

- practicing covenant-love (chapter 1)
- receiving covenant-love (chapter 1)
- understanding my feelings and responses to my partner (chapter 2)
- understanding and being understood by my partner (chapter 3)
- recurring conflicts (chapters 3 and 14)
- maintaining my individuality in the marriage (chapter 4)
- maintaining healthy boundaries around the marriage (chapter 4)
- trusting my partner (chapter 5)
- my partner's lack of trust (chapter 5)
- getting my needs met (chapter 6)
- adjusting to change in the relationship (chapter 7)
- adjusting to changing emotional needs (chapter 8)
- getting my needs met (chapter 9)
- experiencing intimacy (chapter 10)
- communicating with my partner (chapter 11)
- sex (chapter 12)
- leadership issues (chapter 13)
- managing and resolving conflict (chapter 14)

- dealing with in-laws (chapter 15)
- dealing with stepfamily issues (chapter 16)
- my own infidelity (chapter 17)
- my partner's infidelity (chapter 17)
- other _____

After identifying the biggest problem area that you currently experience in your marriage, take another look at the chapter or chapters indicated for that problem area, then list below three actions you intend to take this week to begin changing and healing that problem.

If possible, ask your partner, a counselor, a pastor, priest, rabbi, or a very close and trusted friend to hold you accountable for making those changes in your marriage. Ask that person to pray with you and for you during the week, and to check in with you next week to see how you did.

Renew this commitment from week to week. As you make progress in one area, identify and work on a different problem area in your marriage and ask for prayer and to be held accountable.

It might be helpful to keep a journal or diary of your feelings, progress, setbacks, and accomplishments as you work through the various issues of your marriage. Set a goal point—say, a year from today or your anniversary or New Year's Day—and go over your journal and written exercises you've completed in this book. Odds are, you will have made noticeable, significant progress in your relationship, progress that will encourage you to continue your journey toward deeper and richer intimacy with your partner.

THE END

FOR DISCUSSION GUIDES AND
OTHER HELPFUL MATERIALS, VISIT
THE AUTHOR'S WEB SITE AT
WWW.JAMESOSTERHAUS.COM

ABOUT THE AUTHOR

Jim Osterhaus is a senior partner with TAG. He is a clinical psychologist and a dynamic executive coach and public speaker with extensive experience in helping individuals, couples, families, and organizations move through change, conflict, and reorganization. He brings a depth of understanding of systems and relational network thinking to his work developed from years practicing as a highly respected psychologist in Northern Virginia in addition to consulting. His experience includes a special commission established by the Vice President of the United States to consider the emotional effects of government downsizing, facilitation of the "Organizational Culture" component of the Army Staff Redesign. Recently he has developed a Gettysburg Leadership Experience, taking teams to the battlefield discussing leadership principles. He has worked extensively with the FAA, coaching vice presidents and managers, and leading workshops and seminars on various aspects of leadership. He has been quoted in the *New York Times, Los Angeles Times, Seattle Times,* and many other leading publications.

About Familius

Welcome to a place where mothers are celebrated, not compared. Where heart is at the center of our families, and family at the center of our homes. Where boo-boos are still kissed, cake beaters are still licked, and mistakes are still okay. Welcome to a place where books—and family—are beautiful. Familius: a book publisher dedicated to helping families be happy.

Visit Our Website: www.familius.com

Our website is a different kind of place. Get inspired, read articles, discover books, watch videos, connect with our family experts, download books and apps and audiobooks, and along the way, discover how values and happy family life go together.

Join Our Family

There are lots of ways to connect with us! Subscribe to our newsletters at www.familius.com, to receive uplifting daily inspiration, essays from our Pater Familius, a free ebook every month, and the first word on special discounts and Familius news.

Become an Expert

Familius authors and other established writers interested in helping families be happy are invited to join our family and contribute online content. If you have something important to say on the family, join our expert community by applying at:

www.familius.com/apply-to-become-a-familius-expert

Get Bulk Discounts

If you feel a few friends and family might benefit from what you've read, let us know and we'll be happy to provide you with quantity discounts. Simply email us at specialorders@familius.com.

Website: www.familius.com

Facebook: www.facebook.com/paterfamilius

Twitter: @familiustalk, @paterfamilius1

Pinterest: www.pinterest.com/familius

The most important work

you ever do will be within the

walls of your own home.

CPSIA information can be obtained at www.ICGtesting.com
Printed in the USA
BVOW07s1201300914

368825BV00002B/11/P